"This first copy of the book is humbly dedicated to God."

In Honor of Olympic and Sport Friends:

______________________ 혜존(惠存)

**"Well Wishes!"**

With Heartfelt Appreciation for Your Dedication to the Olympic Movement and Peace Through Sport.

Prof. Rocky Kang-Ro Yoon/윤강로(尹康老)
Seoul, October 2025

"Governance, Grace, and Global Games"

# Thomas Bach: The Olympic Reformer

Rocky Kang-Ro YOON

DKBooks

# Photo Gallery

THOMAS BACH

FRG

**My First Four-Line Poem** (IOC President Thomas Bach)

Change the Olympic Charter to prolong Thomas Bach in the IOC?
June 11, 2024

GIVE PEACE A CHANCE

POST CONFLICT DEVELOPMENT

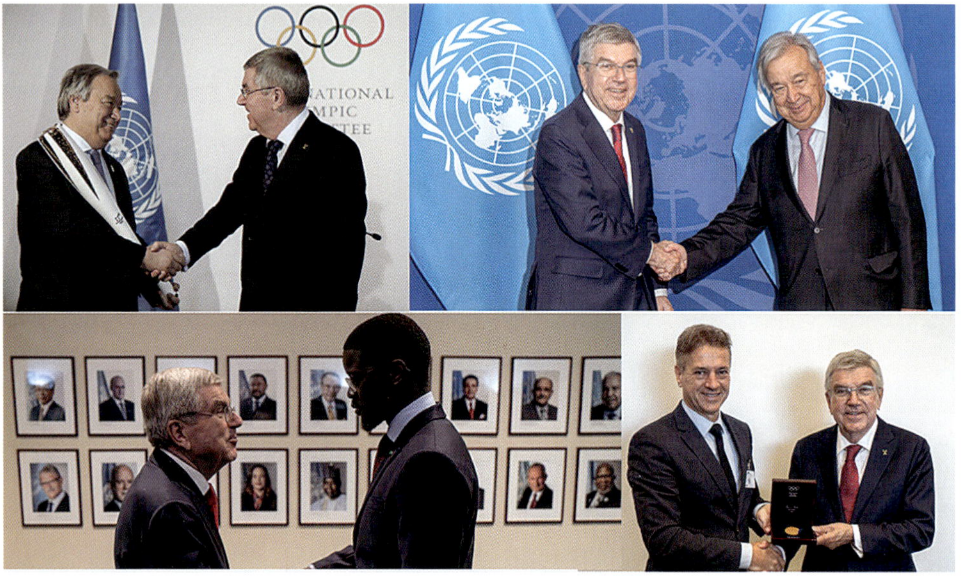

FORUM

PEACE PRIZE
제 15회 서울평화상 시상식

K. SONG I
PRK

COMITE INTERNATIONAL OLYMPIQUE

olympic.org
T. BACH
K. COVENTRY

LE SPORT POUR LE
DÉVELOPPEMENT DURABLE

IOC.org
IOC.org
IOC.org
IOC.org
IOC.org
IOC.org

PRESIDENT
CEREMONY

# Table of Contents

## Chapter 4: Sport and Geopolitics – Navigating a Divided World



## Chapter 5: The Athlete's Advocate



## Chapter 6: Innovation, Inclusion, and the Digital Age



## Chapter 7: Legacy and Leadership

# A. Foreword

**My First Four-Line Poem** (IOC President Thomas Bach)

*(Olympic Gold Medalist at Montreal 1976 Games in Fencing)*

In Honor of Thomas Bach, Ninth President of the International Olympic Committee

In the annals of Olympic history, few leaders have left as indelible a mark as Thomas Bach, the ninth President of the International Olympic Committee. A man of vision, diplomacy, and unwavering commitment to the Olympic ideals, Bach's presidency (2013–2025) was defined by transformation, resilience, and renewal.

An Olympic gold medalist in fencing, Bach brought to the IOC not only the perspective of an athlete but also the wisdom of a statesman. His tenure began with the launch of the groundbreaking Olympic Agenda 2020, a strategic roadmap that reimagined the role of the Olympic Movement in a rapidly changing world. With its emphasis on sustainability, good governance, and youth engagement—and later expanded through Olympic Agenda 2020+5—these reforms reshaped the Games into a more inclusive, cost-effective, and socially responsible global celebration.

Bach's leadership was tested by crises that would have shaken any institution. When the COVID-19 pandemic threatened the very existence of the Tokyo 2020 Games, it was his steady hand and unshakable belief in the power of sport that ensured the Olympics would go on—safely, responsibly, and with dignity. His decision to postpone rather than cancel the Games preserved a vital platform for athletes and inspired a world in isolation.

He also confronted geopolitical tensions with courage and nuance. From the Russian doping scandal to the complexities of war and Olympic neutrality, Bach consistently sought solutions that upheld the integrity of sport while fostering dialogue and peace. His creation of the IOC Refugee Olympic Team—which earned its first medal in Paris 2024—stands as a testament to his belief in the unifying power of sport and the Olympic spirit.

Under his stewardship, the IOC achieved unprecedented financial stability, expanded global partnerships, and deepened its commitment to athletes' rights and well-being. He championed gender equality, digital innovation, and environmental responsibility, ensuring that the Olympic Games would remain relevant and inspiring for generations to come.

Thomas Bach's legacy is not merely administrative—it is transformational. He redefined what it means to lead with principle in a complex world. His presidency will be remembered not only for the Games he helped deliver, but for the values he helped preserve and the future he helped shape.

*"We know that the Olympic Games cannot create peace. But the Olympic Games can create a culture of peace that inspires the world."* — Thomas Bach

In the sacred realm of Olympism, where ideals rise above borders and the torch passes from hand to heart, this book is a personal testament — not just of one leader's legacy, but of two intertwined journeys.

As I stood witness to the vision, resilience, and diplomacy of IOC President Thomas Bach, I did so not as a distant observer, but as a companion in spirit, a communicator entrusted with Olympic narratives, and an advocate for peace through sport. This book is not only a biography of an Architect of Olympic Unity, an Olympic Humanist, Athlete, Torchbearer of Global Peace, Voice of Olympic Reform, and an Olympic Godfather — it is a reflection of shared values, mutual respect, and countless moments where the Olympic flame glowed brighter because of what we experienced together.

In these pages, I offer my voice as someone who walked beside his presidency, echoing his aspirations, bearing witness to transformation, and advocating for the dream of a better world through the power of sport. Through achievements and letters, speeches and ceremonies, through the highlights of Paris and the calls for global unity — I invite readers to join me in reliving those moments.

This book is not a conclusion, but a continuation — of a flame passed, of Olympism shared. Because in truth, Olympism lives in all of us who carry its message. And if you listen closely, you may hear it flicker on each page.

— Author-

# B. Dedication

### (Part I) To: IOC President Thomas Bach

- *"In recognition of your unwavering commitment to peace, unity, and the enduring power of sport. "*
- *"Your legacy has not only shaped the Olympic Movement— it has inspired the world."*

1. Architect of Olympic Unity un Diversity,
2. Olympic Humanist,
3. Torchbearer of Peace through Sport,
4. Champion of Athlete Dignity,
5. Gentleman of Unwavering Conviction,
6. The Olympic Reformer,
7. Olympic Champion,
8. Visionary Leader,
9. Guardian of the Olympism,
10. Diplomat of Global Sport,
11. Custodian of Olympic Legacy
12. Bridge-Builder in Sport and Society,
13. Father of Olympic Refugees,
14. Olympic Godfather, and
15. Hero of heroes of the 21c Olympic Movement

For the moments we shared in quiet reflection and spirited advocacy — for every letter, handshake, and heartfelt exchange that shaped this journey.

*(Courtesy Meeting with IOC President Thomas Bach on 2 April 2025 at Olympic house, Lausanne)*

This tribute is for you and to you. May the Olympic spirit you nurtured continue to light the way for generations to come.

### (Part II) From: 8th UN Secretary General, Ki-moon BAN

Dedication

This book is dedicated to the enduring spirit of peace, friendship, and global progress through sport — values championed by Thomas Bach, former President of the International Olympic Committee.

I also wish to express my deep respect and gratitude to His Excellency Ban Ki-moon, the 8th Secretary-General of the United Nations, also having served IOC Ethics Commission Chair, currently IOC Honor Member since 2025, whose lifelong dedication to diplomacy and humanity and the Olympic Movement continues to inspire me.

Upon requesting a foreword from UN Secretary-General Ban, I received

*(With 8th UN Secretary General Ki-moon Ban and IOC President Thomas Bach)*

the following message — a response so sincere and thoughtful that I felt compelled to share it here, not as a foreword, but as a testament to his integrity and the quiet strength of his character:

Dear Prof. Rocky Kang-Ro YOON,

Thank you for your kind letter.

I sincerely congratulate you on your meaningful work in writing a book about former IOC President Thomas Bach's efforts to promote peace, development, reform, and friendship through sport.

Regarding your request for a foreword, I would naturally wish to honor it, especially considering my relationship with IOC President Bach. However, as a former Secretary-General of the United Nations, I must respectfully decline due to certain unwritten norms I must uphold.

Over the years, I have received many requests — from letters of recommendation for university admissions and employment to endorsements for autobiographies and personal publications — and I have often felt regret at being unable to assist.

I hope you will kindly understand my position.

Wishing you good health during this hot summer season.

Ki-moon BAN
8th UN Secretary General and
IOC Honor Member

His message, though declining the request, reflects the very principles this book seeks to celebrate: humility, duty, and unwavering commitment to ethical standards. I remain deeply honored by his thoughtful reply.

# C. Preface

This book is a tribute to a man whose leadership transcended sport. Thomas Bach, the ninth President of the International Olympic Committee, did not merely guide the Olympic Movement—he redefined it for a new era.

In a time of global uncertainty, Bach stood firm in his belief that sport is more than competition; it is a force for peace, dialogue, and human dignity. His presidency was marked by bold reforms, principled diplomacy, and an unwavering commitment to athletes and the values they represent. From the historic Olympic Agenda 2020 to the courageous staging of the Tokyo 2020 Games during a global pandemic, his decisions shaped not only the future of the Olympics but the role of sport in modern society.

This book is dedicated to honoring that legacy. It is not a biography, nor a chronicle of events alone—but a reflection on the values, challenges, and vision that defined Bach's tenure. Through stories, analysis, and personal reflections, we aim to capture the essence of a leader who believed that the Olympic flame could light more than stadiums—it could illuminate the path to a better world.

Here's a powerful quote from Thomas Bach that would make a fitting close to your foreword:

"We know that the Olympic Games cannot create peace. But the Olympic Games can create a culture of peace that inspires the world." > — *Thomas Bach, Opening Ceremony Address, Paris 2024*

To all who believe in the power of sport to unite and uplift, this book is for you.

- A Dedication that honors Thomas Bach's legacy with grace and bilingual resonance

- A Foreword that captures his achievements and leadership with depth and admiration
- A Preface that invites readers into the heart of your purpose and the spirit of the Olympic Movement

*(IOC President Thomas Bach on 1 January 2025/Photo capture from SportsIn)*

Let's take a look at the comprehensive summary of the key achievements, activities, contributions, and issue-solving examples from Thomas Bach's tenure as the 9th President of the International Olympic Committee (IOC), from 2013 to 2025:

## 1. Overall Achievements (2013–2025)

1) Olympic Agenda 2020 & 2020+5: Bach spearheaded these landmark reform packages to modernize the Olympic Movement. They emphasized sustainability, credibility, and youth engagement.
2) Olympic AI Agenda: Introduced to integrate artificial intelligence into Olympic operations and athlete support.

3) Financial Growth: Under Bach, IOC revenues grew by 60%, with expanded sponsorships (e.g., Airbnb, Alibaba, Intel) and a $7.65 billion broadcast deal with NBC through 2032.
4) Digital Transformation: Promoted e-sports, digital engagement, and virtual Olympic experiences to reach younger audiences.
5) Gender Equality: Advocated for gender parity in Olympic participation and leadership roles.

## 2. Thomas Bach: A Legacy of Reform, Resilience, and Renewal

Thomas Bach, the ninth President of the International Olympic Committee (2013–2025), leaves behind a transformative legacy defined by bold reforms, principled leadership, and steadfast commitment to Olympic values. A former Olympic gold medalist in fencing, Bach brought the perspective of an athlete to the highest echelons of sports governance, becoming the first Olympic champion to lead the IOC.

## 3. His Achievements and Contributions

1) Olympic Agenda Reforms: Bach spearheaded the landmark Olympic Agenda 2020 and its successor, Olympic Agenda 2020+5, which redefined the Olympic Movement's priorities. These reforms emphasized sustainability, cost-efficiency, gender equality, and youth engagement, and were fully embodied in the Paris 2024 Games.
2) Athlete Empowerment: Under his leadership, the IOC significantly

expanded athlete representation, safeguarding, and career support. Initiatives like the IOC Refugee Olympic Team, which won its first medal in Paris 2024, symbolized his commitment to inclusivity and global solidarity.

3) Financial Stewardship: Bach oversaw a 60% increase in IOC revenues, securing long-term broadcast and sponsorship deals, including a $7.65 billion agreement with NBC and expanded partnerships under the TOP Programme.
4) Global Health and Partnerships: He forged strategic alliances with organizations like the World Health Organization to promote physical activity and public health through sport.
5) Cultural and Educational Impact: Bach championed Olympic education and values-based sport, earning numerous honorary doctorates and global honors for his advocacy of peace, diversity, and human dignity.

## 4. Crisis Leadership and Issue-Solving

1) Tokyo 2020 and the COVID-19 Pandemic: Perhaps his most defining challenge, Bach insisted on holding the postponed Tokyo 2020 Olympics despite global uncertainty. His resolve ensured that a generation of athletes could compete, even in empty stadiums. Many credit his leadership with saving the Olympic Movement from a prolonged hiatus.
2) Geopolitical Tensions and Russia: Bach navigated the complex fallout from Russia's state-sponsored doping scandal and its breaches of the Olympic Truce. His decision to allow vetted Russian athletes to com-

pete under a neutral flag at Paris 2024 was seen as a delicate balance between principle and pragmatism.

3) Sustainability and Innovation: He promoted the use of existing venues and temporary infrastructure to reduce the environmental footprint of the Games, a model exemplified by Paris 2024's low-cost, high-impact approach.

Thomas Bach's presidency was marked by a rare blend of vision and tenacity. He modernized the Olympic Movement while preserving its core ideals, guided it through unprecedented global crises, and laid the foundation for a more inclusive, sustainable, and athlete-centered future. His legacy is not merely one of administration, but of transformation.

# D. Author's Reflections

More than anything else, I would like to reiterate my gratitude to 9th IOC President Thomas Bach for safeguarding Korea, through his unwavering philosophy of "**Strictly Politically Neutral Policy**", from the unpredictable and provocative situation prior to the PyeongChang2018 OWG.

Without his insightful leadership and timely intervention, Korea, at that time, almost came near undergoing the similar fate of Ukraine as it is currently.

Not only Korea but also the UN still must owe him a lot for what he has specially done to bring together the "Peace Olympics" on the Korean Peninsula. I indeed trust that God saved us all through him.

I would also take this opportunity to thank him for safeguarding the Olympic Movement from unstable and uncertain global phenomena until quite recently, having overcome risks and dangers threatening the two consecutive Olympic Games of Tokyo 2020 and Beijing 2022.

I have come a long way for 43 years until now since I first joined the Olympic Movement in 1982 at the Korean Olympic Committee, including the period of working at the Seoul1988 Olympic Organizing Committee, for 22 years, and soon after, the PyeongChang Bid Committee for three consecutive OWG Bids 2010-2014-2018, and finally at the PyeongChang2018 OWG Organizing Committee for ensuing 18 long years altogether. In the meantime, I founded and have operated the independent NGO, called the International Sport Diplomacy Institute(2004~Present), and opened the private PyeongSan Sport Museum (2004~2015) in the outskirts of Seoul in order to disseminate the Olympic spirit and values to the general public through the Sport Museum movement. In October 2015, upon request from Gangneung city Mayor (Ice Sport Venue City of PyeongChang2018), I donated all sport and Olympic-related collection items and memorabilia displayed in my private sport museum to the Gangneung Olympic Museum for which then-IOC President Thomas Bach also kindly co-signed the MoU with the Olympic Museum Director and then-Mayor of Gangneung in Lausanne late April 2018

During my 43 year-long career only in the Olympic Movement, I have experienced various kinds of ups and downs, suffered from time to time mostly due to lack of humbleness contextually in line with the Korean culture that I regret, felt a sense of joy from achievements in many cases as well, and nevertheless I now came to realize that I still might have some other missions to be accomplished for the remainder of my life based on my lifelong experiences and knowledge I learned from the Olympic Movement.

It was possible because it was the Olympic Values of "Excellence, Friendship and Respect"

It was possible because of the Olympic Legacy of Sustainable Development Goals(SDGs)

It was possible because I have loved the Olympic spirit toward "Unity in Diversity" as IO globally emphasized.

Sometimes I thought about Dr. Thomas Bach, his role, his responsibilities, and his global contributions as IOC President, and the future of the Olympic Movement, especially in recent years when various difficulties are still being expected in the immediate future and beyond.

Every morning I pray God for my wish to come true to do the job to dedicate myself to and humbly contribute to the Olympic Movement.

# E. Biography: Thomas Bach – Guardian of the Olympic Spirit : "Olympic Godfather"

## MR THOMAS BACH

GER

**[Biography]**

Thomas Bach was born on 29 December 1953 in Würzburg, Germany. Married and a lawyer by profession, he has had a successful career in sports both on and off the field of play. He became an Olympic champion when he won a gold medal in fencing (team foil) at the Games of the XXI Olympiad in Montreal in 1976 and in 2006, he was named as the founding President of the German Olympic Sports Confederation (DOSB).

Thomas Bach was an athletes' representative at the XI Olympic Congress in Baden-Baden (1981) and a founding member of the IOC's Athletes' Commission. He became an IOC member in 1991, was elected as a member of the IOC Executive Board in 1996 and served as an IOC Vice-President for more than 10 years. He has also chaired several IOC Commissions.

On 10 September 2013, Thomas Bach was elected as the ninth President of the IOC. He was re-elected for a second four-year term on 10 March 2021.

### [Education]

Studies in Law and Politics, University of Würzburg (Germany) (1973-1978); Further Law formation (1978-1982); Ph.D. in Law (1983)

### [Career]

Founder of own law firm (1982); Director for Promotion, Adidas (1985-1987); Chairman of the SME Advisory Board of the Federal Minister for Economics (1988-1990); Chairman of the Supervisory Board of Michael Weinig AG (1998-) and Weinig International AG (2000-); Member of the Board of Administration of Siemens Schweiz AG (2000-2009); President of the Ghorfa Arab-German Chamber of Commerce and Industry (2006-2013); Chairman of the Advisory Board of Melius GmbH (2008-2013); Member of the Supervisory Board of Nürnberger Versicherung AG Austria (2009-2013); Chairman of the Advisory Board of Bartec GmbH (2009-2013)

### [Sports practiced]

Fencing, tennis, football

### [Sports Career]

Olympic champion, fencing, men's foil team, Montreal 1976; World Champion, fencing, men's foil team, Montreal 1976 and Buenos Aires 1977

### [Sports Administration]

Chairman of the Athletes' Commission of the German Committee for Competitive Sport in the German Sports Confederation (DSB) (1979-1981);

Athletes' representative at the 11th Olympic Congress, Baden-Baden (Germany) (1981); Founding member of the IOC Athletes' Commission (1981-1988); Individual Member of the National Olympic Committee of Germany (1982-1991); Chairman of the Appeals division of the Court of Arbitration for sport (CAS) (1994-2013); Member of the Supervisory Board of the Organising Committee of the 2006 FIFA World Cup; Founding President (2006-2013) then Honorary President (2013-) of the German Olympic Sports Confederation (DOSB); Chairman of the Board of Trustees of the Organising Committee of the 2011 FIFA Women's World Cup (2007-2011); Chairman of the International Olympic Truce Foundation (IOTF) (2013-)

### [Publications]

Various publications on law, economics, and sports

### [Awards and Distinctions]

Numerous Honorary Professorships in different countries; numerous Doctor Honoris Causa degrees in different countries; numerous orders of Merit from various National Olympic committees and International Sports Organisations; numerous high-level distinctions from various States

### [IOC History]

IOC President (2013-2025); Member (1996-2000) of the IOC Executive Board then Vice-President (2000-2004) and re-elected as Vice-President (2006-2013); Chair of the following Commissions: Evaluation for the XIX Olympic Winter Games (1994-1995), Evaluation for the Games of XXVIII Olympiad (1995-1997), Juridical (2002-2014), Sport and Law (2002-2014),

TV Rights and New Media (2014-2015); member of the following Commissions: Athletes' (1981-1988), Press (1985-1988), Marketing (1992-2014), Juridical (1993-2001), Olympic Collectors (1994-1997), Olympic Movement (1996-1999), Sport and Law (as Athletes' representative, 1995-2001), TV Rights and New Media (2002- 2014), IOC 2000 Reform Follow-up (2002); Coordinator of the Working Group "Role of the IOC" of the "IOC 2000" Commission (1999); Remuneration Working Group (2004); Chair of the board of directors of the Olympic Channel Services S.A., Switzerland (2015-2021)

# Chapter 1:
# *The Athlete Who Became President*

*(Olympic Gold Medalist at Montreal 1976 Games in Fencing)*

The clang of steel echoed through the hall in Montreal, 1976. Under the bright lights of the Olympic fencing piste, a young German athlete named Thomas Bach lunged forward with precision and poise. In that moment—blade extended, heart pounding—he wasn't thinking about politics, diplomacy, or the future of global sport. He was thinking only of the next touch, the next point, the next victory. When the final bout ended, Bach and his teammates stood atop the podium, gold medals around their necks, the West German flag rising behind them. It was a triumph of discipline, teamwork, and belief.

Few could have imagined that this fencer, barely in his twenties, would one day become the most powerful figure in international sport. But even then, the seeds of leadership were there—in his calm under pressure, his strategic mind, and his deep respect for the Olympic ideal.

Born in Würzburg, Germany, in 1953, Thomas Bach grew up in a postwar world where sport offered not just competition, but connection. Fencing, with its blend of intellect and athleticism, became his passion and his path. He studied law while training at the highest level, balancing the rigors of academia with the demands of elite sport. That duality—of mind and body, of principle and performance—would define his life.

After retiring from competition, Bach didn't leave the Olympic world behind. Instead, he stepped into its corridors of influence, serving as an athletes' advocate, legal advisor, and eventually a member of the International Olympic Committee. His rise was steady, marked by diplomacy, multilingual fluency, and a rare ability to listen as well as lead.

When he was elected IOC President in 2013, he became the first Olympic gold medalist to hold the position. It was a symbolic full circle: from the piste in Montreal to the podium in Lausanne. But for Bach, it was never about personal glory. It was about service—to athletes, to the Olympic Movement, and to the ideals that had shaped his life.

## 1. Born for the Arena

*(From 8th IOC President Jacques Rogge to 9th IOC President Thomas Bach on 23 June 2013)*

From the quiet town of Würzburg to the world's grandest stages, Thomas Bach's earliest steps weren't toward podiums, but toward purpose. Born in 1953, his journey began not with fanfare but with dedication — an athlete in heart, in discipline, and in spirit.

Even before his name adorned Olympic history, he was driven not by medals but by meaning. As a young fencer, he learned the language of motion, strategy, and grace — lessons that would echo through his future as a global leader.

In the arena of sport, where triumph is measured in seconds and legacy in decades, few have journeyed as far as Thomas Bach — from Olympic gold medalist to the helm of the world's most emblematic sporting institution.

But for me, his story was never just a headline or a historical note. I saw him. I spoke with him. I walked alongside him through years marked by reform, diplomacy, and unprecedented global upheaval. What unfolded was not only the evolution of a leader, but the unfolding of my own Olympic journey — shaped by dialogue, inspired by leadership, and fueled by a shared belief in the transformative power of sport.

This first chapter begins where all great stories do: with origin. As we explore Thomas Bach's youth, his disciplined ascent through fencing, and his early stirrings of leadership, I invite you to step into both our shoes — his as the athlete with resolve, mine as the witness to that resolve's lasting echo.

Let the journey begin — with footwork, with vision, and with the first step toward the Olympic Presidency.

"Every athlete learns that victory is built not in seconds, but in thousands of hours. That's where leadership begins." — *Author's Reflection*

## 2. Montreal 1976 and the Gold of Legacy

The year was 1976. In Montreal, the German foil team stood tall, and Thomas Bach, with quiet intensity and precision, struck gold. But that victory became more than a medal — it became a signature. A declaration that sport can be elegant, purposeful, and transformative.

For me, this was where Thomas Bach first entered the world stage as more than an athlete — as someone destined for influence beyond the piste. The photo of him lifting his arm in triumph still flickers in my memory as if it happened yesterday.

## 3. From Blade to Briefcase: The Making of a Diplomat

Thomas Bach's journey from Olympic champion to global statesman was not a sudden leap—it was a carefully honed evolution. Even as a young man, he was known not only for his athletic prowess but for his intellect and curiosity. While training with the West German national fencing team, he pursued a law degree at the University of Würzburg, often studying late into the night after grueling practice sessions. His professors noted his analytical mind and his ability to argue with both precision and empathy—traits that would later serve him well in the diplomatic arena.

Bach's upbringing in postwar Germany also played a formative role. He came of age in a country rebuilding its identity, where the scars of conflict were still visible and the yearning for unity was palpable. Sport, in that context, was more than recreation—it was a symbol of reconciliation. Bach internalized this deeply. To him, the Olympic Games were not just a competition of nations, but a rare space where humanity could meet on equal footing, if only for a moment.

After retiring from competitive fencing, Bach quickly became involved in the administrative side of sport. He served as a spokesperson for the German Olympic athletes at the 1980 Olympic Congress in Baden-Baden, where he delivered a powerful address on behalf of his peers. It was a turning point. His voice—measured, articulate, and athlete-centered—caught the attention of IOC members and sports leaders around the world.

From there, his ascent was steady. He joined the IOC in 1991 and took on a variety of roles, including Chair of the Juridical Commission and

Vice-President of the IOC Executive Board. He was instrumental in shaping legal frameworks for sport, advocating for athletes' rights, and navigating the complex intersection of sport, politics, and international law. His ability to build consensus across cultures and ideologies became one of his defining strengths.

But perhaps what set Bach apart most was his unwavering belief in the Olympic ideal—not as a slogan, but as a living philosophy. He often spoke of Olympism as a force for peace, education, and human dignity. And unlike many administrators, he had lived it firsthand. He knew what it meant to stand on the podium, to hear one's anthem, to carry the hopes of a nation. That empathy would become the cornerstone of his leadership.

His transition was seamless yet profound. With each role — athlete, lawyer, diplomat — Bach sharpened not blades but ideas. From sports arbitration to Olympic diplomacy, he became the man who saw sport not as spectacle, but as instrument: of Unity, Peace, and Reform.

I recall receiving his letters: deliberate, thoughtful, and always underscored by a deep respect for the athletes he served. That conviction never wavered. It was what made him more than a president. It made him a steward.

## 4. Rising to the Presidency (2013): A New Era Begins

The election of Thomas Bach as the 9th IOC President was historic — not just for his resume, but for the ethos he carried. He wasn't crowned by circumstance but chosen by vision.

And I had the privilege to see it unfold, not as an observer from afar,

Mr Thomas BACH
GER

*(IOC Presidential Key Handover from Jacques Rogge to Thomas Bach on 23 June 2013)*

but through dialogue, correspondence, and shared reflections. His acceptance speech in Buenos Aires still echoes with humility, courage, and clarity — qualities that would define his entire presidency.

> "Olympism is not just a philosophy. It is a promise." — *Thomas Bach, 2013*

"Many thanks for this symbolic act of handing over the key, which is now a traditional part of IOC history. We both know very well that this handover includes the challenge of taking on the huge demands and responsibility of this office."

"You(Rogge) have left the Olympic Movement a solid foundation and you have every reason to be proud of your great achievement, which has benefited sport worldwide. Here, this evening, we would like to express to you our gratitude, recognition and respect."

The air in Lausanne was thick with anticipation on September 10,

2013. Delegates from around the world had gathered for the 125th IOC Session, where a new president would be chosen to succeed Jacques Rogge. The Olympic Movement stood at a crossroads—facing rising costs, waning public support in some host cities, and growing calls for reform. The world was watching.

When Thomas Bach emerged as the victor after two rounds of voting, he became the first Olympic gold medalist to lead the IOC. His election was more than symbolic—it was a signal that the organization was ready to be led by someone who understood the Games not just from the boardroom, but from the arena.

In his acceptance speech, Bach struck a tone of humility and unity. "Unity in Diversity," he said, quoting the Olympic motto, "will be our guiding principle." He pledged to listen, to modernize, and to protect the values that had made the Olympic Games a beacon for over a century. It was a promise that would soon be tested.

"First of all, I would like to thank from the bottom of my heart all my dear friends and colleagues who voted for me this morning.

This is really an overwhelming sign of trust and confidence.

But I would also like to thank my fellow candidates, who I greatly respect, and all those who did not vote for me this time.

I will also work for and with you in the coming years and want to win your confidence, too."

"I know about the great responsibility of an IOC President."

"This makes me humble.

"I want to lead the IOC according to my motto": 'unity in diversity.'

"I want to be a President for all of you."

"This means I will do my very best to balance well all the different interests of the stakeholders of the Olympic Movement."

"This is why I want to listen to you and to enter into an ongoing dialogue with all of you."

"You should know that my door, my ears, and my heart are always open for you."

From the outset, Bach made it clear that he intended to be a reformer. He launched a sweeping consultation process with athletes, National Olympic Committees, International Federations, and civil society. The result would be the most ambitious reform package in the IOC's modern history: Olympic Agenda 2020.

Bach's manifesto states he wants to keep the Olympic Games "unique" and not "diluted by other events," while ensuring the awarding of the Games is based on "the interest of the IOC in an in-depth review and risk analysis of a bid on the one hand, and the interest of a potential bidder in a social and promotional return on investment in the other.")

But even in those early days, it was evident that Bach's leadership would be defined by more than policy. He brought a calm, deliberate presence to the role—measured in tone, but firm in conviction. He was fluent in multiple languages, comfortable in any diplomatic setting, and adept at navigating the complex web of global sport. Yet he never lost sight of the athlete's perspective. In every decision, he asked: How will this serve the athletes? How will this protect the integrity of the Games?

As the world changed around him—with rising nationalism, digital disruption, and mounting global crises—Bach positioned the IOC not as a passive observer, but as an active force for good. He believed that sport could be a bridge where politics failed, a platform for peace where dialogue had broken down.

And so, with a fencer's precision and a statesman's patience, Thomas Bach began to reshape the Olympic Movement—not for nostalgia, but for the future.

# Chapter 2: *Olympic Agenda 2020+5 – A Vision for the Future*

This chapter will explore the origins, goals, and impact of Olympic Agenda 2020—Thomas Bach's signature reform initiative that reshaped the Olympic Movement for a new era:

When Thomas Bach assumed the Presidency of the International Olympic Committee in 2013, he inherited an institution at a critical juncture. The Olympic Games, though still the world's most celebrated sporting event, were facing mounting skepticism. Host cities were withdrawing bids due to soaring costs and public opposition. Critics questioned the relevance of the Games in a rapidly changing world. The IOC needed not just a leader—it needed a visionary.

Bach responded with boldness and clarity. Within months of taking office, he launched a sweeping consultation process that would culminate in the most comprehensive reform package in the IOC's modern history: Olympic Agenda 2020.

One of the most profound shifts I witnessed was the change in host city selection. President Bach championed legacy — *urging cities to ask: What will remain when the flame goes out?*

Gone were the days of building only to impress. Now, cities embraced reuse, regeneration, and civic harmony. The narrative changed: from cost to contribution, from extravagance to experience.

The Tokyo Metropolitan Government official once confided to me, "This isn't just President Bach's reform — it's a revolution." And that, I believe, was true.

From PyeongChang's creative venues to Paris 2024's gender parity and urban engagement, the touch of Olympic Agenda 2020 was everywhere. It shaped the IOC's DNA. It made the Games smarter, fairer, and closer to their original promise — *"to place sport at the service of humanity."*

For me, this chapter in Thomas Bach's Presidency wasn't just impressive in scale. It was inspiring in its soul. Because every reform spoke not only to a better Olympic movement — but to a better world.

## 1. A Blueprint for Renewal

Unveiled in December 2014 and unanimously approved by the IOC Session in Monaco, Olympic Agenda 2020 was more than a policy document—it was a philosophical shift. Comprising 40 detailed recommendations, it aimed to make the Olympic Movement more sustainable, credible, and youth-focused.

At its core, the Agenda sought to answer a fundamental question: *How can the Olympic Games remain relevant in the 21st century?*

The answers came in the form of sweeping reforms:

1) **Sustainability and Flexibility**: Cities were encouraged to use existing or temporary venues, reducing the financial and environmental burden

of hosting. The rigid model of "build first, justify later" was replaced with a more pragmatic, legacy-driven approach.

2) **Host City Selection Reform**: The bidding process was overhauled to become more collaborative and less adversarial. Dialogue replaced competition, and the focus shifted to aligning the Games with long-term urban development goals.

3) **Good Governance and Transparency**: The IOC committed to publishing financial reports, strengthening ethics oversight, and increasing accountability across all levels of the Olympic Movement.

4) **Athlete-Centered Policies**: From safeguarding and anti-doping to ca-

reer transition support, the Agenda placed athletes at the heart of every decision.

5) **Embracing Youth and Innovation**: New sports like skateboarding, surfing, and sport climbing were introduced to engage younger audiences. Digital platforms were prioritized to connect with fans in real time.

When Thomas Bach stood before the Olympic community as its newly elected President, he didn't inherit an institution satisfied with the status quo. He inherited a challenge — to renew the spirit of Olympism for a world that was changing faster than ever.

The genesis of *Olympic Agenda 2020* was born not from ambition alone, but necessity. The world was restless, cities wary of hosting, and young generations yearning for relevance. President Bach didn't respond with fear — he responded with a vision.

> "We must embrace change, or risk losing our purpose. The Games must remain for the people."
> — *Thomas Bach, 2014*

I remember reading those words, echoed in his early drafts and declarations. It wasn't just policy — it was promise.

## 2. Reimagining the Games – Sustainability, Flexibility, and Good Governance

The reforms came swiftly and thoughtfully. Sustainability wasn't a side note; it was a pillar. The Olympics began shifting away from mega-projects and toward adaptive hosting. Flexibility in bidding, transparency in governance, a newfound respect for local legacy — all guided by Olympic Agenda 2020.

As an Olympic communicator, I saw firsthand how these principles touched not only policy but people — athletes, organizers, even spectators. No longer were the Games a distant spectacle. They were becoming accessible, ethical, and responsive.

"Gigantism gave way to grace. Transparency led to trust."
— *Author's Note*

Olympic Agenda 2020 was not without its skeptics. Some questioned whether the IOC could truly reform itself. But Bach's leadership proved both strategic and inclusive. He built consensus across Continents, Federations, and ideologies—earning trust not through rhetoric, but through results.

The first Games to fully reflect the Agenda's principles—Tokyo 2020 and Paris 2024—demonstrated its power. Costs were contained, public support was higher, and the Games felt more connected to the cities that hosted them. The Olympic Movement had not only survived a period of crisis—it had evolved.

Let's continue to find his brilliant, amazing and charismatic characteristics by exploring how Thomas Bach extended his reformist vision through Olympic Agenda 2020+5, adapting the Olympic Movement to a world reshaped by global crises, digital transformation, and shifting societal values.

## 3. Olympic Agenda 2020+5: Adapting to a Changed World

By the time the world emerged from the initial shock of the COVID-19 pandemic, it was clear that the Olympic Movement—like every global institution—would need to evolve once again. The pandemic had exposed vulnerabilities in international systems, accelerated digital disruption, and deepened conversations around equity, sustainability, and resilience.

Thomas Bach responded not with hesitation, but with foresight. In March 2021, the IOC launched Olympic Agenda 2020+5, a strategic extension of the original Agenda, built around five key themes and 15 recommendations. It was not a departure from his earlier vision—it was a deepening of it, shaped by the lessons of a world in flux.

The five themes were bold and timely:

1) Solidarity and Digitalization: The IOC committed to narrowing the digital divide and using technology to connect athletes and fans more directly. This included expanding Olympic digital platforms, embracing virtual sports, and supporting athletes in the digital economy.
2) Sustainability and Legacy Building on the environmental reforms of Agenda 2020, the IOC pledged to become climate positive by 2024 and to ensure that every Olympic Games would leave a meaningful, measurable legacy for host communities.
3) Credibility and Good Governance Transparency, ethics, and accountability remained central. Bach emphasized that the IOC must lead by example in a world increasingly skeptical of institutions.
4) Economic and Financial Resilience The pandemic had tested the fi-

nancial stability of sport. Olympic Agenda 2020+5 focused on diversifying revenue streams, supporting smaller federations, and ensuring long-term viability without compromising values.

5) Global Solidarity and Peace Perhaps most powerfully, Bach reaffirmed the IOC's role as a bridge-builder in a divided world. He emphasized the Olympic Truce, the Refugee Olympic Team, and the Games as a platform for dialogue and dignity.

## 4. From Reform to Reinvention

Olympic Agenda 2020+5 was not just a policy update—it was a philosophical reaffirmation. It showed that the IOC, under Bach's leadership, was not content to rest on past reforms. It was willing to confront new realities with courage and creativity.

The Paris 2024 Games would become the first to fully embody this expanded vision: gender-balanced participation, climate-conscious planning, and a celebration of youth culture and innovation. The Olympic Village was

*(7th IOC President Juan Antonio Samaranch greeted Thomas Bach as Athlete Representative/ Source: SportsIn)*

powered by renewable energy. Urban sports took center stage. And the message was clear: The Olympics were not just surviving—they were leading.

For Thomas Bach, Olympic Agenda 2020+5 was a culmination of a decade-long journey. It was the proof that reform, when rooted in values and guided by vision, could become reinvention.

## 5. A Movement Reimagined

By the end of his second term, Thomas Bach had done more than implement reforms—he had redefined the very identity of the Olympic Movement. What began as a response to institutional fatigue and public skepticism had evolved into a bold reimagining of what the Games could mean in the 21st century.

Through Olympic Agenda 2020 and its successor, Olympic Agenda 2020+5, Bach positioned the IOC not as a relic of tradition, but as a living, learning institution—capable of listening, adapting, and leading. He proved that reform was not a threat to the Olympic legacy, but its renewal.

The Olympic Games were no longer just a spectacle of sport. They had become a platform for sustainability, inclusion, innovation, and peace. Cities no longer feared hosting them—they aspired to. Athletes no longer felt like participants—they felt like partners. And the world, in moments of division and doubt, still looked to the Olympic flame for a sense of shared humanity.

But the true test of any vision is how it holds up under pressure. And for Thomas Bach, that test came sooner than anyone expected—with a global pandemic that would threaten not only the Games, but the very spirit of international unity they represent.

# Chapter 3:

## *Leading Through Crisis – Tokyo 2020/2021 and the Pandemic*

In March 2020, the world stopped.

Airports emptied. Stadiums fell silent. Borders closed. The COVID-19 pandemic swept across continents with terrifying speed, bringing daily life—and global sport—to a standstill. For the first time since World War II, the Olympic Games faced the unthinkable: cancellation.

The Tokyo 2020 Olympic Games, years in the making and just months from opening, hung in the balance. Athletes were left in limbo, their training disrupted, their dreams uncertain. Host city Tokyo, already deep into preparations, faced mounting pressure from public health officials, governments, and a fearful public. The International Olympic Committee was thrust into the center of a global crisis.

At the helm stood Thomas Bach.

For Bach, the decision was not just logistical—it was existential. The Olympic Games had never been postponed in modern history. To delay them would require unprecedented coordination, diplomacy, and trust. But to cancel them outright would mean extinguishing the hopes of thousands of athletes and sending a message of surrender to a world already gripped by fear.

After intense deliberation with the Tokyo 2020 Organizing Committee, the Japanese government, and the World Health Organization, Bach made the historic call: The Games would be postponed by one year. Not canceled. Not forgotten. Postponed.

It was a decision that required courage, clarity, and compassion.

## 1. The Moment the Flame Paused

Postponing the Games was only the beginning. The logistical challenges that followed were staggering. Venues had to be rebooked. Contracts renegotiated. Broadcast schedules rewritten. Athletes needed clarity, and national Olympic committees needed support. The IOC, under Bach's leadership, mobilized resources, extended funding, and worked around the clock

to ensure that the Olympic flame would still burn in Tokyo.

But the greatest challenge was not technical—it was emotional. How do you inspire the world to believe in the power of sport when the world is in mourning?

Bach's answer was simple: by standing with the athletes.

He launched the #StrongerTogether campaign, emphasizing solidarity and resilience. He held virtual town halls with athletes, listened to their concerns, and reassured them that their voices mattered. He reminded the world that the Olympic Games were not just about medals—they were about meaning.

And when the Games finally opened in July 2021, in a stadium without spectators but with the eyes of the world watching, it was clear that something extraordinary had been achieved. Against all odds, the Olympic spirit had prevailed.

Let's focus on how the Tokyo 2020 Games were reimagined under pandemic conditions—and what they revealed about Bach's leadership style.

No moment in Olympic history had ever resembled the spring of 2020. The world fell silent. Stadiums stood still. Athletes waited. And the Olympic flame, symbol of continuity and hope, flickered in uncertainty.

IOC President Thomas Bach, under immense pressure, didn't flinch — he reflected. Together with Japanese officials, health leaders, and a deeply burdened Olympic community, he made the unthinkable call: to postpone the Tokyo Games.

I recall reading his statement and feeling the quiet weight in every word. It wasn't delay. It was devotion — to athletes, to health, and to the greater human good.

> "This is not cancellation. This is a commitment to everyone — that the Olympic dream endures."
>
> — *Thomas Bach, March 2020*

## 2. The Games That United a Fragmented World

In every broadcast, social post, and medal ceremony — I saw humanity. It was sport, yes. But more than that, it was signal: that we can rebuild, reconnect, and reignite.

Thomas Bach didn't just guide the Olympic ship through stormy seas. He steadied it with calm, vision, and a refusal to let the flame extinguish.

As an Olympic communicator and advocate, I felt pride not only in the outcome, but in the values preserved. The pandemic fractured lives, but through Tokyo, Olympism showed it could still unify.

Let's bring diplomacy and depth into the next chapter of your tribute

— one where sport meets the complexity of geopolitics, and where IOC President Thomas Bach's role becomes not just administrative, but profoundly symbolic.

## 3. Reinventing the Games: Safety, Symbolism, and Solidarity

What the world saw was a change in dates. What it didn't see was the labyrinth of diplomacy behind the decision: daily consultations with the

WHO, negotiations with broadcasters, sponsors, and thousands of stakeholders. Peaceful agreement, in a time of global discord, was nothing short of Olympic diplomacy in action.

I was privileged to correspond with Olympic leaders during this time — messages that reinforced our shared mission and steadiness. We were not just delaying Games. We were preserving meaning.

The Tokyo 2020 Olympic Games—held in 2021—were unlike any in history. There were no roaring crowds, no packed arenas, no jubilant fans waving flags in the streets. Instead, there were masks, daily testing, and strict quarantine protocols. Athletes competed in near silence, celebrated on podiums without handshakes, and returned to the Olympic Village under curfew. It was a Games defined not by spectacle, but by survival.

And yet, it was precisely this stripped-down version of the Olympics that revealed their true essence.

Under Thomas Bach's guidance, the IOC worked closely with Japanese authorities, the World Health Organization, and international experts to create a comprehensive playbook for pandemic-era sport. Every detail—from athlete arrivals to medal ceremonies—was reimagined to prioritize health and safety. The IOC provided financial support to struggling federations and National Olympic Committees, ensuring that no athlete would be left behind due to the crisis.

But beyond logistics, Bach understood the symbolic weight of these Games. In his opening ceremony address, he spoke not of triumph, but of togetherness.

"Today is a moment of hope," he said. "Yes, it is very different from what all of us imagined. But let us cherish this moment because we are finally all here together."

The Tokyo Games became a global catharsis. Viewers around the world watched athletes overcome not just their competitors, but the isolation, anxiety, and uncertainty of the previous year. Stories of perseverance—like Simone Biles prioritizing mental health, or the Refugee Olympic Team marching under the Olympic flag—resonated more deeply than ever.

Bach's decision to hold the Games, despite immense pressure to cancel, was vindicated not by ratings or revenue, but by meaning. The Olympics had become a symbol of human resilience.

## 4. A President Tested—and Proven: Safety, Solidarity, and Symbolism

*(Tokyo2020 Main Stadium)*

When Tokyo finally welcomed the world in 2021, it wasn't with roaring crowds, but with whispered hope. Bubble protocols, empty seats, masks over medals — it wasn't the celebration we expected, but perhaps, it was the one we needed.

IOC President Bach stood at the Opening Ceremony and offered words that carried not just reassurance, but healing. I remember watching from afar, heart heavy and proud, knowing what it took to get there.

"You give the world the most precious gift: hope."

*— Thomas Bach, Tokyo 2021*

And hope it was. Athletes competed with fire. Nations embraced despite distance. The Games, though veiled in silence, roared with resolve.

For Thomas Bach, Tokyo 2020 was the defining test of his Presidency. It demanded every skill he had cultivated over decades: diplomacy, patience, empathy, and resolve. He had to navigate conflicting interests, shifting science, and intense public scrutiny—all while preserving the integrity of the Olympic Movement.

His critics had warned that holding the Games during a pandemic would be reckless. But Bach's response was rooted in principle: the Olympics are not just an event—they are a promise. A promise to the athletes who train in obscurity. A promise to the youth who dream of unity. A promise to the world that even in darkness, there can be light.

And in Tokyo, that promise was kept.

Let's see and focus on a reflection on the legacy of Tokyo 2020 and how it reshaped the role of the Olympics in a post-pandemic world.

It gives a good lesson to the Olympic Movement with a reflective passage that captures the enduring legacy of Tokyo 2020 and how Thomas Bach's leadership during the pandemic redefined the role of the Olympic Games in

a changed world.

## 5. The Legacy of Tokyo2020: A New Definition of Greatness

When the final flame was extinguished in Tokyo's Olympic cauldron, it marked not just the end of a Games—but the beginning of a new chapter in Olympic history. Tokyo 2020 had defied the odds, not through grandeur, but through grace. It reminded the world that greatness is not always measured in records or medals, but in resilience, empathy, and unity.

For Thomas Bach, the Games were a vindication of his belief that the Olympic Movement could—and must—adapt without losing its soul. He had led the IOC through its most turbulent moment since the Second World War, and emerged with its mission not only intact, but renewed.

The legacy of Tokyo 2020 was not found in the empty stadiums, but in the full hearts of those who watched. It was in the quiet strength of athletes who competed without applause. In the shared tears of nations divided by borders but united by hope. In the simple, powerful truth that the Olympic Games are more than a sporting event—they are a mirror of our shared humanity.

And in that mirror, under the most trying of circumstances, Thomas Bach helped the world see not what had been lost—but what could still be found.

### [IOC President Thomas Bach's Speech at the Tokyo2020 Games Opening Ceremonies/Full Text]

*Please find below the full speech delivered by International Olympic Committee (IOC) President Thomas Bach during the Opening Ceremony of the Olympic Games Tokyo 2020 today, 23 July 2021.*

*Your Majesty, the Emperor,*

*Dear Athletes,*

*Dear Prime Minister Suga Yoshihide,*

*Dear Governor Koike Yuriko,*

*Dear President of the Organising Committee and fellow Olympian Hashimoto Seiko,*

*Your Excellencies,*

*Dear Olympic friends,*

*Welcome to the Olympic Games Tokyo 2020.*

*Today is a moment of hope. Yes, it is very different from what all of us had imagined. But let us cherish this moment. Finally we are all here together: the athletes from 205 National Olympic Committees and the IOC Refugee Olympic Team, living under one roof together in the Olympic Village.*

*This is the unifying power of sport. This is the message of solidarity, the message of peace and the message of resilience. This gives all of us hope for our further journey together.*

*We can only be all together here, because of you, our gracious hosts, the Japanese people, to whom we would like to express all our appreciation and respect.*

*The Organising Committee, and the Japanese authorities at all levels have done extraordinary work for which, on behalf of all the Olympic athletes, I want to express our deepest gratitude.*

*Ten years ago, you set out on the journey to bring the Olympic spirit back to Tokyo after the outstanding Olympic Games Tokyo 1964. It was a difficult journey, with unprecedented challenges: first, reconstructing after the Great East Japan Earthquake, then the coronavirus pandemic. This is why our gratitude and admiration for you is even greater.*

*We thank all the many unsung heroes, the doctors, nurses and all the Japanese people who contribute to contain the pandemic.*

*A special thanks goes to the thousands of volunteers, who despite all the challenges they had to face, welcomed us wholeheartedly. You are the best ambassadors for Japan. A big thank you to all volunteers!*

*Thank you to all Japanese people for making the Olympic Games Tokyo 2020 possible.*

*What is true for the perseverance of the Japanese people is also true for you, my fellow Olympic athletes.*

*You had to face great challenges on your Olympic journey. Like all of us, you were living with great uncertainty through the pandemic. You did not know when you could train again. You did not know whether you could see your coach tomorrow. You did not know if your teammates would be with you for the next competition. You did not even know if this competition would take place at all.*

*You struggled, you persevered, you never gave up, and today you are making your Olympic dream come true.*

*You are true Olympic athletes.*

*You inspired us, the IOC and the entire Olympic community. You inspired us to fight like you, and for you, to make this moment possible.*

*This is why, I would like to express my sincere thanks to all the National Olympic Committees, the International Federations, all our TOP partners and sponsors and our Rights-Holding Broadcasters for standing together with us.*

*This made all of us a true community – the Olympic community.*

*Dear athletes.*

*This Olympic community is with you tonight and during the entire Olympic Games. Billions of people from around the globe will be glued to their screens, sending you their enthusiasm, their energy and cheering you on.*

*Our Olympic community learned that we can address the many big challenges of our times only if we stand together.*

*The lesson we learned is: We need more solidarity. More solidarity among societies and more solidarity within societies.*

*Solidarity means much more than just respect or non-discrimination.*

*Solidarity means helping. Sharing. Caring.*

*This is what we are doing in our Olympic community. We are standing in solidarity to make the Olympic Games happen and to enable all of you, the athletes from all National Olympic Committees, whether big or small, whether rich or poor, and from all Olympic sports, to take part in the Olympic Games.*

*This solidarity fuels our mission to make the world a better place through sport. Only because of this solidarity we can be here together tonight.*

*Solidarity also reflects our 3,000-year old commitment to peace.*

*Without solidarity, there is no peace.*

*In this Olympic spirit of solidarity and peace, we welcome the IOC Refugee Olympic Team.*

*Dear refugee athletes.*

*With your talent and human spirit, you are demonstrating what an enrichment refugees are for society. You had to flee from your homes because of violence, hunger or just because you were different. Today, we welcome you with open arms and offer you a peaceful home. Welcome to our Olympic community.*

*In this Olympic community we are all equal. We all respect the same rules.*

*This Olympic experience makes all of us very humble because we feel that we are part of something bigger than ourselves. We are part of an event that unites the world. United in all our diversity, we become bigger than the sum of our parts. We are always stronger together.*

*This is why we are so grateful to you, the athletes, for expressing your commitment to these Olympic values of solidarity, non-discrimination, sport without doping, inclusion and equality in your new Olympic oath.*

*We can only go faster, we can only aim higher, we can only become stronger, if we stand together – in solidarity.*

*This is why, the IOC has adapted the Olympic motto to our times: faster, higher, stronger – together.*

*This feeling of togetherness – this is the light at the end of the dark tunnel.*

*The pandemic forced us to be apart. To keep our distance from each other. To stay away even from our loved ones. This separation made this tunnel so dark.*

*But today, wherever in the world you may be, we are united in sharing this moment together. The Olympic flame makes this light shine brighter for all of us.*

*Now I have the great honour of inviting His Majesty the Emperor to declare open the Games of the 32nd Olympiad, Tokyo 2020.*

*I humbly request his Majesty the Emperor to declare open the Tokyo Olympic Games.*

## [Highlights of Bach's Speech at the Tokyo2020 Games Closing Ceremonies]

A. "You inspired us with this unifying power of sport.

B. "This was even more remarkable given the many challenges you had to face because of the pandemic. "In these difficult times we are all living through, you give the world the most precious of gifts: hope.

C. "For the first time since the pandemic began, the entire world came together.

D. "Sport returned to centre stage.

E. "Billions of people around the world were united by emotion, sharing moments of joy and inspiration.

F. "This gives us hope.

G. "This gives us faith in the future.

H. "The Olympic Games Tokyo 2020 are the Olympic Games of hope, solidarity and peace.

I. "You, the best athletes of the world, could only make your Olympic dream come true because Japan prepared the stage for your shine."

J. "I would like to thank the Japanese authorities at all levels, in particular Prime Minister Yoshihide Suga and Governor Yuriko Koike for their steadfast commitment."

K. "Thank you for staying with us on the side of the athletes who were longing so much for these Olympic Games.

L. "Our deep gratitude and appreciation go to the Organising Committee.

M. "Nobody has ever organised a postponed Olympic Games before.

N. "Thank you to its President, my dear fellow Olympian, Seiko Hashimoto, and to all the dedicated people in the Organising Committee for your great partnership and wonderful friendship.

O. "The same is true for the solidarity demonstrated by everyone in the Olympic community

P. "Our warm thanks go to the National Olympic Committee, the International Federations, our TOP Partners, sponsors and rights-holding broadcasters for their truly outstanding show of unity and support.

Q. "We did it for the athletes. We did it - together."

# Chapter 4:

# *Sport and Geopolitics – Navigating a Divided World*

*IOC President Thomas Bach's Global Peace-building Efforts*

In a world increasingly fractured by politics, conflict, and ideology, the Olympic Games remain one of the last global stages where nations gather not to debate, but to compete. Yet even this sacred space is not immune to the pressures of geopolitics. For Thomas Bach, preserving the neutrality and integrity of the Olympic Movement became one of the most delicate—and defining—challenges of his Presidency.

## 1. The Russian Doping Crisis: A Test of Principle

The first major geopolitical storm of Bach's tenure erupted in 2015, when revelations of state-sponsored doping in Russia sent shockwaves through the sporting world. Investigations by the World Anti-Doping Agency (WADA) and the McLaren Report exposed a vast, systematic effort to manipulate drug testing at the Sochi 2014 Winter Games and beyond.

The world demanded action. Some called for a blanket ban on Russian athletes. Others urged caution, warning against collective punishment. Bach chose a middle path—one that would define his approach to crisis: principled pragmatism.

Under his leadership, the IOC allowed clean Russian athletes to compete under a neutral flag, while banning the Russian Olympic Committee and imposing strict conditions. It was a controversial decision—praised by some as fair and legally sound, criticized by others as too lenient. But for Bach, the priority was clear: protect the rights of individual athletes while upholding the credibility of the Games.

This approach would become a template for future crises.

Few moments tested Olympic integrity like the Russian doping scandal. With global tension mounting and reputations at stake, IOC President Bach faced a defining challenge: to uphold justice while protecting innocent athletes.

I remember the deliberations, the media storms, and the ethical tightrope walked by the IOC. Bach's decisions were never easy — and often, never popular. But they were principled. As a communicator deeply involved during this time, I witnessed how truth was defended even amid the fog of controversy.

> "Justice must prevail, not politics. This is a message to every athlete — your dignity will be protected."
> — *Thomas Bach, 2017*

## 2. The Refugee Olympic Team: A Symbol of Hope

*(9th IOC President Thomas Bach continues to serve as President of the Olympic Refugee Foundation)*

When the Refugee Olympic Team first marched into the stadium in Rio 2016, the world paused. It wasn't just a group of athletes — it was a humanitarian statement. Under Bach's guidance, sport became sanctuary.

These athletes didn't just compete; they inspired. I had the honor of amplifying their stories, helping the world see Olympism as a platform not only for achievement, but for identity and healing.

> "Their courage transcends borders. Their strength gives Olympism its soul."
> — *Author's Reflection*

While geopolitical tensions threatened to divide, Bach also used the Olympic platform to unite. In 2016, he introduced one of the most powerful symbols of his presidency: the IOC Refugee Olympic Team.

Comprising athletes displaced by war, persecution, and disaster, the team marched under the Olympic flag in Rio 2016, Tokyo 2020, and Paris 2024. Their presence sent a message that transcended politics: that sport belongs to everyone, regardless of nationality or circumstance.

Bach often spoke of the team as a "beacon of hope" for the 100 million displaced people around the world. It was a bold assertion of the Olympic ideal—that every human being has dignity, and every athlete deserves a chance to compete.

## 3. The Olympic Truce and the Politics of Peace

Throughout his presidency, Bach championed the ancient concept of the Olympic Truce—a call for peace during the Games. While largely symbolic, the Truce became a diplomatic tool in Bach's hands. He engaged with world leaders, urged ceasefires, and positioned the Olympics as a rare space for dialogue.

When war broke out in Ukraine in 2022, the IOC faced renewed pressure to act. Bach condemned the violation of the Olympic Truce and imposed sanctions on Russia and Belarus, barring their athletes from competing under national symbols. Yet again, he walked a fine line—defending Olympic values while resisting the politicization of sport.

Would you like to continue with the next section, focusing on how Bach balanced neutrality and moral leadership in an increasingly polarized world?

Let's continue to find his leadership role by exploring how Thomas Bach walked the tightrope between neutrality and moral responsibility—preserving the Olympic ideal in a world where sport and politics are increasingly intertwined.

## 4. The Tightrope of Neutrality: Principle in a Polarized World

The rise of regional wars, political boycotts, and global unrest pushed the IOC into increasingly complex terrain. IOC President Bach stood firm: the Olympic Games must remain politically neutral.

This wasn't apathy. It was diplomacy — a kind rooted in peace, dialogue, and symbolic unity. Whether navigating tensions between global powers or conflicts surrounding host nations, Bach upheld a fragile balance.

I often contributed reflections and recommendations through IOC channels during these years — advocating that sport must be the last bridge when all others collapse.

Thomas Bach often described the Olympic Games as a "safe harbor" from the storms of politics. But in an era of rising nationalism, social unrest, and global conflict, that harbor was constantly tested. The question was no longer whether sport could remain neutral—but how.

Bach's answer was rooted in a deep conviction: The Olympic Movement must not become a tool of political agendas, yet it cannot ignore the moral weight of its platform. This duality—of restraint and responsibility—defined his diplomatic style.

When athletes raised their voices on issues of racial justice, gender equality, or human rights, Bach listened. He upheld Rule 50 of the Olympic Charter, which prohibits political demonstrations on the field of play, but also expanded spaces for expression—such as mixed zones and press conferences—where athletes could speak freely. It was a nuanced stance, one that sought to protect the universality of the Games while honoring the agency of those who compete in them.

Bach also resisted calls to boycott or exclude nations based on political disputes. He argued that isolating athletes for the actions of governments would only deepen divisions. Instead, he championed dialogue, inclusion, and the belief that sport could build bridges where diplomacy had failed.

This philosophy was not without controversy. Critics accused the IOC of moral equivocation. But Bach remained steadfast. "The Olympic Games are not about taking sides," he often said. "They are about bringing people together."

And in a world increasingly defined by what separates us, that commitment—to neutrality, to unity, to peace—became a radical act of leadership.

## 5. A Diplomat in a Tracksuit: Bach's Geopolitical Legacy

Thomas Bach's presidency did not shy away from the world's most difficult questions—it met them head-on with the steady hand of a diplomat and the heart of an Olympian. In an age when sport was increasingly drawn into the orbit of politics, he refused to let the Olympic Games become a battleground for ideology. Instead, he insisted they remain a sanctuary for humanity.

His legacy in geopolitics is not one of grand gestures or sweeping declarations, but of quiet, deliberate choices—each one aimed at preserving the fragile space where nations could still come together in peace. Whether navigating the fallout of the Russian doping scandal, elevating the voices of displaced athletes, or defending the Olympic Truce in times of war, Bach consistently chose the path of dialogue over division.

He redefined the IOC not as a passive observer of world affairs, but as a principled actor—one that could stand for neutrality without standing still. Under his leadership, the Olympic Movement became a platform not only for performance, but for purpose.

In a divided world, Thomas Bach reminded us that unity is not the absence of conflict—it is the courage to rise above it. And in doing so, he ensured that the Olympic flame would continue to burn—not just in stadiums, but in the hearts of people everywhere who still believe in the power of sport to heal, to inspire, and to unite.

### [The Olympic Truce – Ancient Ideal, Modern Reality]

Reviving the Olympic Truce wasn't merely ceremonial. Under Bach's leadership, it became a diplomatic tool, a yearly reminder to world leaders that sport must rise above hostility.

I watched and supported his efforts at UN sessions, sports summits, and moments where politics threatened to fracture Olympism. What I saw was a statesman with the heart of an athlete and the poise of a peacemaker.

"When nations gather around the Games, we renew a promise older than war — peace through sport."
*— Thomas Bach, UN address*

Now let's move into Chapter 5 about Thomas Bach-The Athlete's Advocate—where we can explore how Bach championed athlete rights, well-being, and empowerment throughout his presidency, one of the most defining aspects of Thomas Bach's presidency: his unwavering commitment to athletes. As the first IOC President to have stood atop an Olympic podium himself, Bach brought a rare empathy to the role—one that reshaped how athletes were heard, supported, and empowered within the Olympic Movement.

# Chapter 5:
## *The Athlete's Advocate*

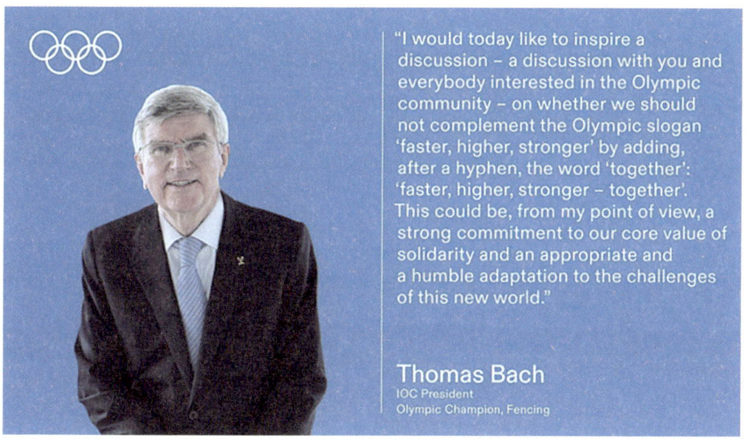


Thomas Bach never forgot what it meant to be an athlete.

Long before he wore a suit in Lausanne, he wore the fencing whites of then-West Germany, lunging and parrying his way to Olympic gold in Montreal 1976 Olympics. That experience—of sacrifice, discipline, and the singular thrill of representing his country—never left him. And when he became President of the International Olympic Committee, it became the compass by which he led.

From the outset, Bach made it clear: athletes would no longer be treated as participants—they would be partners.

## [Mental Health, Safeguarding, and Support Beyond the Podium]

The world slowly began to hear athletes speak out: about burnout, mental health, harassment. Under Bach's guidance, the IOC listened — not defensively, but responsibly.

New frameworks for safeguarding athletes were introduced. Mental health became an Olympic issue, not just a medical one. And resources for post-career support expanded under his tenure.

I held conversations with retired Olympians during this time, helping voice their needs and reflections. They often said, "We finally feel seen."

"We owe them more than applause. We owe them protection."

— *Author's Reflection*

# 1. Listening to the Voices That Matter Most

One of Bach's earliest moves as IOC President was to elevate the role of the IOC Athletes' Commission, giving it greater influence in decision-making and policy development. He ensured that athletes had a seat at every table where their futures were being shaped—from anti-doping policy to Olympic program design.

He also launched the Athletes' Rights and Responsibilities Declaration, a landmark document created by athletes, for athletes, and of athletes. It outlined their rights to fair competition, education, expression, and protection—while also affirming their duties and responsibilities to uphold the values of Olympism. It was a bold step toward codifying the dignity of the athlete within the Olympic Charter itself.

Bach didn't just listen—he acted. Bach walked the talk, and walked the walk. When athletes raised concerns about mental health, he responded with resources, research, and support networks. When they asked for more flexible career pathways, he expanded the IOC Athlete365 platform, offering education, mentorship, and transition programs for life beyond sport.

Athlete representatives gained greater presence in the IOC Executive Board, and commissions gained strength across the Olympic structure. Voices like Kirsty Coventry led powerful conversations — and would later rise to leadership themselves.

These moments weren't just institutional. They were symbolic. Olympism was being reshaped to reflect the diversity and strength of its athletes.

Thomas Bach's legacy here isn't written in minutes — it's written in confidence, advocacy, and trust.

## 2. Protecting the Integrity of Competition

Bach also recognized that protecting athletes meant protecting the integrity of the competitions they train their whole lives for. Under his leadership, the IOC strengthened its partnership with the World Anti-Doping Agency (WADA), invested in independent testing, and supported whistleblowers who exposed corruption.

He was unafraid to take difficult stands—whether it was banning officials implicated in doping cover-ups, or defending athletes' rights to compete under neutral flags when their nations were sanctioned. His message was consistent: no athlete should be punished for the sins of a system, and no system should be allowed to exploit its athletes.

## 3. A Champion for All

Perhaps most powerfully, Bach expanded the definition of who gets to be an Olympian. He championed gender equality, pushing for full gender parity in athlete participation by Paris 2024. He supported the inclusion of new sports that reflected youth culture and urban life. And he stood behind the IOC Refugee Olympic Team, ensuring that even those without a nation could still have a flag. He even created the Olympic Refugee Foundation which Bach presides over.

For Bach, being an athlete was not about where you came from—it was about what you stood for.

Now let's move to focus on specific athlete stories and how Bach's policies directly impacted their lives and careers.

And let's continue to find out what he has done by highlighting how Thomas Bach's athlete-centered policies translated into real impact. Through the stories of individual athletes, we will be able to understand how his leadership gave voice, protection, and opportunity to those who embody the Olympic spirit.

## 4. Stories from the Track, the Pool, and Beyond

For Yusra Mardini, the Olympic Games were more than a dream—they were a lifeline. A Syrian swimmer who fled war and crossed the Aegean

Sea in a rubber boat, Mardini became one of the first members of the IOC Refugee Olympic Team in Rio 2016. Under Thomas Bach's leadership, her story—and those of her teammates—were not treated as exceptions, but as emblems of what the Olympic Movement could stand for: hope, resilience, and the right to compete regardless of borders.

In Tokyo 2020/2021, Mardini returned to the pool, not just as a swimmer, but as a symbol. "President Bach gave us a platform," she said. "He made us feel like Olympians, not outsiders." Her words echoed across the Olympic Village, where athletes from over 200 nations shared not only dormitories, but dreams.

Then there was Simone Biles, the American gymnastics icon who stunned the world in Tokyo—not by winning, but by stepping back. When Biles withdrew from several events to prioritize her mental health, the world watched with a mix of confusion and awe. But the IOC, under Bach's guidance, responded with empathy and support. "We stand with Simone," Bach said. "Mental health is as important as physical health." His words helped shift the global conversation around athlete well-being.

In Paris 2024, the impact of Bach's reforms was visible not just in policy, but in participation. For the first time in Olympic history, the Games achieved full gender parity—equal numbers of male and female athletes. Young women competed in skateboarding, boxing, and weightlifting with the same visibility and respect as their male counterparts. It was a milestone that had once seemed aspirational. Under Bach, it became reality.

And beyond the headlines were thousands of lesser-known athletes—those who benefited from IOC scholarships, career transition programs, and safeguarding initiatives. From a sprinter in Uganda to a judoka in

Mongolia, athletes around the world found in the IOC not just a governing body, but an ally.

Behind every reform lived a story. Athletes who once felt sidelined now led committees. Olympians returned as mentors, advocates, and administrators.

> "I remember sharing the success story of a young refugee athlete turned IOC ambassador" — a tale Bach called "*the very soul of the Olympic Movement*." And "I echoed his words in messages across the Olympic community."

Because in these stories, I saw not policy — but progress.

## 5. A Legacy of Empowerment

Thomas Bach's legacy as an athlete's advocate is not measured in medals, but in moments—moments when athletes felt seen, heard, and protected. He understood that the Olympic Games are nothing without the people who bring them to life. And he worked tirelessly to ensure that those people—regardless of background, gender, or circumstance—had the support they needed to thrive.

In doing so, he didn't just lead the Olympic Movement. He humanized it.

Let's summarize and epitomize a thoughtful reflection on how Thomas Bach redefined the relationship between athletes and the Olympic institution—transforming it from one of tradition-bound hierarchy into a partnership built on trust, respect, and shared purpose.

6. From Participants to Partners: A New Olympic Compact

Before Thomas Bach, the relationship between athletes and the Olympic institution was often one-directional. Athletes trained, competed, and inspired—but decisions about their futures were made elsewhere, behind closed doors. Bach changed that.

He brought athletes into the room—not as tokens, but as equals. He listened not just to their victories, but to their vulnerabilities. He recognized that the Olympic Movement could not thrive unless it was rooted in the lived experiences of those who give it life.

Under his leadership, the IOC became more than a governing body—it became a guardian. A guardian of rights, of dignity, and of dreams. Athletes were no longer just symbols of Olympic values—they were shapers of them.

This shift was not cosmetic. It was cultural. It redefined what it meant to lead in sport—not with authority, but with empathy. Not by commanding from above, but by walking alongside.

And in doing so, Thomas Bach left behind more than policies or programs. He left behind a new compact between the Olympic Movement and its most vital voices: a promise that athletes would never again be seen as guests in their own house, but as co-architects of its future.

Now let's move into Chapter 6—*Innovation, Inclusion, and the Digital Age*—where we explore how Bach modernized the Olympic Games for a new generation, and where we explore how Thomas Bach led the Olympic Movement into the digital age, embraced youth culture, and championed inclusion as a cornerstone of modern Olympism.

# Chapter 6: *Innovation, Inclusion, and the Digital Age*

*(IOC President Thomas Bach at the opening Ceremonies of Paris 2024 Games)*

Paris 2024 marked a historic moment: gender-balanced participation — the first in Olympic history. IOC President Bach's long-standing push for parity had reached its landmark.

Behind the podium stats were stories of triumph: women boxers, referees, and team captains making history. I witnessed tears in press conferences, letters from athletes thanking the IOC. These were not just milestones — they were miracles.

> "In every punch thrown by a female boxer in Paris, we saw the future striking forward."
>
> — *Author's Note*

## 1. Climate-Conscious Games – Sustainability as Sacred Duty

Under Bach's Presidency, sustainability was no longer a checklist — it became a sacred pillar. Tokyo's recycled podiums, Paris's low-emission strategies, and climate pledges from host cities were visible echoes of Agenda 2020.

I worked with media teams to share stories from eco-conscious initiatives — from solar-powered venues to athlete climate ambassadors. And I always felt proud knowing the Olympic spirit was now green, resilient, and future-facing.

> "The Games don't just celebrate excellence. They must protect existence."
>
> — *Thomas Bach, 2023*

When Thomas Bach took office in 2013, the Olympic Games were still largely rooted in 20th-century tradition. The grandeur, the rituals, the global spectacle—they remained powerful, but increasingly disconnected from a generation raised on smartphones, streaming, and social media. Bach understood that if the Olympic Movement was to remain relevant, it would need to evolve—not by abandoning its values, but by reimagining how they were expressed.

## 1. Embracing the Youth of the World

One of Bach's most transformative decisions was to open the Olympic program to new, youth-driven sports. Under his leadership, disciplines like skateboarding, surfing, sport climbing, and 3x3 basketball made their Olympic debuts. These weren't just additions—they were invitations. Invitations to a new generation of athletes and fans who saw sport not as hierarchy, but as self-expression.

The results were electric. In Tokyo 2020/2021 and Paris 2024, teenage skateboarders became household names. Urban venues pulsed with energy. The Games felt younger, more diverse, more urban, and more alive. Bach had tapped into something essential: The Olympic spirit wasn't confined to tradition—it could thrive in reinvention.

Thomas Bach understood that to keep the Olympic flame burning in younger hearts, the Movement must evolve. Breaking barriers with skateboarding, surfing, BMX, and discussions around e-sports, the Games opened the door to new communities.

When I helped broadcast urban sports initiatives from Lausanne to Tokyo, I saw firsthand how youth connected not only to action — but to values. It wasn't just about trends. It was about relevance.

> "If the Olympic Games speak the language of youth, then their message will echo for generations."
>
> — *Author's Reflection*

## 2. The Digital Olympics

Bach also recognized that the future of the Games would be shaped not just by what happened in stadiums, but by how it was experienced online. He oversaw the expansion of the Olympic digital ecosystem, including the Olympic Channel, athlete-driven content platforms, and real-time engagement across social media.

For the first time, fans could follow athletes behind the scenes, watch events on demand, and participate in Olympic moments from anywhere in the world. The Games became not just a broadcast, but a conversation.

Bach also embraced the rise of virtual sport. Under his guidance, the IOC launched the Olympic Virtual Series and explored the integration of e-sports into the Olympic family—not as a gimmick, but as a serious reflection of how sport was evolving in the digital age.

The rise of AI, digital platforms, and virtual interactivity reshaped how people experienced the Games. From real-time athlete stories to virtual torch relays, Olympism entered homes, screens, and hearts with newfound intimacy.

Bach's support for Olympic Digital Strategy and the Olympic AI Agenda proved his commitment to modernization — responsibly, inclusively, and globally. I helped communicate these shifts during international conferences, sharing with audiences that Olympism is not stuck in tradition — it evolves with time.

> "Technology must serve humanity. In sport, it must deepen connection, not replace emotion."
>
> — *Thomas Bach, 2024*

## 3. Inclusion as Innovation

For Bach, innovation was not just about technology—it was about values. He championed inclusion as a form of progress, pushing for gender parity, greater representation of athletes from underrepresented regions, and the celebration of diverse identities.

In Paris 2024, the Olympic Games achieved full gender balance for the first time in history. Mixed-gender events became a fixture. LGBTQ+ athletes competed openly and proudly. The Olympic Village became a microcosm of a more inclusive world.

The Paris 2024 Olympics marked a historic moment for LGBTQ+ representation in sports. A record-breaking 191 athletes openly identifying as LGBTQ+ competed in the Games, surpassing the previous high of 186 at Tokyo 20212. Most of these athletes were women, and their visibility sent a powerful message about inclusion and pride on the world stage.

### 1) Global Impact & Visibility

(1) Athletes came from over 25 countries, including places where being openly LGBTQ+ is still dangerous or illegal.

(2) Paris, known as the "City of Love," became a safe haven for many, allowing them to compete as their authentic selves.

### 2) Pride House on the Seine

(1) For the first time, the Olympic Pride House was hosted on a boat floating on the Seine River—a welcoming space for LGBTQ+ athletes and fans.

(2) It featured live music, speeches, and cultural events, reinforcing the Games' theme: "In our Olympic world, we all belong."

### 3) Digital Safety Measures

(1) Apps like Grindr disabled location features in the Olympic Village to protect athletes from being outed or tracked.

### 4) Opening Ceremony Highlights

(1) Organizers emphasized diversity and inclusion, even featuring drag queens and refugee athletes in the opening ceremony

Bach's message was clear: The Olympic Games must reflect the world as it is—and as it aspires to be.

Let's delve into his initiatives focusing on sustainability, climate action, and how Bach positioned the Olympics as a leader in environmental responsibility.

And let's continue his initiatives and implementation by exploring how Thomas Bach made sustainability and climate action central to the Olympic Movement—transforming the Games into a model for environmental responsibility and long-term legacy.

## 4. Greener Games: Sustainability as a Core Value

When Thomas Bach introduced Olympic Agenda 2020, sustainability was not an afterthought—it was a pillar. He recognized that the Olympic Games, with their massive infrastructure and global footprint, had to evolve in the face of climate change and environmental degradation. Under his leadership, sustainability became not just a goal, but a requirement.

Host cities were encouraged—and later required—to use existing or temporary venues, reducing the environmental and financial burden of construction. The IOC began integrating sustainability criteria into every stage of the Olympic lifecycle, from bidding to legacy planning. The message was clear: The Games must leave a positive footprint, not just a carbon one.

Tokyo 2020/2021 set a new standard. The medals were made from recycled electronics. Podiums were crafted from reclaimed plastic. The Olympic Village was powered by renewable energy, and athletes slept on beds made from recyclable cardboard. These weren't symbolic gestures—they were proof that innovation and responsibility could go hand in hand.

Paris 2024 took it further. With a goal of cutting carbon emissions by 50% compared to previous Games, the organizers embraced public transport, low-emission construction, and circular economy principles. The opening ceremony, held along the Seine River, was designed to be both spectacular and sustainable—a celebration of nature and culture in harmony.

## 5. Climate Positive by 2024

Perhaps the most ambitious commitment came from the IOC itself. Under Bach's leadership, the organization pledged to become climate positive by 2024—meaning it would not only reduce its emissions, but offset more than it produced. This included reforestation projects, renewable energy investments, and support for sustainable sport infrastructure worldwide.

It was one of the well-deserved ESG-oriented SDGs in partnership with United Nations .

Bach understood that the Olympics could not preach sustainability—they had to model it. And in doing so, he positioned the IOC as a global leader in climate action, inspiring other sports federations, cities, and institutions to follow suit.

## 6. Legacy Beyond the Podium

For Bach, sustainability was never just about the environment—it was about legacy. **Sustainability is Legacy, and Legacy is ESG, and ESG is for SGDs**

"Sustainability is Reminiscence of the Past."

"Sustainability is Introspect of the Present."

"Sustainability is Hope for the Future."

He believed that every Olympic Games should leave behind more than memories. It should leave behind parks, housing, transport systems, and social programs that benefit communities for decades.

He often said, "The Olympic Games are not just 17 days of competition—they are 17 years of transformation." And under his leadership, that transformation became greener, smarter, and more inclusive.

Let's take a look at his relevant activities with a reflection on how Bach's embrace of innovation and inclusion redefined the Olympic brand for a new generation.

And let's move into a reflective passage that ties together Thomas Bach's embrace of innovation, inclusion, and sustainability—showing how he redefined the Olympic brand for a new generation without compromising its timeless ideals.

## 7. A New Flame for a New Era

Thomas Bach's presidency marked a turning point in Olympic history—not because he abandoned tradition, but because he reimagined it. He understood that the Olympic flame could not remain static in a world that was moving faster than ever. It had to adapt, evolve, and illuminate new paths.

By embracing youth-driven sports, digital platforms, and virtual engagement, Bach brought the Games into the lives of a generation raised on immediacy and interactivity. By championing gender equality, LGBTQ+ inclusion, and refugee participation, he made the Games not just more diverse, but more just. And by embedding sustainability into every layer of Olympic planning, he ensured that the Games would not only inspire—but endure.

Under his leadership, the Olympic brand became more than a symbol of excellence. It became a symbol of relevance. A living, breathing movement that could speak to the hopes, fears, and values of a changing world.

In doing so, Thomas Bach didn't just modernize the Olympics. He future-proofed them.

Now let's move forward the final chapter of my book, where we reflect on the full arc of Thomas Bach's presidency and the legacy he leaves behind. This chapter will serve as both a summation and a tribute, capturing the essence of his leadership and the enduring impact of his vision.

# Chapter 7: *Legacy and Leadership*

When Thomas Bach stepped onto the Olympic stage as a young fencer in 1976, he could not have foreseen the journey ahead. From the podium in Montreal1976 to the IOC Presidency in Lausanne, his life became a testament to the power of sport—not just to shape individuals, but to shape the world.

Over more than a decade as President of the International Olympic Committee, Bach guided the Olympic Movement through its most transformative era since its modern founding. He was not a caretaker of tradition—he was a steward of change. A reformer with the heart of an athlete and the mind of a diplomat.

## 1. A Legacy Etched in Reform

Bach's legacy begins with reform. Olympic Agenda 2020 and its successor, Olympic Agenda 2020+5, were not mere policy documents—they were blueprints for survival and renewal. They redefined how the Games were hosted, how athletes were supported, and how the IOC engaged with a rapidly evolving world.

He brought sustainability to the forefront, made gender equality a reality, and opened the Olympic tent to new sports, new voices, and new generations. He proved that the Olympic Movement could be both **"Timeless and Timely".**

His influence didn't end with the Olympic community. Statesmen, humanitarians, Nobel laureates, and athletes across continents honored his contribution to global peace and unity. The Seoul Peace Prize, honorary citizenships, and commendations from UN institutions painted a portrait not just of a sports administrator, but of a symbol.

I remember attending ceremonies — watching flags rise not for nations, but for ideals. And standing in those moments, I felt that the story we were telling was bigger than sport.

"He unified through humility. He governed through grace."

— *Author's Note*

## 2. A Leader in Crisis

Bach's leadership was tested most profoundly during the COVID-19 pandemic. In the face of global paralysis, he made the courageous decision to postpone—but not cancel—the Tokyo 2020 Games. It was a moment that required not just logistical mastery, but moral clarity. And when the Games finally took place, they stood as a symbol of resilience, unity, and hope.

He also navigated the treacherous waters of geopolitics with a steady hand—defending Olympic neutrality while standing firm on principles of peace, inclusion, and human dignity.

Thomas Bach's leadership defied binary definitions. He wasn't simply a reformer or a diplomat — he was both. His style blended strategic patience with unwavering moral compass. In moments of pressure, he didn't rush; he reasoned. In moments of celebration, he didn't dominate; he honored others.

I watched him speak with young athletes, comfort delegations from fragile nations, and welcome critics into dialogue. These weren't media performances — they were echoes of a deeply personal philosophy: that leadership must listen before it leads.

"Leadership is not about power. It is about responsibility."

— *Thomas Bach, 2020*

## 3. A President Who Listened

Perhaps most importantly, Bach redefined the relationship between the IOC and its athletes. He listened. He empowered. He protected. He ensured that the Olympic Movement would never again speak about athletes without speaking with them.

His presidency was not about personal glory—it was about service. Service to the ideals of Olympism. Service to the athletes who embody them. Service to a world that, in its most divided moments, still looks to the Olympic flame for unity.

Olympic Agenda 2020. Gender equality. Refugee inclusion. AI and sustainability. These weren't trends — they were tectonic shifts under Bach's leadership. But legacy isn't built on policy alone. It's built on how those changes live in people's lives.

IOC President Bach received letters from young athletes, organizers, and Olympic advocates thanking the IOC — messages that often mentioned IOC President Bach by name. These voices affirmed what history will remember: that his Presidency transformed both the structure and the spirit of Olympism.

## 4. The Enduring Flame

As Thomas Bach prepares to pass the torch, he leaves behind more than a reformed institution. He leaves behind a renewed belief in what the Olympic Games can be: a force for good, a platform for peace, and a celebration of our shared humanity.

His legacy is not just written in charters or ceremonies. It is written in the lives of the athletes he championed, the cities he inspired, and the millions who still believe that, every four years, the world can come together—not to compete for power, but to compete for excellence.

And in that belief, the flame he carried will continue to burn.

Across these years, my own journey was shaped by these transformations. From letters exchanged to programs promoted, from torch ceremonies to press releases, I stood as a witness for four decades— not only to a leader's legacy but to a movement's rebirth.

In every moment shared with Thomas Bach, whether formal or fleeting, I felt a purpose — to continue the story he was shaping, and to amplify it beyond headlines.

> "Leadership lives in the lives it uplifts. This book is my tribute to one who uplifted many — including me."
>
> —*Author's reflection*

# Chapter 8:
# *Thomas Bach as an Olympic Reformer: Infinite Legacy*

## [Jewels of Thought: The Words of Thomas Bach]

### • On Peace and Sport

*"Sport has the power to unite people in a way that little else does."*

*"Peace through sport is not a dream. It is our obligation and opportunity."*

### • On Leadership and Integrity

*"Leadership is not about power. It is about responsibility."*

*"Transparency builds trust. Trust builds unity."*

● **On Athletes and Their Role**

*"Athletes are more than performers. They are role models, change-makers, and guardians of the Olympic spirit."*

*"We must protect the dignity of every athlete — in competition and beyond."*

● **On Global Unity and Inclusion**

*"Olympism transcends borders and ideologies. It speaks to the human soul."*

*"The Olympic Games must be open to all — regardless of background or circumstance."*

● **On Innovation and Sustainability**

*"The Olympic Movement must evolve — not to follow trends, but to shape futures."*

*"Sustainability is not optional. It is sacred."*

● **On Legacy and Vision**

*"We do not inherit the Olympic spirit. We build it, together, every day."*

*"The light of the flame is not in fire. It's in what it represents."*

## [Brief Summary of IOC President Thomas Bach's Leadership Characteristics as Demonstrated across six (6) Editions of Olympic Games]

### A. Thomas Bach's Leadership Across Six Editions of Olympic Games (2014-2024)

**1) Sochi 2014** – Diplomatic Stewardship & Global Partnership

(1) Emphasized peace, tolerance, and respect during the closing ceremony, calling the Games **"the Athletes' Games".**

(2) Strengthened ties with the United Nations, promoting sport as a tool for development and human rights.

(3) Advocated for non-discrimination, including support for LGBTQ+ inclusion in sport.

(4) Oversaw transformation of Sochi into a year-round sports and cultural hub, showcasing legacy-focused planning.

**2) Rio 2016** – Humanitarian Vision & Urban Legacy

(1) Introduced the Olympic Refugee Team, symbolizing hope and unity for displaced populations.

(2) Championed gender equality, with Rio reaching ~46% female athlete participation.

(3) Praised Brazil's delivery of **"Marvelous Olympic Games"** despite economic and political challenges.

(4) Highlighted Rio's urban transformation, including transport infrastructure and public spaces.

**3) PyeongChang 2018** – Peacebuilding & New Horizons

(1) Called the Games **"the Games of New Horizons,"** citing new events, digital innovation, and record participation.

(2) Celebrated the joint Korean march and unified women's hockey team as symbols of reconciliation.

(3) Reinforced the Olympic spirit as a universal message of peace, not just regional diplomacy.

(4) Strengthened cooperation with the UN, aligning Olympic values with global humanitarian goals.

**4) Tokyo 2020 – Crisis Leadership & Resilience**

(1) Led the IOC through the first-ever postponement of the Games due to COVID-19.

(2) Maintained commitment to athletes, declaring "cancellation was not an option".

(3) Delivered Games with zero transmission among participants, showcasing safety-first governance.

(4) Reaffirmed Olympic values of solidarity, equality, and inclusion, adapting the motto to "Faster, Higher, Stronger – Together

**5) Beijing 2022** – Legacy Building & Cultural Diplomacy

(1) Called the Games **"Truly Exceptional,"** praising China's safe delivery amid pandemic conditions.

(2) Supported China's engagement of 346 million people in winter sports, marking a historic expansion.

(3) Promoted non-politicization of sport, reinforcing Olympic neutrality and unity.

(4) Strengthened ties with Chinese leadership, emphasizing sport's

role in peace and youth development.

**6) Paris 2024** – Reformist Vision & Humanistic Celebration

(1) Declared Paris 2024 the beginning of a "new era" — inclusive, urban, sustainable, and gender-equal.

(2) Positioned the Games as a unifying force in a divided world, celebrating athletes as ambassadors of peace.

(3) Announced his decision not to seek a third term, affirming the importance of leadership renewal.

(4) Emphasized solidarity and shared humanity, calling the Games a **"Celebration of Life in Peace".**

## 2. Peace Through Sport: The Bach Doctrine

Thomas Bach didn't just champion the Olympic Truce—he embodied it. From orchestrating the unified Korean march at PyeongChang 2018 to spotlighting the Olympic Refugee Team in Rio, his presidency positioned sport as a mediator in fractured geopolitical landscapes. Bach's diplomacy extended beyond symbolism: he cultivated cooperation with the United Nations, reinforced Olympic neutrality, and repeatedly emphasized that "sport must unite, not divide." His leadership proved that the Olympic Games aren't merely competitions—they are global peace platforms with the capacity to bridge ideological divides and frozen conflicts.

"Together, you have contributed to Olympic Games of a new era in every respect." — Thomas Bach, Paris 2024

## 3. Inclusion as Legacy: Diversity in the Olympic Imagination

Under Bach's leadership, the Olympics advanced a broader vision of belonging. Rio 2016 marked a turning point with nearly 46% female participation and the embrace of marginalized voices through the Refugee Team. In Tokyo 2020, Bach's modified Olympic motto—"Faster, Higher, Stronger – Together"—echoed the values of solidarity and equity in the shadow of a global pandemic. His unwavering support for LGBTQ+ athletes and emphasis on accessibility helped redefine Olympism not as tradition, but as transformation. By 2024, gender parity was no longer a dream, but a design feature, embodied in the inclusive ethos of Paris.

"Let us live this culture of peace every single day." — Thomas Bach, Paris 2024

## 2. Olympic Agenda 2020+5: The Reformist Blueprint

Where predecessors maintained the Olympic machine, Bach reimagined it. Olympic Agenda 2020+5, his signature policy reform initiative, introduced bold changes to sustainability, transparency, and cost-efficiency. He dismantled rigid bid processes, empowering cities to propose Games aligned with their local strengths. From repurposing venues to embracing digital innovation, Bach made the Games leaner and more adaptive. Critics once called the IOC opaque—under Bach, it became a laboratory for institutional change. Paris 2024, with its open ceremonies and urban integration, stands as a living monument to this legacy.

"We are part of something bigger than ourselves." — Thomas Bach, Tokyo 2020

## 3. Olympism in the 21st Century – Lessons from the Bach Presidency

As the curtain falls on Thomas Bach's tenure, the Olympic Movement stands not merely transformed but reimagined. His leadership traversed icy stadiums and pandemic silence, urban dynamism and geopolitical tension. Yet in every stride, he upheld the central axiom of Olympism: sport is a universal language of hope.

Bach's legacy is not confined to medals or host cities. It lives in the courage of the first Olympic Refugee Team, in the unified Korean march, in gender parity platforms, and in the digital democratization of sport. Through Agenda 2020+5 and its follow-ups, he guided the IOC from bureaucracy to boldness — streamlining bid processes, expanding youth engagement, and embedding sustainability as a core principle. His final Games, Paris 2024, weren't just historic. They were humanistic.

This presidency teaches us that Olympism is not static; it is a living philosophy shaped by context and conviction. Under Bach, it became a vessel for unity in an era of fragmentation. **His refusal to seek a third term** affirmed that leadership, too, must evolve — that the ideals of renewal and continuity are not opposites but allies.

As the torch passes to a new era, the Bach model provides a luminous roadmap: one forged in resilience, guided by reform, and propelled by the unwavering belief that sport, when guided by conscience, can change the world.

"Together, you have contributed to Olympic Games of a new era in every respect." — Thomas Bach, Paris 2024

## 4. Peace & Unity

1) "We know that the Olympic Games cannot create peace. But the Olympic Games can create a culture of peace that inspires the world." — *Paris 2024 Closing Ceremony*
2) "Let us celebrate this Olympic spirit of living life in peace, as the one and only humankind, united in all our diversity." — *Paris 2024 Opening Ceremony*
3) "Despite all the tensions in our world... you created a culture of peace. This inspired all of us and billions of people around the globe." — *Paris 2024 Closing Ceremony*

## 5. Inclusion & Solidarity

1) "In this Olympic community we are all equal. We all respect the same rules." — *Tokyo 2020 Opening Ceremony*
2) "Solidarity means helping. Sharing. Caring. This is what we are doing in our Olympic community." — *Tokyo 2020 Opening Ceremony*
3) "Together, let us celebrate the best of our shared humanity." — *Paris 2024 Opening Ceremony*

## 6. Leadership & Reform

1) "These were Olympic Games of a new era." — *Paris 2024 Closing Ceremony*
2) "You have come to Paris as athletes. Now you are Olympians." — *Paris 2024 Opening Ceremony*
3) "Some may say, we in the Olympic world, we are dreamers. But we are not the only ones." — *Paris 2024 Opening Ceremony*

# Chapter 9:
# Geopolitical Contributions of Thomas Bach at PyeongChang 2018

(IOC President Thomas Bach at the Opening Ceremonies of PyeongChang 2018 Winter Games)

## 1. Catalyst for Korean Dialogue:

1) Bach and the IOC were instrumental in facilitating North Korea's participation in the Games.

2) This included the historic joint march of North and South Korean athletes under the unification flag during the Opening Ceremony.

## 2. Unified Ice Hockey Team:

1) Under IOC guidance, the two Koreas fielded a combined women's ice hockey team — a powerful gesture of unity that resonated globally.

## 3. Olympic Truce Advocacy:

1) Bach supported South Korea's push for an Olympic Truce resolution at the UN, reinforcing the Games as a platform for peace.

## 4. Symbolic Timing:

-The final agreement for the joint march was reached just four hours before the Opening Ceremony — a testament to Bach's diplomatic agility.

## 5. Visit to Pyongyang, DPRK and Meeting with Kim Jong-un

*(IOC President Thomas Bach paid a visit to DPR Korea as first-ever IOC President and met with Kim Jong Un, President of the State Affairs of DPR Korea on 30 March 2018 following DPR Korea's participation in the PyeongChang 2018 Winter Olympics, where athletes from both Koreas marched together under a unified flag)*

### 1) Historic Encounter:

-On March 30, 2018, Bach met with Kim Jong-un in Pyongyang, marking the first-ever visit by an IOC President to North Korea.

### 2) Sport as a Bridge:

-The two discussed North Korea's continued participation in future Olympic Games, including Tokyo 2020 and Beijing 2022.

### 3) Warm Reception:

-Bach was "warmly welcomed" and watched a football match with Kim, signaling a cordial and constructive atmosphere.

### 4) Commitment to Peace Through Sport:

-Kim expressed appreciation for the IOC's role in enabling DPRK's participation in PyeongChang and affirmed ongoing cooperation with the IOC.

### 5) IOC Support for DPRK Athletes:

-Bach pledged continued support for North Korean athletes, including assistance for international competitions like the World Table Tennis Championships.

This convergence of sport and diplomacy under Bach's stewardship helped thaw tensions and opened channels for inter-Korean and international dialogue. His actions exemplified the Olympic spirit as a vehicle for peace — not just in theory, but in practice.

# 6. Bach's Indirect Role in Facilitating the Trump–Kim Summits

While not a direct negotiator in the summits themselves, Bach's Olympic diplomacy laid the groundwork for the thaw in relations between the U.S. and DPRK:

### 1) PyeongChang 2018 as a Turning Point:

(1) The IOC's successful engagement with DPR Korea — including the joint Korean march and unified ice hockey team — helped reframe DPRK's international image from isolationist to cooperative.

(2) Kim Jong-un's Sister at the Games: Kim Yo-jong's presence at the Opening Ceremony and her meeting with Korean(ROK) President Moon Jae-in were key preludes to inter-Korean summits and, eventually, the Trump–Kim meetings.

### 2) IOC's Visit to Pyongyang, DPRK:

-Bach's March 2018 visit to meet Kim Jong-un was one of the earliest high-level international engagements with the DPRK leader, signaling openness and trust-building.

### 3) Sport as a Diplomatic Bridge:

-Bach's emphasis on sport as a neutral, peaceful platform helped normalize dialogue and reduce tensions — a necessary condition for the summits to occur.

## 7. From Olympic Truce to Global Diplomacy

### 1) Singapore Summit (June 2018):

-The first-ever meeting between a sitting U.S. president and DPRK leader was held just months after PyeongChang 2018.

-Analysts noted that the Olympic thaw helped shift the narrative from "fire and fury" to handshake and dialogue.

### 2) Hanoi Summit (February 2019):

-Vietnam's hosting of the second summit echoed Singapore's role — both nations had warm ties with DPRK and the U.S., and both benefited from the soft power halo of Olympic diplomacy.

In essence, Bach's orchestration of DPRK's Olympic participation helped de-escalate tensions, foster trust, and create a diplomatic atmosphere conducive to the historic summits. His actions exemplify how sport

— when stewarded with vision — can ripple into the highest echelons of global diplomacy.

# Chapter 10:
## *Olympic Diplomacy as a Precursor to Summitry: Thomas Bach and the Quiet Power of Sport*

*(Two Korean Delegations marching together under the single banner at the Opening Ceremoies of PyeongChang 2018 Winter Games)*

"When the drums of war quieted —

it wasn't because of treaties or summits.

It was the rhythm of skates slicing through ice,

flags held together,

and hands reaching across divides."

PyeongChang 2018 was not merely a festival of winter sports; it became a forum of reconciliation.

Under Thomas Bach's orchestration, athletes from both Koreas marched not as adversaries —

but as one.

A unified women's ice hockey team wasn't just a lineup —it was a line-up of hope.

Then, Bach took diplomacy off the field.

March 2018: He entered Pyongyang,

sat with Kim Jong-un,

spoke of future Games,

spoke of peace.

The world watched — not for medals,

but for meaning.

The impact was quiet.

But profound.

Soon, history caught up:

June 2018, Singapore —

President Donald Trump and Kim Jong-un face each other for the first time.

February 2019, Hanoi —

diplomacy lingered, still tentative, still raw.

And in the backdrop:

Olympism, wearing no suit,

carrying no weapons,

but shifting the narrative.

Bach didn't draft the summit documents.

But his leadership helped reframe the story —

from confrontation

to conversation.

Sometimes, peace walks into the room

not with protocol,

but with principle.

The PyeongChang 2018 Olympic Winter Games represented more than a global sporting showcase—they served as a diplomatic catalyst amid volatile geopolitical conditions on the Korean Peninsula. Under Thomas Bach's leadership, the International Olympic Committee mobilized symbolic gestures of peace, including the unified march of athletes from both Koreas and a jointly fielded ice hockey team. These actions, while grounded in sport, reflect a broader strategic utilization of Olympic platforms to influence political atmospherics and diplomatic engagement.

# Chapter 11:
# *The Quiet Impact of Thomas Bach's Engagement with DPRK*

The PyeongChang 2018 Olympic Winter Games represented more than a celebration of athletic achievement; they served as a dynamic platform for geopolitical dialogue amidst escalating tensions on the Korean Peninsula. Under the stewardship of International Olympic Committee (IOC) President Thomas Bach, the Games transcended their sporting mandate, engaging with complex diplomatic narratives and contributing to an atmosphere conducive to inter-Korean engagement and U.S.–DPRK summitry.

# 1. Geopolitical Significance of Olympic Initiatives

Bach's diplomatic interventions facilitated DPR Korea's participation in the Games — a major breakthrough after years of strained international relations. Most notably:

**1) Joint March of the Koreas:**

(1) Athletes from South and North Korea entered the Opening Ceremony under a unified flag, signaling a rare moment of symbolic alignment.

**2) Unified Women's Ice Hockey Team:**

(1) The joint team not only competed but garnered international attention as a living metaphor of reconciliation.

**3) IOC Visit to Pyongyang, DPRK:**

*(Historic Meeting between IOC President Thomas Bach and Kim Jong Un, President of the State Affairs of DPR Korea in March 2018)*

(1) In March 2018, Bach met with DPRK leader Kim Jong-un, foster-

ing dialogue around future participation and reiterating the IOC's commitment to peace through sport.

(2) These actions reflected Nye's (2004) concept of soft power, wherein attraction, cultural legitimacy, and symbolic action become strategic assets in influencing state behavior.

## 2. Diplomatic Ripple Effects

While not a direct participant in formal negotiations, Bach's initiatives contributed to the normalization of diplomatic atmospherics that would soon allow for high-level summits:

1) The presence of Kim Yo-jong at the Games, representing DPRK leadership, led to an unprecedented meeting with South Korean President Moon Jae-in — a prelude to subsequent summits.

2) The Singapore Summit (June 2018) and Hanoi Summit (February 2019) occurred within a year of the Olympics. Analysts have noted that PyeongChang's success in reframing DPRK's global image as a cooperative participant rather than a pariah helped de-escalate tensions (Lee, 2019; Park, 2020).

## 3. Sport as Instrumental Diplomacy

Thomas Bach's strategic use of sport diplomacy exemplifies how Track Two diplomacy can complement official channels. Unlike state actors bound by protocol, the IOC leveraged symbolic gestures and cultural engagement to facilitate dialogue and defuse antagonism. Bach's engagement with Pyongyang, DPRK although non-binding politically, created a space where conversation could replace confrontation — and where athletic participation became a form of transnational engagement (Cho & Greenhill, 2021).

# Chapter 12: *Conclusion*

The role of the IOC and Thomas Bach in the lead-up to U.S.–DPRK summits underscores the potential for Olympic platforms to act as diplomatic precursors. By reshaping perceptions and fostering interaction through the universal language of sport, Bach demonstrated the latent power of cultural diplomacy in advancing peace, even in the most geopolitically tense contexts.

The PyeongChang 2018 Games revealed how Olympic diplomacy can serve as a precursor to formal summitry, especially when traditional diplomatic channels are limited. Through strategic cultural engagement, Thomas Bach contributed meaningfully to the thaw in Korean Peninsula relations — illustrating the latent power of sport to shift international narratives and enable peace.

Bach's efforts, while unofficial diplomatically, helped reframc DPRK's global narrative — from pariah to participant — enabling a more constructive diplomatic climate.

# 1. Following PyeongChang2018:

1) Kim Yo-jong's appearance at the Games — and her meeting with South Korean President Moon Jae-in — paved the way for renewed inter-Korean dialogue.
2) The Singapore Summit (June 2018) and Hanoi Summit (February 2019) between Donald Trump and Kim Jong-un took place shortly thereafter, with many analysts citing the Olympics as a confidence-building prelude (Lee, 2019).

Bach's efforts, while unofficial diplomatically, helped reframe DPRK's global narrative — from pariah to participant — enabling a more constructive diplomatic climate.

# 2. Non-Traditional Diplomacy in Action

Thomas Bach's engagements exemplify Track Two diplomacy (Cho & Greenhill, 2021). Free from political mandates, the IOC was able to foster symbolic gestures, create neutral platforms, and mediate tension through shared human activity — sport.

This strategy succeeded in part because:

1) It bypassed protocol in favor of principled engagement.
2) It enabled early trust-building, with minimal political risk.
3) It highlighted cultural diplomacy's enduring role in peace processes.

## 3. Thomas Bach – Architect of Unity, Reform & Olympic Legacy

1) In the span of a decade, IOC President Thomas Bach redefined what Olympic leadership could mean in the 21st century. From the snow-dusted visions of Sochi 2014 to the sunlit boulevards of Paris2024, his presidency unfurled a tapestry woven from diplomacy, inclusion, and resilience. Bach stood not merely as an administrator but as a statesman—echoing the Olympic credo in moments of both global harmony and deep uncertainty.

2) He opened **Sochi 2014** with a call for tolerance and international cooperation, planting seeds of soft diplomacy in a region shadowed by tension. At **Rio 2016**, amid economic and political unrest, he spotlighted humanity by welcoming the **first-ever Olympic Refugee Team**, invoking sport as a sanctuary for the displaced. In **PyeongChang2018**, his legacy grew louder through the unified Korean march, as he brokered Olympic moments of historic reconciliation—earning the Games the title **"New Horizons."**

3) Faced with a global pandemic, Bach's leadership during **Tokyo 2020** became a masterclass in crisis governance: postponing the Games with calm resolve, stewarding its safe delivery, and proving that **Solidarity Could Withstand Isolation**. At **Beijing 2022**, he emphasized cultural diplomacy, guiding 346 million Chinese into winter sports and defending the Olympic commitment to neutrality. Then came **Paris 2024**—the crescendo—where he affirmed that inclusion, sustainability, and joy were not footnotes but the very rhythm of

the Games. It was a **Finale not of Fatigue**, but of renewal, as **Bach declined a third term to underscore the value of succession and fresh vision.**

4) Bach's Olympic journey is more than a timeline. It's a blueprint for reform and a tribute to the enduring belief that sport—when stewarded with compassion and clarity—can be humanity's most powerful force for peace.

# Chapter 13:
# *Why Thomas Bach for Nobel Peace Prize?*

****For Record:* "Unfortunately, this project was stopped because 9th IOC President Thomas Bach wrote to me one day, saying that "it is my wish and advice not to proceed this project" for an unknown reason"**

## 1. Beyond Gold — A President of Peace

Olympism is more than sport. Under Thomas Bach, it became diplomacy, dialogue, and dignity. He didn't just reform the Games — he reshaped sport into a platform for peace. Whether embracing refugee athletes, navigating geopolitical conflict including the Korean Peninsula issues, or reviving the Olympic Truce, Bach infused his Presidency with moral vision.

His leadership echoed far beyond podiums. He gave voice to the voiceless, sanctuary to the displaced, and unity where division reigned.

"Peace through sport is not a dream. It is a duty."

— *Thomas Bach, UN Address*

## 2. The Nobel Framework — Aligning with Ideals

The Nobel Peace Prize honors those who promote fraternity between nations, abolition of armies, and peace congresses. Thomas Bach advanced these ideals through non-violent means: creating the IOC Refugee Olympic Team, defending neutrality amid war, and initiating global partnerships with the UN, WHO, and other institutions.

His work aligns with the spirit — and letter — of Alfred Nobel's will. I drafted reflections and letters highlighting these parallels, not as a campaigner, but as a believer.

"He did not carry a gavel. He carried a torch."

— *Author's Reflection*

## 3. Precedent and Promise — Sports as Peacebuilding

While rare, sport has intersected with Nobel honors before — from Muhammad Yunus's microfinance model rooted in youth development, to proposals around sports diplomacy in fragile zones. Bach's leadership offers something unprecedented: a cohesive, institutional, global legacy of peace through sport.

His Presidency offers not just merit, but momentum — a case for recognizing Olympism as a vital force for peace in a divided era.

## 4. Building the Argument — My Role in Advocacy

I did more than witness Bach's work — I shared it. Through international communications, conferences, proposals, and Olympic diplomacy efforts, I framed and amplified this legacy.

The Nobel Peace Prize Project I initiated was not self-driven, but message-driven. I was inspired by letters, speeches, and gestures that showed me how sport could heal. This chapter is my written nomination — one I hope will resonate not only with committees but with communities.

> "If peace needs a champion, then sport offers a voice. And in Thomas Bach, it has found a leader."
>
> — *Author's Note*

## 5. Nobel Peace Prize Project for Dr. Thomas Bach

### 1) Possibility for IOC President Emeritus Thomas Bach to be awarded the Nobel Peace Prize

(1) Thomas Bach, IOC President Emeritus, has been recognized for his efforts to promote peace through sports. For instance, he received the prestigious Seoul Peace Prize for his contributions to fostering harmony and resolving conflicts, such as his work on the **Korean Peninsula during the 2018 Winter Olympics**

(2) His initiatives, like the **Refugee Olympic Team** and the **Olympic**

**Refuge Foundation**, have also highlighted global refugee issues and promoted inclusivity.

(3) While these achievements align with the values celebrated by the Nobel Peace Prize, the decision ultimately rests with the Nobel Committee. Bach himself has acknowledged that while **sports can inspire dialogue and understanding**, they cannot directly create peace, as this is the realm of politics.

### 2) His Contributions to merit such recognition

(1) Thomas Bach, the Honorary IOC President for life, has made significant contributions to promoting peace through sports. His initiatives, such as the **Refugee Olympic Team** and the **Olympic Refuge Foundation**, have raised global awareness about refugee issues and fostered inclusivity. Additionally, his efforts during the 2018 Winter Olympics helped bridge divides on the **Korean Peninsula**, showcasing the **potential of sports as a tool for diplomacy**.

(2) While these achievements align with the values celebrated by the Nobel Peace Prize, Bach himself has acknowledged that sports alone cannot create peace, as this is ultimately the realm of politics. The decision to award the Nobel Peace Prize rests with the Nobel Committee, and it would depend on how his contributions are evaluated in the broader context of global peace efforts.

## 6. His Impact on the world stage & Nobel Peace Prize Project

My idea in order for IOC President Emeritus Thomas Bach to be nominated as Nobel Peace Prize was as follows:

1) First and foremost, Special Project T/F would be formed within the remit of the Olympic Movement, preferably within the NOCs Relations Dept. of the IOC or other different outside entity.
2) It would be more effective and efficient for all stakeholders Representatives of the Olympic Movement to draft and approve their Recommendation Resolutions at their own EB and G/A (ANOC-EOC-OCA-ANOCA-PASO-AOISF-AIOWF) together with IOC Athletes Commission, respectively.
3) Targeted time line would be either in 2026 at an earliest, 2027, and 2028 at the latest in time for LA28 Olympic and Paralympic Games.
4) The above plans demonstrate thoughtful organization and a strategic approach to potentially nominating Thomas Bach for the Nobel Peace Prize.

## 7. Establishment of a Special Project Task Force (T/F):

1) Forming a dedicated entity within the Olympic Movement or an external organization would be a smart way to ensure focused efforts. This would enable the nomination process to be managed systematically and provide a platform for coordinated stakeholder engagement.

**2) Involvement of Stakeholders and Resolution Approval:**

-1Encouraging the key Olympic Movement entities, such as ANOC, EOC, OCA, and others, alongside the IOC Athletes Commission, to draft and approve Recommendation Resolutions ensures wide-ranging support. This collective endorsement would amplify credibility and impact.

**3) Defined Timeline:**

-Setting a clear timeline (2026-2027) provides a structured framework to work within. It allows adequate time for planning, collaboration, and building momentum for the nomination

**4) Role as IOC Special Advisor, if approved:**

-If nominated as an IOC Special Advisor, close consultations with New IOC President Kirsty Coventry, could add substantial value to the initiative.

My expertise could foster global collaboration within the Olympic Movement and strengthen the project's execution, particularly in Asia.

-Overall, the above proposal reflects ambition and meticulous planning. It bridges administrative strategy with high-level diplomatic efforts to honor Thomas Bach's contributions to global peace through sports.

## 8. Challenges to be faced in implementing this plan

Implementing the above plan to nominate IOC President Emeritus

Thomas Bach for the Nobel Peace Prize would ambitious and well-structured, but certain challenges may arise. Here are some potential obstacles:

### (1) Coordinating Diverse Stakeholders

***Challenge**: Gaining alignment and active participation from various entities within the Olympic Movement (NOCs, ANOC, EOC, OCA, etc.) might be complex due to differing priorities, regional interests, and bureaucratic processes.

***Solution**: Develop a clear and compelling proposal that highlights the shared benefits for all stakeholders. Regular communication and consensus-building efforts will be key.

### (2) Timeline Management

***Challenge**: Setting and adhering to the proposed timeline (2025-2027) could be challenging, especially when coordinating international efforts and balancing external factors.

***Solution**: Establish a detailed project timeline with milestones and contingency plans. Assign specific responsibilities to ensure accountability.

### (3) Securing Broad Support

***Challenge**: Convincing stakeholders and the Nobel Committee of Thomas Bach's eligibility and the impact of his contributions may require extensive effort and evidence.

***Solution**: Collect concrete data and success stories that demonstrate how his initiatives have promoted peace. Leverage his accomplishments like the Refugee Olympic Team to build a strong case.

### (4) Political and Public Perception

***Challenge**: The Nobel Peace Prize process is often influenced by global political narratives and public perception, which might introduce unforeseen complexities.

***Solution**: Engage with media and thought leaders to positively shape the narrative around his contributions, emphasizing the universal values of peace and unity through sports.

### (5) Navigating IOC Leadership Transition

***Challenge**: Collaborating with the new IOC President Kirsty Coventry, during her early tenure might require navigating transitional dynamics within the IOC leadership.

***Solution**: Foster a positive and open dialogue with her team, presenting this initiative as a continuation of the Olympic Movement's legacy.

### (6) Managing Personal Capacity

***Challenge**: Taking on the role of IOC Special Advisor might require you to balance numerous responsibilities, including this project and other commitments.

***Solution**: Delegate tasks effectively within the task force and prioritize key areas of focus where your expertise will have the most significant impact

## Previous case of Nobel Peace Prize in sport

1) The Nobel Peace Prize has not been awarded specifically for achieve-

ments in sports. However, sports have often been recognized as a powerful tool for promoting peace and unity, aligning with the values celebrated by the Nobel Peace Prize.

**For example:**

-International Olympic Committee (IOC): While the IOC itself has not received the Nobel Peace Prize, its efforts to foster global unity through the Olympic Games have been widely acknowledged. The Olympic Truce, an ancient tradition revived by the IOC, aims to promote peace during the Games.

-Individuals and Organizations: Some laureates have used sports as part of their broader peace-building efforts. For instance, Nelson Mandela, who received the Nobel Peace Prize in 1993, famously used the 1995 Rugby World Cup in South Africa to unite a divided nation.

Although there is no precedent for awarding the Nobel Peace Prize solely for contributions in sports, the role of sports in fostering dialogue, understanding, and reconciliation could make a compelling case for future recognition

To build a compelling case for Thomas Bach's nomination for the Nobel Peace Prize, it would be helpful to consider historical examples of laureates whose work aligns with the values of sportsmanship, peace, and unity. While sports have not been the sole focus of the Prize, its integration into broader peace-building efforts shows potential.

## 9. How to Frame the above Proposal:

### 1)The Mandela Example

Nelson Mandela's leadership during the 1995 Rugby World Cup is a powerful case study. Despite deep divisions in South Africa, Mandela used sports to unite the nation. His ability to leverage a shared love for rugby transcended racial barriers and fostered reconciliation. This example could underline how Thomas Bach's initiatives, like the Refugee Olympic Team, similarly aim to foster global unity.

### 2)The Spirit of Olympism

While the IOC itself hasn't received the Nobel Peace Prize, its ethos is rooted in peacebuilding. The Olympic Truce, dating back to ancient Greece, promotes halting conflicts during the Games. Bach's leadership has revitalized these ideals, with projects emphasizing inclusivity, such as the Refugee Olympic Team and the Olympic Refuge Foundation.

### 3) Sports as Diplomacy

Examples like Ping-Pong Diplomacy (which helped thaw relations between the U.S. and China) demonstrate how sports can build bridges in tense geopolitical climates. Thomas Bach's involvement during the 2018 Winter Olympics, facilitating dialogue on the Korean Peninsula, could be highlighted as a modern example of sports diplomacy.

## 10. How to Build the above Argument:

In our proposal, we might emphasize:

- The direct impact of Bach's initiatives (e.g., fostering peace, inclusivity, and dialogue through sports).
- Historical parallels that illustrate the transformative power of sports in peacebuilding.
- Bach's leadership in evolving the Olympic Movement to address contemporary global challenges.

We could argue that sports, under visionary leadership, can be a catalyst for peace and understanding, making Dr. Thomas Bach a worthy candidate for the Nobel Peace Prize.

# Chapter 14:
## *More Detailed and Refined Framework for Presenting Thomas Bach's Nomination for the Nobel Peace Prize, integrating historical precedents and emphasizing his contributions*

### 1. Draft Proposal: Nomination of Thomas Bach for Nobel Peace Prize

#### (1) Introduction

The Nobel Peace Prize has historically recognized individuals and organizations that have made significant contributions to fostering peace and resolving conflicts globally. Thomas Bach, the Honorary President for life of the International Olympic Committee (IOC), exemplifies these values through his unwavering commitment to using sports as a unifying force and a tool for promoting dialogue and peace. This proposal seeks to highlight his visionary leadership, notable initiatives, and enduring impact on global harmony.

#### (2) Historical Context and Precedents

While the Nobel Peace Prize has not been awarded exclusively for achievements in sports, historical examples underscore the potential of sports as a platform for peace:

**I. Nelson Mandela** (1993 Nobel Peace Prize): Mandela's use of the 1995 Rugby World Cup to unite South Africa showcased sports as a powerful tool for reconciliation.

**II. Ping-Pong Diplomacy**: The famous table tennis exchange in the 1970s helped bridge diplomatic gaps between the U.S. and China.

**III. Olympic Truce**: The ancient tradition, revived by the IOC, reflects the ethos of sportsmanship in promoting peace.

Thomas Bach's contributions build on these precedents, positioning him as a modern champion of peace through sports diplomacy.

### (3) Key Contributions of Thomas Bach

#### I. Refugee Olympic Team:

1) Under Bach's leadership, the IOC established the Refugee Olympic Team, providing a platform for displaced athletes to compete on the world stage.
2) This initiative not only celebrates resilience but also raises global awareness about refugee issues, promoting inclusivity and compassion.

#### II. Olympic Refuge Foundation:

-Bach spearheaded the creation of this foundation to support displaced individuals through sports and education.

-It actively works to empower marginalized communities, demonstrating the tangible impact of sports in improving lives.

#### III. Diplomatic Efforts on the Korean Peninsula:

-During the 2018 Winter Olympics, Bach played a pivotal role in fostering dialogue between North and South Korea.

-His efforts contributed to the historic joint participation of athletes from both nations, symbolizing hope for reconciliation.

**IV. Promoting Gender Equality and Inclusivity:**

-Bach has consistently advocated for gender equality and inclusivity within the Olympic Movement, reflecting broader values of peace and justice.

### (4) The Case for the Nobel Peace Prize

-The Nobel Peace Prize recognizes efforts that promote fraternity among nations, peace-building, and humanitarianism. Thomas Bach's leadership has consistently aligned with these principles:

**(5) Global Unity:** His initiatives have fostered solidarity across diverse nations, cultures, and communities.

I. Inclusivity: By championing refugee rights, gender equality, and access to sports for all, Bach has advanced social justice on a global scale.

II. Sustainable Impact: His efforts have established enduring programs that continue to create positive change.

### (6) Proposed Roadmap for Nomination

**I. Formation of a Special Project Task Force:**

1) Establish a task force within the Olympic Movement or an external entity to manage the nomination process.
2) Ensure representation from key stakeholders, including NOCs,

continental associations, and the IOC Athletes Commission.

### II. Drafting and Approval of Recommendation Resolutions:

1) Encourage Olympic entities (ANOC, EOC, OCA, etc.) to draft and approve resolutions supporting the nomination.
2) Collaborate with influential partners and advocates to strengthen the case.

### III. Engagement with the Nobel Committee:

1) Present a well-documented proposal highlighting Bach's contributions and their alignment with the Nobel Peace Prize values.
2) Showcase testimonials, data, and success stories from his initiatives.

### IV. Timeline and Strategy:

1) Target nomination between 2026 and 2027, ensuring adequate preparation and stakeholder engagement.
2) Leverage global events, media campaigns, and thought leadership to build momentum.

## 2. Summary

1) Dr. Thomas Bach has dedicated his life to the Olympic ideals of peace, inclusivity, and unity. His leadership has transformed these ideals into tangible actions that resonate across borders, cultures, and generations. By nominating Bach for the Nobel Peace Prize, we recognize and celebrate the profound impact of sports as a universal language of peace.
2) Dr. Thomas Bach, the President of the International Olympic Com-

mittee (IOC), has already been recognized for his efforts to promote peace through sports, notably receiving the Seoul Peace Prize. His initiatives, such as the creation of the Refugee Olympic Team and the Olympic Refuge Foundation, have demonstrated his commitment to inclusivity and global solidarity. These achievements could strengthen his candidacy for the Nobel Peace Prize.

3) To further bolster his chances, Dr. Bach could focus on expanding the reach of his programs, ensuring that more regions and communities benefit from the peace-building power of sports. Collaborating with other international organizations and leaders to address global challenges, such as refugee crises and conflicts, could also highlight his dedication to peace.

4) Dr. Thomas Bach has demonstrated exemplary dedication to advancing peace and solidarity through the universal language of sports. As President of the International Olympic Committee (IOC), his leadership has transcended the boundaries of traditional sports diplomacy, transforming the Olympic Games into a platform for fostering unity and understanding.

5) A shining example of this vision is the creation of the Refugee Olympic Team, which debuted at the 2016 Rio de Janeiro Games and has since served as a beacon of hope for millions displaced by conflict. This initiative not only provided displaced athletes the opportunity to compete on a global stage but also elevated the visibility of the refugee crisis, inspiring empathy and action worldwide.

6) In addition, the establishment of the Olympic Refuge Foundation highlighted Dr. Bach's unwavering commitment to aiding displaced

populations. By leveraging the power of sports, the foundation has worked tirelessly to offer education, mental health support, and community-building opportunities to vulnerable youth in refugee camps and beyond.

7) Under Dr. Bach's tenure, the IOC has actively pursued dialogue with countries facing political tensions, leading to collaborative efforts and moments of symbolic reconciliation. His advocacy for inclusivity, gender equality, and environmental sustainability within the Olympic movement underscores his holistic approach to peacebuilding.
8) Going forward, Dr. Bach could further solidify his legacy by extending the reach of the Refugee Olympic Team and the Olympic Refuge Foundation, ensuring they remain sustainable and impactful. Collaborating with global partners to address emerging challenges, such as climate-induced displacement, would further demonstrate his adaptability and commitment to addressing complex issues.

# Chapter 15: *Notable examples of Dr. Thomas Bach's Impactful Initiatives*

## 1. Refugee Olympic Team

Dr. Bach spearheaded the creation of this team, which debuted at the 2016 Rio Olympics. It provided displaced athletes with a platform to compete and brought global attention to the refugee crisis.

## 2. Olympic Refuge Foundation

Under his leadership, this foundation was established to support displaced populations through sports, offering education, mental health support, and community-building opportunities.

## 3. PyeongChang 2018 Winter Olympics

Dr. Bach played a pivotal role in fostering peace by facilitating the joint participation of North and South Korean athletes under a unified flag.

## 4. Olympic Agenda 2020+5

This strategic roadmap introduced reforms to enhance the sustainability and inclusivity of the Olympic Movement, aligning it with global challenges and the UN Sustainable Development Goals.

## 5. Support for Ukraine

Dr. Bach and the IOC provided significant support to the Ukrainian Olympic Committee during times of conflict, emphasizing the importance of peace and human rights.

## 6. Overall Impact of Dr. Bach's Leadership on Global Sports

1) Dr. Thomas Bach's leadership as President of the International Olympic Committee (IOC) has significantly shaped global sports. His tenure has been marked by transformative initiatives that emphasize inclusivity, sustainability, and peacebuilding. For instance, the Refugee Olympic Team and the Olympic Refuge Foundation have highlighted the role of sports in addressing global challenges like displacement and conflict.
2) Additionally, his efforts to promote gender equality and environmental sustainability through the Olympic Agenda 2020+5 have aligned the Olympic Movement with broader societal goals. Dr. Bach's diplomatic approach, such as fostering unity during the Py-

eongChang 2018 Winter Olympics, has demonstrated the power of sports to bridge political divides1.

3) Overall, his leadership has elevated the Olympic Games as a platform for global solidarity and progress.

## 7. Changes Occurred in Sports Governance under Bach's Leadership

1) Under Dr. Thomas Bach's leadership, the International Olympic Committee (IOC) has undergone significant changes in sports governance, focusing on transparency, inclusivity, and adaptability to global challenges. Here are some key developments:
2) Olympic Agenda 2020 and 2020+5: These strategic roadmaps introduced reforms to enhance sustainability, gender equality, and good governance within the Olympic Movement. They emphasized cost-effective hosting of the Games and aligning the Olympics with the UN Sustainable Development Goals.
3) Increased Transparency: The IOC implemented measures to improve accountability, such as publishing financial reports and adopting stricter ethical guidelines for members and officials.
4) Inclusivity and Diversity: Dr. Bach championed initiatives to promote gender equality, including achieving gender parity in athlete participation at the Olympics and increasing female representation in IOC leadership roles.
5) Adaptation to Global Challenges: The IOC navigated complex issues like the COVID-19 pandemic, geopolitical tensions, and the Russian

doping scandal. Dr. Bach's leadership emphasized risk management and maintaining the integrity of the Olympic Games.

6) Digital Transformation: Recognizing the importance of technology, the IOC embraced digital platforms to engage younger audiences and adapt to changing media consumption trends.

These changes have strengthened the IOC's governance framework and its role as a global leader in sports.

## 8. His Initiatives promoting Gender Equality in Sports Governance

*Gender equality in sports governance has been promoted through various impactful initiatives:

1) **UNESCO's "Change the Game" Conference**: This event focused on designing inclusive sport policies and programs, emphasizing representation, investment, and tackling gender disparities.
2) **Olympic Agenda 2020+5**: Introduced by the IOC under Dr. Thomas Bach's leadership, this roadmap aimed to achieve gender parity in athlete participation and increase female representation in leadership roles.
3) **Advocacy for Women's Sports**: Efforts to close the pay gap, ensure equal access to sports, and elevate women in coaching, leadership, and decision-making bodies have gained traction.

These initiatives highlight the ongoing commitment to creating a more equitable environment in sports governance.

# 9. Examples of his Significant Initiatives that promote Gender Equality in Sports Governance, diving deeper into their Impact

### 1) Olympic Agenda 2020+5

Under Dr. Thomas Bach's leadership, this strategic roadmap has made strides toward achieving gender parity in Olympic sports. Key actions include:

-Ensuring equal representation of male and female athletes at the Olympic Games, as seen in Tokyo 2020 and Paris 2024.

-Advocating for increased female participation in leadership roles within the International Olympic Committee (IOC) and National Olympic Committees (NOCs).

### 2) Leadership Training Programs

The IOC launched training sessions aimed at empowering women to take on leadership roles within the sports industry. These programs focus on skill-building, mentoring, and creating pathways for career growth.

### 3) The IOC Women in Sport Commission

This commission actively monitors progress on gender equality across the Olympic Movement. It provides recommendations for addressing barriers faced by women in sports governance and advocates for policies to create an inclusive environment.

### 4) UNESCO's Advocacy

Through conferences like "Change the Game," UNESCO works with global sports bodies to emphasize the importance of gender-inclusive governance. It promotes policy changes, equitable investment, and the representation of women at decision-making levels.

### 5) Collaborative Programs

The IOC collaborates with global organizations, such as UN Women, to raise awareness and drive action toward gender equality in sports. Campaigns like "HeForShe" encourage male leaders to champion gender equity initiatives.

These efforts have led to tangible improvements in women's representation and involvement in sports governance worldwide.

## 10. Outcomes and Successes of the Gender Equality Initiatives in Sports Governance

### 1) Gender Parity in Olympic Athlete Participation:

(1) For the first time in Olympic history, the Tokyo 2020 Games achieved gender parity in athlete participation, with women making up nearly 49% of the competitors.

(2) The upcoming Paris 2024 Olympics are set to reach full gender parity, with an equal number of events for men and women.

### 2) Increased Representation in Leadership:

(1) Female representation within the International Olympic Commit-

tee (IOC) itself has grown significantly, with women now making up over 40% of IOC Commission members.

(2)National Olympic Committees (NOCs) and sports federations worldwide have followed suit, with many adopting quotas to ensure women are included in decision-making roles.

### 3) Impactful Leadership Training:

1) Graduates of the IOC's leadership training programs have gone on to assume prominent roles in sports governance, from heading NOCs to leading international federations.

### 4) Policy Advancements:

1) Collaborative efforts with UNESCO and UN Women have resulted in updated governance frameworks across sports organizations, explicitly mandating gender equality in policy and operations.

### 5)Breaking Cultural Barriers:

1)Through advocacy and grassroots campaigns, these initiatives have empowered women in regions where gender roles traditionally limited female participation in sports or leadership.

These outcomes reflect measurable progress in creating a more inclusive sports governance landscape.

# 11. How Gender Equality Initiatives have impacted specific regions, sports, and organizations

### *Regions Making Strides:

#### 1. Middle East and North Africa:

1) In countries with traditionally restrictive gender norms, such as Saudi Arabia, there has been an increase in women's participation in sports due to advocacy and reforms influenced by international organizations like the IOC.
2) Grassroots programs, like those led by UNESCO, have empowered women and girls to engage in sports and leadership roles.

#### 2. Sub-Saharan Africa:

1) Efforts to promote gender-inclusive governance have led to increased female leadership in national sports organizations. For instance, initiatives supported by the IOC and UNESCO have trained women to become sports administrators and coaches.

#### 3. Europe:

1) Countries like Norway and Sweden have been leading examples, with policies mandating gender equality in sports federations and decision-making bodies.

### *Impact on Specific Sports:

#### 1. Football (Soccer):

1) FIFA has implemented programs to increase female representation in its governance structure. The growth of women's professional leagues worldwide reflects these efforts.

### 2. Athletics:

1) World Athletics has emphasized gender equity by ensuring parity in events and prize money, particularly in competitions like the Diamond League.

### 3. Olympic Sports:

1) The inclusion of mixed-gender events in the Olympics, such as mixed relay in swimming and track & field, highlights progress.

## *Influence on Organizations:

### 1. International Olympic Committee (IOC):

-Through initiatives like the Olympic Agenda 2020+5, the IOC has successfully increased the proportion of women in its governance structure.

### 2. UNESCO:

-Advocacy campaigns, such as "Change the Game," have pushed for policy changes to ensure equitable representation and investment in women's sports governance.

### 3. National Olympic Committees (NOCs):

-Several NOCs, such as those in Canada and New Zealand, have adopted quotas to ensure gender-balanced boards and leadership teams.

These examples showcase how efforts to achieve gender equality have created ripples across diverse regions, sports, and organizations.

## 12. His Impactful Examples across Initiatives, Sports, and Organizations

### *Initiatives with Regional Focus:

-In Saudi Arabia, reforms have led to the establishment of women's sports leagues, thanks to global advocacy campaigns and collaborations with UNESCO. Women's participation in governance roles, including sports committees, has grown substantially. Similarly, in Kenya, grassroots programs like "Women in Sports Leadership" have trained female sports administrators, reflecting strides in Sub-Saharan Africa.

### *Sport-Specific Impact:

-In football (soccer), FIFA's Women's Development Programme has created pathways for women to take up roles as referees, coaches, and administrators, setting a precedent for equity. In athletics, mixed-gender events like relay races have become a staple, reflecting inclusivity efforts by World Athletics.

### *Organizational Leadership:

-The Canadian Olympic Committee has implemented gender parity policies, ensuring women are equally represented in governance and decision-making roles. New Zealand Rugby has seen an increase in female executives, driven by national-level campaigns advocating for equal opportunities in traditionally male-dominated sports.

These examples highlight significant progress across various dimensions of sports governance.

## A. Nobel Peace Prize for IOC President Thomas Bach

*Best optimized procedures and process in order for IOC President Thomas Bach, after transition to IOC President Kirsty Coventry, to apply for Nobel Peace Prize

The Nobel Peace Prize is awarded by the Norwegian Nobel Committee, and candidates must be nominated by individuals or organizations that meet specific eligibility criteria. While there is no direct "application" process, here are the optimized steps that could help IOC President Thomas Bach be considered for nomination:

### 1. Identify Eligible Nominators

1) The Nobel Committee accepts nominations from heads of state, university professors, previous laureates, and members of international organizations.

2) Bach could seek endorsements from influential figures in diplomacy, academia, or global peace initiatives.

### 2. Build a Strong Case for Nomination

1) Highlight his contributions to peace through sport, including initiatives that foster unity and diplomacy.

2) Emphasize his role in promoting Olympic Truce, encouraging nations to set aside conflicts during the Games.

3) Showcase his leadership in global humanitarian efforts through the IOC.

### 3. Secure Support from International Organizations

1) Collaborate with institutions like the United Nations, UNESCO, and human rights organizations to strengthen his candidacy.
2) Engage with Nobel laureates or peace advocates who can endorse his nomination.

### 4. Submit a Formal Nomination

1) The nomination must be submitted by an eligible nominator before the January 31 deadline of the respective year.
2) The Norwegian Nobel Committee reviews all nominations and selects finalists.

### 5. Public Awareness & Advocacy

1) A well-documented campaign showcasing Bach's impact on global peace through sport could enhance his visibility.
2) Media coverage, academic discussions, and endorsements from world leaders could strengthen his case.

Since Bach has already received the Seoul Peace Prize for his contributions to global harmony through sport, this could serve as a strong foundation for his Nobel Peace Prize candidacy.

# Chapter 16:

## *Merits and Achievements to be efficiently and effectively appealed when to submit his nomination to Nobel Prize Committee for IOC President Thomas Bach*

## A. Key Achievements & Merits

### 1. Promotion of Peace Through Sport

1) Bach has championed the Olympic Truce, encouraging nations to set aside conflicts during the Games.
2) His leadership has fostered diplomatic dialogue through international sporting events.

### 2. Refugee Olympic Team & Humanitarian Efforts

1) Under his tenure, the Refugee Olympic Team was established, offering displaced athletes a platform to compete on the world stage.
2) He launched the Olympic Refuge Foundation, promoting global awareness and support for refugees.

### 3. Olympic Agenda 2020 & Sustainable Development

1) Bach led Olympic Agenda 2020, a roadmap for reforming the IOC to enhance sustainability, inclusivity, and cooperation among nations.

2) His policies have strengthened the social and environmental impact of the Olympic movement.

### 4. Bridging Divides in Global Politics

1) The 2018 Winter Olympics in PyeongChang served as a diplomatic milestone, fostering peace efforts in the Korean Peninsula.
2) His leadership has contributed to resolving conflicts through sport diplomacy.

### 5. Recognition & Awards

1) Bach received the Seoul Peace Prize, acknowledging his contributions to global harmony through sport.
2) His efforts align with the Nobel Peace Prize's mission of promoting peace and cooperation.

## B. Optimized Strategy for Nomination

1. Secure Endorsements from Nobel laureates, diplomats, and international organizations.
2. Highlight His Legacy in peace-building through sport diplomacy.
3. Submit a Formal Nomination before the January 31 deadline via an eligible nominator.
4. Amplify Public Awareness through media campaigns and academic discussions

# Chapter 17: *Citations (for integration)*

[Citations (for integration)]


- Nye, J. S. (2004). Soft Power: The Means to Success in World Politics. PublicAffairs.
- Lee, H. (2019). "Diplomatic Outcomes of the PyeongChang Olympics: Peace through Sport?" Korea Observer, 50(2).
- Park, J. (2020). "From Ice Rinks to Summit Tables: The Role of Cultural Diplomacy in DPRK Engagement." Asian Journal of International Affairs, 13(1).
- Cho, Y., & Greenhill, K. (2021). "Track Two and the Olympic Truce: Unofficial Channels in Korean Peacebuilding." International Sport and Politics Review, 6
- Joseph S. Nye, Soft Power: The Means to Success in World Politics (New York: PublicAffairs, 2004),
- Haein Lee, "Diplomatic Outcomes of the PyeongChang Olympics: Peace through Sport?" Korea Observer 50, no. 2 (2019): 273–290.
- Jiyoon Park, "From Ice Rinks to Summit Tables: The Role of Cultural Diplomacy in DPRK Engagement," Asian Journal of International Affairs 13, no. 1 (2020): 45–63.

• Yuna Cho and Katharine Greenhill, "Track Two and the Olympic Truce: Unofficial Channels in Korean Peacebuilding," International Sport and Politics Review 6, no. 3 (2021): 112–134

[Endnotes & References]

1) Thomas Bach, Paris 2024 Closing Ceremony Speech, 11 August 2024: "We know that the Olympic Games cannot create peace. But the Olympic Games can create a culture of peace that inspires the world."

2) Thomas Bach, Tokyo 2020 Opening Ceremony Speech, 23 July 2021: "This is the message of solidarity, the message of peace and the message of resilience."

3) United Nations General Assembly Resolution A/RES/70/4 (2015): "Building a peaceful and better world through sport and the Olympic ideal."

4) Thomas Bach, Tokyo 2020 Opening Ceremony Speech: "In this Olympic community we are all equal. We all respect the same rules."

5) IOC Press Release, Paris 2024 Games Achieve Full Gender Parity, 2024: "The first Olympic Games with full gender parity on the field of play."

6) Olympic Agenda 2020+5, IOC Strategic Roadmap (2021): Section on "Strengthening the role of sport in society."

7) IOC, Olympic Agenda 2020, December 2014: Strategic recommendations for sustainability, transparency, and legacy.

8) Thomas Bach, Paris 2024 Opening Ceremony Speech, 26 July 2024: "These were Olympic Games of a new era."

9) IOC, Olympic Agenda 2020+5, March 2021: Follow-up reforms including digital engagement and youth empowerment.

10) IOC website

# Chapter 18:
# *Reminiscences, Episodes & Highlights (40)*

## 1. The Measure of a Legacy

In the end, the legacy of a leader is not measured by titles held or speeches given. It is measured by the lives touched, the ideals upheld, and the future made possible by their vision.

Thomas Bach's time as President of the International Olympic Committee was not without challenge. He led through turbulence, through transformation, and through times when the very relevance of the Olympic

Games was questioned. But he never wavered in his belief that sport could be a force for unity in a fractured world.

He reminded us that the Olympic flame is not just a symbol—it is a promise. A promise that excellence can coexist with humility. That competition can coexist with compassion. That nations can come together not to divide, but to inspire.

And as the torch passes to a new generation, that promise endures.

## 2. Acknowledgments

This book would not have been possible without the insights, encouragement, and generosity of many individuals who share a deep belief in the Olympic spirit.

To the athletes, coaches, and Olympic officials who shared their stories—thank you for your candor and your courage. To the scholars, journalists, and historians whose work informed these pages—your dedication to truth and context is invaluable.

To the International Olympic Committee and its archives—thank you for preserving the legacy of a movement that continues to shape the world.

And to Thomas Bach—

*"Thank you most awfully for your leadership, your vision, your unwavering belief in the unifying power of sport to unite humanity, and more importantly for me, your insightful wisdom, and kind, thoughtful and unforgettable gesture, allowing me to be awarded such a prestigious IOC Pierre de Coubertin Medal at first hand through an official awarding ceremony held in Seoul in October 2022 as well as*

*the valued nomination of membership of IOC Culture and Olympic Heritage Commission rendered to me at the time of Gangwon 2024 Youth Olympic Winter Games in January 2024."*

*(IOC President Thomas Bach awarded to me the IOC's Pierre de Coubertin Medal in October 2022 in Seoul)*

## 3. Author's Note

Writing this book has been both a privilege and a journey. In tracing the arc of Thomas Bach's presidency, I have come to appreciate not only the complexity of global sport, but the quiet strength required to lead it with integrity.

This is not a biography. It is a tribute—to a man, to a movement, and to the enduring idea that even in our most divided moments, we can still find common ground in the pursuit of excellence, respect, and peace.

May the Olympic flame continue to light the way, now under the amazing new IOC leadership by his successor, current IOC President Kirsty Coventry with her "Ubuntu philosophy"

# 4. Author's Special Note of Reminiscences (DPR Korea)

*(IOC President Thomas Bach paid a visit to DPR Korea as first-ever IOC President and met with Kim Jong Un, President of the State Affairs of DPR Korea on 30 March 2018 following DPR Korea's participation in the PyeongChang 2018 Winter Olympics, where athletes from both Koreas marched together under a unified flag)*

Upon carefully recalling Thomas Bach's 12-year-long brilliant and inimitable contribution and accomplishments to World Peace in his capacity as IOC President, it has occurred to me that he must be the perfect role model, being the best-optimized global winner-candidate to be awarded the Nobel Peace Prize for the first time in the history of the Olympic Movement.

First thing that comes to my mind is that he is the first-ever, one and only IOC President having paid a visit to Pyongyang, DPR Korea, known as Hermit Kingdom, and having met historically with DPR Korean leader Mr. KIM, Jeong-eun in order to bring peace to the Korean Peninsula along the PyeongChang2018 OWG through thick and thin.

*"Discussions will focus on the further development of sport in the DPRK after the successful participation of athletes at the Olympic Winter Games Pyeongchang 2018, and the preparation of athletes from the NOC of the DPRK with the objective of qualifying for and participat-*

*ing in the Olympic Games Tokyo 2020 and Olympic Winter Games Beijing 2022, as well as the Youth Olympic Games 2020 and 2022." (IOC Statement dated 29 March 2018)*

Of course, it would be most probably not possible for anyone to enumerate and specify such a great deal of historic, large-scale achievements that he has accumulated during his 12-year long tenure, including but not limited to the peace through sport and the Olympic Movement brought to the Korean Peninsula through PyeongChang 2018 OWG, resulted in DPR Korean Delegation's participation, a joint-marching of two Korean Delegations at its opening ceremonies and the first-ever inter-Korean unified Olympic team of Women's Ice Hockey.

In addition, his unwavering and firm determination not to decide to extend his term of office as IOC President, under those circumstances that were favorable and available with the full support of the IOC EB and the IOC Session at that time, was evaluated not only as exemplary but also remarkable determination in comparison with other successful predecessors such as the 2nd IOC President Baron de Pierre de Coubertin, having served 29 years, and the 7th IOC President Juan Antonio Samaranch, having served 21 years, who could have been named and referred to as most successful and respected IOC Presidents in the 131 years of the IOC's history. It was an unexpected anti-climactic global news at the end of the IOC Session in Paris. Bach is such a different human enabler in demonstrating, implementing, practicing, and showcasing the real, good governance by himself. It surprised the whole world including but not limited the Olympic Movement. **"The Olympic Movement is best served by a change in leadership."**

As recently as on 21-23 October 2024, the KSPO (Korea Sports Promotion Foundation) as the living legacy entity of Seoul 1988 Games organized, at Seoul Olympic Park, the 2024 Seoul Olympic Legacy Forum represented by more than 20 developing countries form Asia-Pacific Rim also attended by Mme. Chair Khunying Patama Leeswadtrakul of the IOC Culture and Olympic Heritage Commission and IOC Member for Thailand (now Badminton World Federation President) including various groups of participants from local sport legacy entities. As already well known, it was initiated by 1st Seoul Olympic Legacy Forum highlighted by IOC President Thomas Bach's presence in 2022. I also had an opportunity to give the participants a special lecture as a form of Mega-Sport

Consulting Class on the legacies of Seoul 1988 and PyeongChang2018 with new concept and vision for the Olympic Movement quoting some of his philosophy including his words of jewel as well.

*(With Mme. Chair , Khunying Patama Leeswadtrakul of the IOC Culture and Olympic Heritage Commission and IOC Member for Thailand (now Badminton World Federation President)*

At its farewell reception on 23 October, I was asked to propose a toast:

*"As one and only person who has been deeply engaged and involved both in the Seoul1988 Olympic Organizing Committee and the PyeongChang2028 Olympic Winter Games Organizing Committee, I am very delighted to propose a toast for all participants attending the 2024 Seoul Olympic Legacy Forum.*

*As Aristotle once said, we are what we repeatedly do, Excellence, then, is not an act, but a habit. Legacy is a form of sustainable habit. So we belong to Excellence group.*

*The fundamental values in the new era would be Resilience, Adaptability, Creativity, Flexibility, a high rate of learning, and certainly Familiarity of the tools, such as AI and state-of-the art technology equipment.*

*As the old saying dictates, "When it comes to M.S. and the Speech, the shorter, the better.*

*Sustainability is Legacy, and Legacy is ESG. ESG is for SGDs. Therefore, now I propose a toast. When I say "ESG-oriented SDGs, then you say "Legacy"!*

As I wrote to him previously, it would be appropriate for the IOC to elect a new IOC member from DPR Korea sooner than later in order to accomplish the IOC's "Unfinished Symphony" for Peace in the Korean Peninsula which was evidently initiated and orchestrated by 9th IOC President Thomas Bach. Of course, I would like to be part of the relevant Task Force, when selected, to propel the project for the good cause, which would strongly support the first-ever proposal to recommend him representing the global Olympic Movement as the most outstanding and certainly acceptable candidate for the Nobel Peace Prize Winner. Bach is obviously a role model of strictly politically neutral IOC President, and that is one of so many reasons that he should be nominated as a most appropriate and justifiable candidate for the Nobel Peace Prize. In so many contexts of his IOC leadership (2013~2025), no one will dispute the fact that he deserves more than Nobel Peace Prize Winner

Alas, at the end of the day, 9th IOC President Thomas Bach finally declined my offer to become a candidate for Nobel Peace Prize winter. He is a man of humility as well.

As far as I remember, he has always "Walked the Talk, and Walked the Walk."

"Give Peace a Chance", "Give Peace through Sport a Chance!"

*(With Mr. Ung CHANG, DPR Korean IOC Member<1996~2018>, now IOC Honorary Member)*

## 5. Peace through Sport for DPR Korea (From my Letter to IOC President Thomas Bach on 17 September 2024)

As for DPR Korea, there is yet no IOC member since Mr. Ung CHANG, now IOC Honorary Member, left in 2018 due to his age limit of 80 years old.

Kirsty Coventry and Thomas Bach with Guk Kim Il. © IOC / Quinton Meyer

*(Coventry, Il-Guk KIM, Bach/22 June 2025)*

In this context, I would like to humbly presume that it would be about time for the IOC, preferably within the time frame of your term as IOC President to recruit one most suitable IOC member candidate from DPR Korea (North Korea) as appropriate for the sake of safeguarding peace through sport on the Korean Peninsula.

As you emphasized, "Give Peace a Chance."

As you are probably aware, Mr. Ung CHANG and myself have been in good and trust-worthy relationship for more than 20 years including but not limited to the period when he had served Secretary General and Vice President of DPR Korean NOC before he had been elected IOC membership in Atlanta1996 together with the late Kun-Hee LEE (former Samsung Chairman). I also used to have overall good relationship with many other DPR Korean NOC and sport people on many occasions so far.

With a future-oriented aim and objective to re-build peace through sport in mind, I was beginning to think that it would be just fitting and proper that such a personality as myself should serve as the next IOC member for Republic of Korea(South Korea) side by side in order to achieve the long-awaited peace mission, still remaining as an unfinished symphony initiated and orchestrated by yourself as IOC President at the time of PyeongChanag2018 OWG in the Korean Peninsula as well as by the global Olympic Movement with a common goal to build a better global society through sport. “Sport has a power to unify the people.” This unifying power of sport brings people together, anywhere, anytime, anyhow, as you mentioned.

In accordance with the Olympic Agenda 2020+5(“**This Olympic Agenda 2020 is like a jig-saw puzzle**”), it is stipulated that the IOC is allowed to implement a targeted recruitment process of IOC members, within the remit of the Olympic Movement, with a maximum of five special case exceptions for those who deserve their skillsets, e.g., sport management expertise, etc.

As I will be 68 years old by the time of the 144th IOC Session next March, I think I might still have an opportunity to be proposed as IOC member candidate and, when elected, to be granted the **4 further years of extension beyond the current age limit of 70** at your insightful discretion and with your approval for the good cause.

As you mentioned, “There is ‘**No One-Size-Fits-All**’ Solution.”, “**Success is the best reason for change**”, “The Olympic Games are **a symbol of hope and for peace**” “Charge boldly through the clouds and do not be afraid. The future belongs to you.”,

At this juncture, may I take this opportunity to cordially ask for your kind and thoughtful determination to reconsider my IOC membership case, once and for all, in order to safeguard the Olympic values of "Excellence, Friendship, and Respect".

## 6. IOC President's Key-Handover Ceremony from, 8th IOC President the late Jacques Rogge in 2013 and from 9th IOC President Thomas Bach to 10th IOC President Kirsty Coventry (23 June 2025)

1) "Many thanks for this symbolic act of handing over the key, which is now a traditional part of IOC history. We both know very well that this handover includes the challenge of taking on the huge demands and responsibility of this office."
2) "You(Rogge) have left the Olympic Movement a solid foundation and you have every reason to be proud of your great achievement, which has benefited sport worldwide. Here, this evening, we would like to express to you our gratitude, recognition and respect."

*(IOC Presidential Key Handover Ceremony from 8th IOC President Rogge to 9th IOC President Bach in 2013 and from 9th IOC President Bach to 10th Current IOC President Kirsty Coventry on 23 June 2025)*

## 7. Highlights of Bach's Acceptance Speech of the Election of the 9th IOC President in the 125th IOC Session in Buenos Aires on 10 September 2013

1) "First of all, I would like to thank from the bottom of my heart all my dear friends and colleagues who voted for me this morning.
2) This is really an overwhelming sign of trust and confidence.
3) But I would also like to thank my fellow candidates, who I greatly respect, and all those who did not vote for me this time.
4) I will also work for and with you in the coming years and want to win your confidence, too."
5) "I know about the great responsibility of an IOC President."

6) "This makes me humble.

7) "I want to lead the IOC according to my motto": 'Unity in Diversity.'

8) "I want to be a President for all of you."

9) "This means I will do my very best to balance well all the different interests of the stakeholders of the Olympic Movement."

10) "This is why I want to listen to you and to enter into an ongoing dialogue with all of you."

11) "You should know that my door, my ears, and my heart are always open for you."

(Bach's manifesto states he wants to keep the Olympic Games "unique" and not "diluted by other events," while ensuring the awarding of the Games is based on "the interest of the IOC in an in-depth review and risk analysis of a bid on the one hand, and the interest of a potential bidder in a social and promotional return on investment in the other.")

## 8. "Thomas Bach's Ten Commandments" for the Olympic Movement (Ref.: The Sports Examiner)

1) Bidding for Olympic Games should not create losers, who waste millions for absolutely no return.
   (The IOC now selects its hosts through a mostly-private discussion process.)
2) An Olympic Games must conform to the city, region or country where it is held, and not require unnecessary expenditures.
3) It is considered best if no new venues or permanent constructions are undertaken for a Games, unless as part of an otherwise useful

local development plan.

4) Sport must go to where the people are, not require people to come to it.

(This was successfully demonstrated at the 2018 Youth Olympic Games in Buenos Aires at the free, open-air opening ceremony at the iconic Obelisk, and transferred to Paris 2024 with its opening on the Seine.)

5) Sport must appeal to youth, or in Olympic-speak, "be more urban" and "youth-oriented."

(Thus the inclusion to the permanent program of skateboarding, sport climbing and surfing from 2028 and the IOC moving toward its own "e-sport Olympics.)

6) Sport governance through the "solidarity model," in which money is distributed through National Olympic Committees for development projects and athlete support, rather than simply paying ath-

letes directly through prize money.

7) Strict requirements for gender equality in terms of the number of men's and women's athletes competing, which will be reached at Paris 2024.

8) Strenuous anti-doping measures, preferably handled by an independent agency; the IOC created the International testing Agency in 2018, which has quickly absorbed most of the anti-doping programming for Olympic-sport federations.

9) Athletes are not responsible for the actions of their government, so long as they are not affiliated with their government.

10) The IOC should respect, follow and implement the directives and regulations of the United Nations.

## 9. Presentation Ceremony of the Pierre de Coubertin Medal to Rocky Kang-Ro YOON(Author) by IOC President Thomas Bach /Seoul, October 2022

"It is with great pleasure to inform you that the IOC Executive Board, which met today, has decided to award you the Pierre de Coubertin Medal for blending culture and sport in such a unique way in your publishing" (Letter by IOC President Thomas Bach about the decision by IOC Executive Board dated 9 September)

Dear friends,

For our founder, Pierre de Coubertin, the Olympic Games were always much more than just a sporting event. He wanted to make the world a bet-

ter place through sport and its values. This remains the overarching mission of the IOC and the entire Olympic Movement to this day.

Dear Rocky,

Having known you for such a long time, I can say from personal observation that during all these many years, your commitment to the Olympic Movement has always been a reflection of this vision of our founder.

Making the world a better and more peaceful place through sport has always been your guiding principle throughout your illustrious career.

At the Korean Olympic Committee, as the Korean Sport and Olympic Committee was formerly known, you were deeply involved in the successful organisation of the Olympic Games Seoul 1988. These Games left a remarkable sporting legacy to the people of Seoul and the Republic of Korea.

My personal connection to Seoul and Korea also began during these Games. At the time, I was the athletes' representative on the Games' steering committee. Ever since then, Seoul and its people have a very special place in my heart.

After the closing of the Olympic Games Seoul 1988, promoting the legacy of these Games has been the guiding theme of your career. As Standing Advisor to the Korea Sports Promotion Foundation, you have taken part in long-term projects including the Seoul Olympic Legacy Forum, which is taking place this week right here in Seoul.

You spent more than two decades as an official delegate for the NOC of the Republic of Korea, serving the development of sport and spreading the Olympic values throughout the country. During this time, your outstanding dedication to the athletes is reflected in the fact that you were a leading member of the South Korean delegation for an incredible ten editions of the Olympic Games.

Over the years, you have always shown a desire to share and pass on your extensive Olympic experience. Most recently you did so by providing guidance and counsel to the Organising Committee of the Olympic Winter Games PyeongChang 2018 in your capacity as senior advisor to the OCOG President. I am very grateful to say that the IOC, through its Evaluation Commission for the Olympic Games Beijing 2008, has also benefited your deep expertise.

Your belief in the power of sport has also guided you in your current role as President of the International Sport Diplomacy Institute. In this capacity, you are continuing to keep the legacy of Seoul 1988 alive, in particular through your active engagement with young people. With your lectures at renowned universities, you are inspiring the new generation with our shared Olympic values.

Perhaps nothing illustrates your passion for sport better than the creation of the Pyeongsan Sports Museum close to your home town, where thousands of Olympic artifacts and memorabilia are on display, many from your private collection.

Having just recently published the book "True Record and Stories of Korea Sports Diplomacy" you show no signs of slowing down. On the contrary, your unwavering commitment and enthusiasm for the Olympic Games continues to reach new heights. This is why today, we salute and honour your unique contribution and deep-rooted attachment to the Olympic values.

Dear Mr. Yoon Kang-Ro, dear Rocky,

In recognition of your outstanding achievements in supporting the cause of world sport and your faithfulness to the Olympic ideal as illustrated by Pierre de Coubertin, reviver of the Olympic Games, it is an honor and pleasure to present you with the Pierre de Coubertin Medal.

## 10. Rocky YOON's Thank-you Note to IOC President Thomas Bach at the IOC Pierre de Coubertin Medal Awarding Ceremony (Seoul, 21 Oct. 2022)

Honorable IOC President, Dr. Thomas Bach,

Distinguished guests who are present here today to attend the Awarding Ceremony of this prestigious Baron Pierre de Coubertin Medal out of busy schedule.

Very good morning!

First and foremost, I am deeply touched by and grateful to IOC President Thomas Bach who is sharing this space with us at this present time and made this possible at the IOC EB held on 9 September for his generous and insightful decision and consideration to award to me the Coubertin Medal.

When I receive his letter, I could not believe my eyes, but soon I realize that this is really happening to me.

I am very much excited, tremendously honored, incredibly privileged, and enormously and immeasurably pleased not only to become a recipient of this medal but also to receive it at first hand from IOC President Thomas Bach who has come a long way for this ceremony as well, on the auspicious occasion of the first Seoul Olympic Legacy Forum as a key-note speaker, which ended yesterday.

This medal is so important in giving me a sense of encouragement and motivation and inspiration to move forward together to build a better society concerned with the preservation of human dignity during the rest of my life.

Blending sport with culture and education, Olympism seeks to create a way of life based on the joy, found in efforts and educational value of good example based on the universal, fundamental and ethical principles.

No one will dispute the fact that IOC President Thomas Bach is by far the greatest global leader in the 21st century Olympic Movement with vision, wisdom, ability and inspiration to upgrade and re-design the modern Olympic Movement with his brain child masterpiece, Olympic Agenda 2020+5, ensuring and realizing transparency, sustainability, good governance, cost-effectiveness, best possible efficiency of the Olympic Games as well as equal and balanced opportunities in a spirit of the Olympic values of Excellence, Friendship and Respect.

Coubertin was a pioneer and forefather with a crystal clear vision for the initial Olympic Movement above and beyond time and space toward universality and sportsmanship with values of Olympic motto of Faster, Higher, Stronger, and recently strengthened with one simple but very meaningful and unifying word "Together" by IOC President Thomas Bach. Baron Pierre de Coubertin devised and designed Best Optimized Olympic Concept and vision suggesting to revitalize human values from teenagers, youth to produce a better and more peaceful world through sport.

In full alignment of the vision of Baron Pierre de Coubertin and the Olympic Agenda 2020+5, President Bach's vision is well reflected and echoed in his connotative and implicative words of "Unity in Diversity", Unifying Power of Sport and Olympics to bring together people, cultures, ideas, and lifestyles over Five Rings around the world. I would like to define it as a new revolution of the modern Olympic Movement in order to discharge prejudice and discrimination of any kind.

On each and every occasion of his speech, IOC President Thomas Bach impressed the world with his own expressions, such as "There is no one-size-fit-all solution", "This world is run by politics and not by sports organizations" as a reason why sport stay on neutrality, to say the least.

In order to eliminate mal practices, danger and risk factors of the past

Olympic Host City selection process, he reformed it and created the new age Olympic Host selection system by creating "FHC" system, thereby enabling IOC to choose best optimized Olympic Host Cities "whenever timing is right". I think he must be an Olympic genius and here of heroes in the 21st century Olympic Movement.

During the 128 years of the Olympic Movement, in my judgment, I can say there have been three most outstanding and greatest IOC Presidents, Firstly, Baron Pierre de Coubertin who served 21 years. Secondly, Juan Antonio Samaranch who also served 21 years. Thirdly and most importantly for the vast majority of the global stakeholders, I believe, the current IOC President Thomas Bach who has served 9 years so far and will serve only 3 more years, but I believe his term should be extended likewise in accordance with his achievements and role to play in order to overcome on-going and rapidly approaching crisis facing the global Olympic Movement including but not limited to pandemics.

Once again, I would like to reiterate my profound gratitude to IOC President Thomas Bach for his generous and insightful decision awarding this prestigious Pierre de Coubertin Medal to me in person. Thank you for your attention. And may God bless you and the Olympic Movement.

## 11. Quotations (76) from IOC President Thomas Bach's Speech at the 130th Extraordinary IOC Session in Lausanne on 11 July 2017

"Charge boldly through the clouds and do not be afraid. The future belongs to you."

"Let us show that sport is also always about ambition and optimism

"Let us not rest on our current position of strength."

"Let us make sure that we can enjoy such stability also in the years to come"

1) "A warm welcome to all of you to this extraordinary IOC Session."
2) "It is an extraordinary meeting because we are at an important juncture for the Olympic Movement."
3) "Our discussions and decisions today will chart the course of the Olympic Games for the foreseeable future."
4) "We will be discussing two separate but related decisions."
5) "Both will affect the future of the Olympic Games in profound ways."
6) "In this respect, now is a moment to shape the future of our Movement. "
7) "This is why I am looking forward to an interesting debate today."
8) "We can have this discussion from a position of strength and stability."

9) "You will see this when the audited accounts will be presented and we can hopefully approve the financial figures."

10) "This gives us the opportunity to once more look at our governance structures."

11) "The financial figures are not only audited by our external auditors, but they are also always closely monitored by our Audit Committee and our Internal Auditor."

12) "Let me thank the members of our Audit Committee under the great leadership of its Chair, Pierre-Olivier Beckers-Vieujant, for their hard work and good advice they are giving us on this matter throughout the year."

13) "This Audit Committee is of course further supported by the Finance Commission who again monitor the financial flows and operations of the IOC."

14) "Let me also acknowledge and thank all its members and its Chair, Ser Miang Ng, for their valuable contribution."

15) "The financial figures take into account the record amount that we have distributed to Rio 2016. "

16) "We have made a tremendous effort, together with the IFs and NOCs, with additional financial contributions and savings at the same time, to make the first Olympic Games in South America a reality, despite all the unprecedented challenges of our Brazilian friends."

17) "As you approve the audited accounts, I hope you take all this into consideration."

18) "Following the approval, we can then proceed to publish the Annual Report."

19) "As always, the Annual Report will provide an in-depth account of our activities, making all the IOC's financial flows fully transparent and demonstrating that we are distributing 90 per cent of all our revenues for the development of sport worldwide."
20) "This very high percentage of redistribution to support world sport is something that we can be very proud of."
21) "Our strong and stable financial situation allows us to focus almost all our energy on the overarching mission of the IOC, to make the world a better place through sport."
22) "This is the solid foundation that we can build on for our future."
23) "This strong position of the Olympic Movement is also demonstrated by a great opportunity that we will discuss today."
24) "This is about awarding the Olympic Games 2024 and 2028 at the same time in Lima this September."
25) "As you have seen and heard this morning, and as confirmed by the report of our Evaluation Commission, we have two outstanding candidatures for 2024."
26) "With Los Angeles and Paris, there are two fantastic cities from countries with a profound Olympic history."
27) "The two candidate cities are enthusiastic and dynamic."
28) "They are promoting the Olympic Games and the Olympic spirit in a great way."
29) "The Candidate Cities for the Olympic Games 2024 are the first to fully benefit from the significant changes that resulted from Olympic Agenda 2020."
30) "The Evaluation Commission has come back with praise for both

candidatures."

31) "Both cities have really embraced Olympic Agenda 2020, in particular by using a record number of existing and temporary facilities."
32) "This is something we have not seen in this dimension in the history of the Olympic Games."
33) "Such proposals lead to significant cost reductions in the organization of the Olympic Games."
34) "This sets a precedent to make the Games more sustainable and more feasible for the future."
35) "It is exactly this spirit of Olympic Agenda 2020 that we are promoting."
36) "As you can see, this is a golden opportunity."
37) "It is hard to imagine something better."
38) "This is why the Executive Board asked the IOC Vice-Presidents to study how the Olympic Movement could make the most of this unique constellation."
39) "The Executive Board is unanimously supporting their recommendation not to miss this golden opportunity."
40) "The Vice-Presidents will give you even more reasons why this double allocation should happen and how we can make it happen."
41) "We can create a win-win-win situation for the entire Olympic Movement, for Los Angeles and the United States of America, and for Paris and France."
42) "While the allocation the Olympic Games 2024 and 2028 at the same time is about seizing an opportunity, the next decision is about addressing a challenge."

43) "This decision is about reforming our current candidature procedure with a view to the Olympic Winter Games 2026."

44) "The challenges that we face here are both external and internal."

45) "Firstly, there is a profound change in the decision-making process in many Western countries."

46) "In the past, when we saw that a candidature enjoyed the support of the government, of the opposition, of business and of the sport community, then we were sure that the candidature had broad public support."

47) "This has changed dramatically, in particular in Europe."

48) "Today, when people see that the government, the opposition, business and the sport community, in other words, when the entire establishment is united behind one project, then the people immediately have mistrust and conclude that something must be terribly wrong."

49) "In many countries, populist movements are on the rise."

50) "As we have seen in the recent past, these populist movements can be very effective, even if they might still be too small to run a government."

51) "But they have a strong influence over policy and political decision making."

52) "The New York Times described this quite well recently when they wrote:

53) "Western populism may be entering something like its awkward teenage years – able to borrow the car but not own it, have an influence on the household but too young to run it."

54) "We may not like this new political reality, but we cannot ignore it. "

55) "This is the external challenge."

56) "But we have to acknowledge that internally, with our candidature procedure, we have given some arguments to this public scepticism and mistrust."

57) "In a nutshell, the candidature procedure, which worked very well in the past, has become too expensive and too onerous for some potential candidate cities today."

58) "We have been asking too much too soon from the candidate cities."

59) "For all these reasons, it is extremely difficult for sport and government authorities in many countries today to come back with a second candidature, when a first one was not successful."

60) "In particular, this is limiting the number of potential candidates for Olympic Winter Games, where for geographic reasons, but increasingly also because of climate change, we had and continue to have a much smaller number of potential candidate cities."

61) "Because of the fact that the Olympic Winter Games 2014, 2018 and 2022 are all held in completely new winter sport destinations, there is a public perception that this trend will continue."

62) "It is therefore in our best interest to demonstrate that traditional winter sport

destinations in the Americas, Europe or Asia are most welcome as Olympic hosts."

63) "The world is changing at an ever-faster pace."

64) "It has changed in profound ways even in the time since we passed Olympic Agenda 2020."

65) “It has changed in profound ways even in the last few months, even in the last weeks and days.”

66) “We need to continue to address this change.”

67) “The Vice-Presidents will share the details of the proposal, unanimously supported by the Executive Board, for a new approach for the Olympic Winter Games 2026.”

68) “As you can see, these two decisions before us will have far-reaching implications for the future of the Olympic Games.”

69) “One is an opportunity, the other one a challenge.”

70) “Both are an occasion to remind ourselves of our founder, Pierre de Coubertin who once said:

71) “Charge boldly through the clouds and do not be afraid. The future belongs to you.”

72) “Let us take courage from his words.”

73) “Let us show that sport is also always about ambition and optimism.”

74) “Let us not rest on our current position of strength.”

75) “Let us make sure that we can enjoy such stability also in the years to come.”

76) “In this spirit of ambition and optimism, I wish us all fruitful discussions and a successful Extraordinary Session.”

## 12. IOC President Thomas Bach's Secret of the Success of the PyeongChang2018 Winter Games

1) “The secret of PyeongChang2018's success in encouraging North

Korean participation was due to political neutrality."

1) "It would be "naïve" and "unrealistic" to believe the Olympic Games can ignore wider political developments."
2) "It would only be possible to be able to this while remaining strictly neural."
3) "This world is run by politics and not by sports organizations."
4) "Therefore, to preserve the autonomy, we have to have a partnership and mutual respect."
5) "On the one hand, our respect for the priorities of politics, and on the other hand, their respect of the politics for the autonomy of the IOC, making them aware that we can only accomplish our mission if we have this autonomy, if we are politically strictly neutral."
6) "And what this means, you can see from the Korean issues."
7) "If we would not have been strictly politically neutral, we could never have achieved the joint march behind the one flag nor the joint women's ice hockey team."

# 13. IOC President Thomas Bach's Acceptance Speech for Seoul Peace Prize

Seoul Peace Prize

Acceptance speech

Seoul, 26 October 2020

It is a great privilege to receive the prestigious Seoul Peace Prize, today.

The fact that I can only address you virtually and not in person is itself a reflection of the unprecedented situation the entire world is facing because of the global coronavirus crisis.

As you can imagine, it is a huge personal disappointment that I could not be there with you today to receive it in Seoul, which is a great Olympic City that holds such a strong place in my heart.

It is with much gratefulness and appreciation that I humbly accept this distinction, and I would like to thank the Seoul Peace Prize Cultural Foundation for this honour. This prize belongs to the entire IOC and the whole of the Olympic Movement, because without the support of so many around the globe, the achievements for peace through sport could never have been accomplished.

It is very humbling to join the illustrious ranks of previous recipients, who include extraordinary personalities like my predecessor Juan Antonio Samaranch, Professor Muhammad Yunus, with whom we are working closely together to empower athletes around the world, or former UN Secretary-General Ban Ki-moon, who is now the Chair of the IOC Ethics Commission.

Although I could not attend the ceremony in person, I am comforted by the fact that His Excellency Mr Ban Ki-moon is present to collect the award trophy on my behalf today.

The close Olympic connection of the prize, in commemoration of the unforgettable Olympic Games Seoul 1988, gives this ceremony today even more significance. My personal connection to Seoul also began during the Olympic Games Seoul 1988. At the time, I was the first-ever athletes' representative on the Games' steering committee. This was the beginning of a precious bond that I share with Seoul and the Korean people. After becoming an honorary citizen of Seoul in 2018, today's distinction adds another chapter to this special relationship for which I will always be grateful.

The country I come from, Germany, shares a history with Korea of being a divided country. Because of this shared history, we have another common bond, and that is the wish for peace.

This wish for peace in the world is also a driving force behind the mission of the International Olympic Committee and the Olympic Games.

## [The peace mission of the IOC]

Already over 3,000 years ago, the foundation for the ancient Olympic

Games to take place in peace was a sacred truce – the ekecheiria, or the Olympic Truce. The ekecheiria ensured a halt to hostilities, allowing athletes and spectators to travel safely to Olympia and home again. In this way, there was already in Ancient times an inseparable link between the Olympic Games and peace.

When the founder of the International Olympic Committee, Pierre de Coubertin, revived the Olympic Games, he saw it as a way to promote peace among nations and people. Always the visionary, he said: "Should the institution of the Olympic Games prosper, it can become a potent factor in securing universal peace."

The purpose of the IOC was always to promote peace through sport. When Coubertin founded the IOC in 1894 at the University of Sorbonne in Paris, he did so in the presence and with the full support of leading figures of the international peace movement of the time. At this founding moment, six of the first thirteen future winners of the Nobel Peace Prize were present to support Coubertin's vision. This demonstrates that, for the IOC, sport and peace were intricately intertwined from its first moment of existence.

In our increasingly confrontational and fragile world, we see how relevant our mission of building a more peaceful world through sport is in our times.

Ideals are by definition impossible to fully achieve. Like other peace movements, the Olympic Movement has sometimes fallen short of achieving our ideals. In our efforts to build a more peaceful world through sport, sometimes we have failed, and have been failed. 3

But being in sport, this only encourages me to strive even harder. As every athlete knows, if you do not make it at first, try again. And again. Because it is only by striving that we make progress; that we go beyond and finally achieve the impossible. This is what motivates and drives me day after day.

While we are determined to strive for our ideals, we have to be realistic about our limitations. We know very well that sport alone cannot create peace. We cannot take decisions on war and peace – this is the realm of politics, and not of sport.

And yet, knowing that we operate within these limitations, navigating between what sport can and cannot do, opens up a unique pathway for us. This pathway is about finding those areas where the power of sport as a force for good can unfold. In order to adapt our mission to our modern age, we need to look beyond the Olympic Games as a singular event and take a holistic view of how sport as a whole can best contribute to make the world a better place.

To contribute to peace through sport, we have to look at why human conflict happens in the first place. Conflicts occur for many different reasons: aggression, discrimination, prejudice, inequality, social disparity, competition for limited resources, just to name a few.

The Olympic Movement cannot address all these political and social challenges. But the Olympic Games can set an example for a world where everyone respects the same rules and one another. They can inspire us to solve problems in friendship and solidarity. They can build bridges, leading to better understanding among people. In this way, they can open the door to peace.

The pathway of sport to best unfold its peace-building power is by addressing roots of conflict in a holistic way. This holistic approach to the role of sport in society forms the thinking behind Olympic Agenda 2020, the reform programme that we initiated in 2014, shortly after my election as IOC President.

The overarching goal of Olympic Agenda 2020 is to strengthen the role of sport in society so that we can pursue our mission in our rapidly changing times.

We are living in an age of global crises, division and discrimination. We are seeing many societies driven by egoism and nationalism. The zeitgeist in many parts of the world is one of narrow self-interest gaining ground over solidarity, shared values and common rules. This leads to more confrontation and to the politicisation of all aspects of life.

Olympic Agenda 2020 is our answer to the challenges of our times, giving a renewed sense of purpose to the Olympic Movement. Our mission requires us to stand against this zeitgeist of division, of nationalism and of discrimination. More than ever, in our troubled times, we need to stand up for the ideals that define us. Olympic Agenda 2020 defines the pathway for sport to be a force of good in the world. This is why Olympic Agenda 2020 is focused on promoting universality, solidarity, inclusivity, sustainability and credibility in and through sport.

## [Universality and political neutrality]

The power of the Olympic Games is their universality – uniting the entire world in peaceful competition. To ensure that this unifying power of the Olympic Games can unfold, our relationship with politics must be based on solid principles. Navigating a values-based organisation like ours through a highly political and commercialised world requires the IOC to be strictly committed to political neutrality. Only this principle of political neutrality ensures that the Olympic Games can stand above and beyond the political differences that exist in our world.

Therefore, the Olympic Games are governed by the IOC, not by governments. The IOC issues the invitation to National Olympic Committees to participate in the Olympic Games, the invitations do not come from the government of the host country. It is the NOCs which then invite their political authorities to accompany their athletes to the Games.

At the same time, the IOC needs to be in constant dialogue with politics in order to advance its mission. In this dialogue, we always need to build understanding and to gain respect for the role of the Olympic Games and for our principle of political neutrality. Only in this way can we be truly inclusive.

The Olympic Games are the only event that brings the entire world together in peaceful competition. They are a celebration of the unity of humanity in all our diversity, uniting the best athletes of all 206 National Olympic Committees and the IOC Refugee Olympic Team. The Olympic athletes personify the values of excellence, friendship, respect and solidarity. They are competitors in sport, but at the same time, they live peacefully together under one roof in the Olympic Village. At the Olympic Games, there is no discrimination, everyone respects the same rules, regardless of social background, gender, religion or political belief. At the Olympic Games, we are all equal.

In this way, the Olympic Games show us that despite all our differences it is possible for humankind to live together in peace and harmony.

## [Olympic Winter Games PyeongChang 2018]

The Olympic Winter Games PyeongChang 2018 are an illustration of these principles in action. We all remember the incredible moment at the Opening Ceremony, when the athletes from the NOCs of the Republic of Korea and the Democratic People's Republic of Korea marched as one team behind one flag, the Korean Unification Flag. This moment sent a powerful message of peace from Korea to the world.

This moment did not happen by chance. It was the result of a long process of negotiations and high-level government engagement by the IOC that began back in 2014 and lasted until four hours before the Opening Ceremony.

When we started the talks with North Korea and support for its athletes in 2014, we were facing many political obstacles. Even the South Korean government at the time showed little interest in the participation of the North Korean athletes, to put it diplomatically.

This changed after President Moon Jae-in was elected. When I met with President Moon, shortly after he took office in May 2017, we agreed that the participation of athletes from North Korea in PyeongChang would be a priority and task for the IOC, while President Moon and his government would support the IOC initiative on the political side. This cooperation was a good example of how politics and sport can work together if the political neutrality of sport is respected.

But the political tensions on the Korean Peninsula escalated significantly during the second half of 2017. There was aggressive rhetoric from all sides. The thought of North Korean participation or of both Korean teams marching peacefully at the Olympic Games together seemed illusionary: we were facing missile launches, nuclear tests and threats of war on the 6 Korean Peninsula. We were indeed confronted with the fundamental question of whether the Olympic Games could take place at all under such circumstances.

Throughout even these most difficult times of political tensions, the IOC always kept the door open for the participation of North Korean athletes in PyeongChang. We continued to engage both sides in dialogue, without taking a political side.

We did so out of our firm belief in the universality of the Olympic Games. We did so out of our unshakeable conviction that athletes from all NOCs in the world should be able to participate in the Olympic Games without any discrimination, regardless of their background. We did so based on our strict commitment to political neutrality.

When the commitment of North Korea for its participation was expressed in the 2018 New Year's message by the North Korean leader, Kim Jong-un, I immediately called for a meeting on 20 January 2018 in Lausanne, chaired by the IOC, with the two NOCs, the two Korean governments and the Organising Committee of the Games.

The meeting resulted in all parties signing the "Olympic Korean Peninsula Declaration". This declaration contained exceptional decisions of the IOC to make the participation and joint activities of the two teams possible.

If somebody thought that with this agreement everything was sorted, they were wrong. The delicate political discussions came up again two days before the Opening Ceremony. On the evening before the Opening Ceremony, North Korea indicated that they may not participate in the Olympic

Games at all. This is why I had to resume the talks with them again. Just four hours before the Opening Ceremony, we finally had an agreement again to respect the conditions contained in the "Olympic Korean Peninsula Declaration".

The road was finally clear. When then the athletes from the NOCs of both North and South Korea entered the Olympic stadium as one team, under the name Korea and behind the Korean Unification flag, it sent a powerful message of peace from the Korean Peninsula to the world. When the unified women's ice hockey team played in a crowded arena with incredible support from the spectators, it showed the world the unifying power of sport. For the first time in their Olympic history, the two NOCs united to compete as one team in a sport. And all this 7 on Korean soil. There was an extremely positive response to these actions from almost every corner of the world.

With these powerful symbols and gestures, we have seen how the Olympic Games can open the way to dialogue, how the Olympic values can open the way to a more peaceful future.

We were happy and proud to see all our efforts become reality. But we also knew that sport alone cannot create peace. The political tensions would not disappear overnight. But, as we saw in PyeongChang, the Olympic Games can open the door to a more peaceful future.

This power of the Olympic Games to open doors is obviously also on the minds of the political actors. For example, within the past few days, the US administration expressed its hope for a resumption of peace talks with North Korea on the occasion of the Olympic Games Tokyo 2020 next year.

There are many other examples of our peace efforts. Over the years, the IOC has mediated between governments, building bridges through sport and opening the door to peace and reconciliation. This has been the case in the last couple of years for our negotiations, for example, with the governments of India, Pakistan, Serbia, Kosovo, Spain, Tunisia, Israel, Palestine, Iran, Ukraine, Russia, Armenia, Azerbaijan and others. Our negotiations were always restricted to sport and always took place with strict political neutrality. Only in this way, could we be successful.

If the Olympic Games can bring together athletes from bitter political rivals and enemies today, this shows that our ideal of promoting a peaceful world through sport continues to have much compelling power.

In our fragile world that is drifting apart, the enduring relevance of our mission could not be clearer.

## [Solidarity and inclusivity]

Uniting the world in peace requires more than political neutrality. The Olympic Games can only unite the entire world through sport if everyone can participate. For us, universality also means solidarity and inclusivity. This is why we not only respect but wholeheartedly embrace diversity.

Guided by Olympic Agenda 2020, we contribute to peace by actively promoting solidarity, inclusivity and diversity.

We do this through our Olympic solidarity model which benefits all athletes in the world. The IOC distributes 90 per cent of all its revenues for the benefit of the athletes and the development of sport and Paralympic sport around the globe. With this solidarity model, the equivalent of 5 billion US dollars during the past Olympiad went to support athletes and sports organisations worldwide. Because of the long-term commercial stability of the Olympic Movement, which is thanks to the great confidence and loyalty our commercial partners are demonstrating, we can expect this figure to increase significantly during the current Olympiad. This financial support benefits not just a few countries, or a few sports. It benefits all the athletes from all 206 NOCs, from the IOC Refugee Olympic Team and from all Olympic sports, whether popular or less popular, thereby ensuring true universality and diversity.

We also demonstrate solidarity through the IOC Refugee Olympic Team, which we created for the Olympic Games Rio 2016. For the first time in Olympic history, refugee athletes competed side by side with the teams from all 206 NOCs, sending a message of hope and inclusion to all refugees in the world. With half the world's population watching coverage of these Olympic Games, the refugee athletes demonstrated to a global audience that we are all part of the same humanity. Their participation was a clear signal that refugees are our fellow human beings – that they are an enrichment to society just as they are an enrichment to our Olympic community.

Unfortunately, the reasons why we created this team continue to persist. This is why we will have once again an IOC Refugee Olympic Team for the Olympic Games Tokyo 2020 next year. In this way, we want to continue to raise awareness about the magnitude of the ongoing global refugee crisis. 9

Furthermore, we launched the Olympic Refuge Foundation in 2017, which brings together all our many refugee activities, from grassroots support to the IOC Refugee Olympic Team. The goal of the Olympic Refuge Foundation is to support the protection and empowerment of vulnerable displaced people through sport and through the creation of safe sports facilities. In the relatively short time of its existence, the Olympic Refuge

Foundation has already reached over 200,000 displaced young people and their host communities. This is another example of how we contribute to peace through the power of sport.

We promote inclusivity through our cooperation with the International Paralympic Committee, having taken it to a new level with a long-term partnership. This cooperation ensures the organisation of the Paralympic Games and gives financial stability to the IPC as the governing body of Paralympic sport. With our partnership, we are increasing the visibility of the Paralympic Games and the IPC, with which we share so many of the same values and objectives. Enhancing the cooperation between the Olympic and Paralympic Movements was in fact one of the key recommendations of Olympic Agenda 2020.

Guided by Olympic Agenda 2020, we are also advancing gender equality on and off the field of play. We will achieve gender-balance at the Olympic Games for the first time at the postponed Olympic Games Tokyo 2020 next year, with about 49 per cent of the athletes being female. We achieved this by establishing the necessary qualification and athletes' quota systems and by including more mixed sports events in the programme. We also modified the Olympic competition schedule to better balance the visibility of men and women's events. Furthermore, we have changed the rules to allow NOCs to nominate a female and a male athlete to jointly bear their flag during the Opening Ceremony. We are also aiming to have, for the first time ever at the Olympic Games, at least one female and one male athlete in each and every one of the 206 Olympic teams.

Off the field of play, we are also putting our commitment into action. We have elected more female IOC members, increasing female membership to 37.5 per cent, up from 21 per cent at the start of my presidency. On the IOC Executive Board, female representation has grown from 20 per cent to 33.3 per cent. We have appointed many more female IOC commission members, increasing female membership to currently 47.7 per cent – more than double from only 20 per cent. 10

## [Sustainability and good governance]

In a world where conflicts arise far too often over struggles for limited resources, we want sport to contribute to positive change in the area of sustainability as well. This is why sustainability is a key pillar of Olympic Agenda 2020 and we have made sustainability an integral part of all IOC activities. In this regard, climate change is a challenge of unprecedented proportions for all humankind – and it requires an unprecedented response. This is why we want to ensure that sport contributes to the global efforts to address climate change. The IOC as an organisation is already carbon neutral, as the Olympic Games Tokyo 2020 should also be. Our aim is to make both the IOC and the Olympic Games climate positive even before 2030, which is the year targeted by the international community to achieve their climate goals.

Another concrete example of how we make sustainability a central element in all our activities is our Olympic House, the new IOC headquarters. Inaugurated in 2019, Olympic House is one of the most sustainable buildings in the world.

We know that our ability to make a difference in the world rests on our credibility and integrity. For this reason, good governance is a central feature of Olympic Agenda 2020. As a values-based organisation, we have the double-duty to uphold good governance and integrity in everything we do. This is why, through the Olympic Agenda 2020 reforms, we have put in place a robust system of governance and transparency. We have established advanced control and risk management processes. Our accounts are audited at a much higher standard than legally required. We publish an annual report where we make all our flows of money transparent. We have an organisational excellence programme in place to ensure best-in class operations. We have strong rules in place to prevent misconduct as well as to swiftly sanction such behaviour. We are monitored by a well-respected and independent Ethics Commission. We are honoured that this IOC Ethics Commission is chaired by former UN Secretary-General Ban Ki-moon, who has made integrity a hallmark of his illustrious career in public service. He summarised this IOC approach in an excellent way when he said: "Sport is a unique vehicle for peace, but it can only be efficient if it has credibility."

## [Opportunities]

The universal Olympic Games show us what the world could look like, if we were all guided by the ideals and values of sport. We know that our ideals are not shared by everyone in this world, they are contrary to the zeitgeist. But a disregard of our Olympic ideals does not negate their inherent value. On the contrary: it demonstrates the importance of our mission, to strive to uphold these values and ideals in a world where peace and solidarity are under threat.

Building peace is an ongoing effort. This is why I accept this Seoul

Peace Prize, not as a reward, but as an encouragement to continue to work towards our Olympic ideals. Our journey to achieve our mission of uniting all of humanity in peace at the Olympic Games goes on. This is why we will carry forward Olympic Agenda 2020 in light of the new challenges that the world and sport are facing today. This updated agenda will address the deteriorating political environment as well as the far-reaching political, social and economic consequences of the global coronavirus crisis. But this crisis also offers an opportunity. An opportunity for us to emphasise one important lesson that I hope we have all learned from this crisis – and this lesson is: we need more solidarity. Solidarity within societies and solidarity between societies. The post-coronavirus world will need sport and its values. We are ready to contribute to shaping it with our Olympic ideals.

Just as this prestigious distinction will strengthen the peace efforts of the IOC, it is my sincere hope that it will encourage all Koreans to continue your journey of building peace through sport. With the Winter Youth Olympic Games Gangwon 2024, you have every opportunity to again build peace through the power of sport. Inspired by this prize, I can assure you that the IOC will continue to be on your side for every step of this journey. We will continue to build bridges through sport and in this way open the door to peace.

Once again, I thank you from the bottom of my heart for the recognition of this award. I hope to see you all soon, in person, in Seoul, to renew the special bond I have with this great city and with your great Olympic nation

# 13. From Seoul1988 to PyeongChang2018: Korea's Olympic Legacy and Vision "Unity in Diversity on New Horizons"

**[Keynote Speech at the time of International Seminar as part of Cultural Olympiad of Milan Cortina 2026 OWG held in Treviso, Verona, and Venice on 5 June 2025 as IOC Member of Culture and Olympic Heritage Commission]**

It is my great honor and privilege to continue to serve in the global Olympic Movement since I joined the Korean Olympic Committee in 1982. As we now look forward to the Milano Cortina 2026 Olympic and Paralympic Winter Games, it is an opportune moment to reflect on the profound impact of sport and education as catalysts for international unity in diversity, economic progress, and youth empowerment.

Today, I am also privileged to share Korea's Olympic journey and its significant role in promoting these ideals.

## 1. Seoul 1988: A Turning Point for Korea and the World

The Seoul 1988 Olympic Games were a milestone not only for Korea but for the global Olympic movement. As the first Olympic Games hosted in Korea, Seoul 1988 symbolized a nation's total transformation—bridging cultures, fostering international collaboration, and opening new opportunities for overall development for Korea. It showcased the **unifying power of sport** in breaking down barriers and connecting people across the world with its slogan of "World to Seoul, Seoul to the World" together with "Peace and Harmony" and "Hand in Hand"

The Seoul 1988 Olympics marked a pivotal moment in global history, serving as a bridge between Cold War tensions and the transformative geopolitical changes that followed.

### 1) German Reunification (1990)

Three years after the Seoul Olympics, East and West Germany unified into a single nation. The Olympics symbolized a platform for dialogue and cooperation, showcasing the possibility of unity amidst division. The Games brought together athletes from both German states, fostering a sense of shared identity and mutual respect. This spirit of collaboration, coupled with the fall of the Brandenburg Gate & Berlin Wall in 1989, paved the way for reunification in 1990.

### 1) Dissolution of the Soviet Union (1991)

Similarly, the Soviet Union's participation in the Seoul Olympics was one of its last appearances as a unified entity. The Games highlighted the diversity within the USSR, as athletes from various republics competed under one flag. However, the political and economic strains within the

Soviet Union intensified in the years following the Seoul Olympics. By 1991, the USSR dissolved into the Commonwealth of Independent States (CIS), with each republic asserting its independence with the policy of **Gorbachev's Perestroika and Glasnost.**

### 2) The Role of the Olympics

The Seoul Olympics played a subtle yet significant role in these global transformations. It was the last Games where countries like **East Germany** and the **Soviet Union** competed as separate entities. The event symbolized the potential for peaceful coexistence and cultural exchange, even amidst ideological divides. It also demonstrated the **unifying power of sport diplomacy** in fostering dialogue and understanding.

These changes were driven by broader political, economic, and social factors, but the Olympics provided a unique stage for nations to reflect on **unity**, **identity**, **sustainability** and **the possibility of change**. "**Change or Be Changed**"

Through its groundbreaking achievements, including the introduction of table tennis and tennis as Olympic sports, Seoul 1988 left an indelible mark on Olympic history and reaffirmed the value of international participation and "**Unity in Diversity**" as reiterated by IOC President Thomas Bach

## 2. PyeongChang 2018: Embracing Innovation and Sustainability

Fast forward to the PyeongChang 2018 Winter Games, Korea again demonstrated its ability to lead on the global stage, thanks to the unsparing efforts and contribution to world peace and **Peacebuilding on the Korean Peninsula** by IOC President **Thomas Bach's unwavering policy** of **"Staying strictly politically neutral"**. As a result, PyeongChang 2018 Games were highlighted, spotlighted and celebrated not only by Joint marching and parade of two Korean delegations at its Opening Ceremonies but also realizing its **first-ever Olympic inter-Korean single team** at women's Ice Hockey competition. These Games were celebrated for their innovative approach, including advanced technologies like 5G and eco-friendly initiatives that emphasized sustainability—a key pillar of modern Olympism.

PyeongChang also highlighted the **"Unifying Power of Sport"**. The participation of athletes from both South and North Korea under one Korean Peninsula flag sent a strong message of **Peace and Hope** to the world. It remains a testament to how sport can transcend political divides and foster dialogue and understanding **in a true spirit of Olympic Movement**.

### 3. The Role of Sport in Education and Business Development

In Korea, sports have consistently been intertwined with education and business development. From grassroots programs that teach teamwork and leadership to industry sectors that thrive on the opportunities provided by global sporting events, the Olympic movement has become a cornerstone of both our social and economic growth. The legacy of Seoul 1988 and PyeongChang 2018 continues to inspire our youth and drive innovation.

### 4. Vision for the Future: Inspired by #Gen26

As we look to Milano Cortina 2026, we are reminded of the shared Olympic values: **Excellence, Friendship, and Respect**. Korea's Olympic experiences exemplify how these values can pave the way for lasting positive change. Inspired by the **GenerAZIONE2026 Project**, our focus remains on creating meaningful opportunities for young people—empowering them to dream, connect, and lead as global citizens.

Ladies and gentlemen, Korea's Olympic legacy is not just a collection of milestones—it is a living example of how sport and Olympic Movement can unite nations, transform lives, and shape a brighter future. Let us continue to share our stories, exchange ideas, and collaborate in the spirit of **Olympic Unity and Solidarity**.

Thank you for your attention, and I look forward to engaging further in this inspiring dialogue. Grazie mille.

## 15. Foreword for my Book by IOC President Thomas Bach

INTERNATIONAL
OLYMPIC
COMMITTEE

Thomas Bach President

[Foreword for True Records and Stories of Korea Sport Diplomacy "The New Horizons"]

It only seems like yesterday that we were celebrating a world united by sport in peaceful competition at the Olympic Winter Games PyeongChang 2018. The magic of Olympic sport on snow and ice, the unforgettable performances by the athletes and the wonderful hospitality of the Korean people and will live on in our hearts forever. The Olympic Winter Games PyeongChang 2018 also sent a powerful message of peace from the Korean Peninsula to the world. That moment came when the athletes from the National Olympic Committees of the Republic of Korea and the Democratic People's Republic of Korea entered the Olympic stadium as one team, behind one flag, the Korean Unification flag. This one moment demonstrated the unique power of sport to unite the whole world in peace. To me, this is the most powerful message of the Olympic Games. With these powerful symbols in PyeongChang, we have seen how the Olympic Games can open the way to dialogue. This moment did not happen by chance. It was the result of a long process of negotiations and high-level government engagement by the International Olympic Committee that began back in 2014 and lasted until a few hours before this unforgettable Opening Ceremony. We know that sport alone cannot create peace. But as we saw in PyeongChang, the Olympic Games can open the way to a more peaceful future. This power of sport to unite the world in peaceful competition is a central theme in this insightful book that chronicles the history of the Olympic Movement in the Republic of Korea. My personal connection with the Korean people began during the Olympic Games Seoul 1988. At the time, I was the athletes' representative on the Games' steering committee. This early contact with the Koreans and the Korean culture left a lasting impression on me that continues to this day. It is in this context that I got to know and appreciate Rocky Kang-Ro Yoon as a leading figure in Korean sport. Building on his great knowledge on the Olympic Movement, he is ideally placed to share his many accounts of the rich Korean sporting history and the role that sport can play to make the world a better place. In order to shape the future, one needs to understand the past. This is why this book is a timely contribution to inspire the next generation of sport leaders with the lessons of the past, as they shape our way forward.

## 16. New Year's Message for 2019 by IOC President Thomas Bach IOC

### New Year's Message 2019

### Where we are coming from

"Where will destinies lie 100 years from now in 2018? Armed as we are with the indefinite applications of growing knowledge, human evolution has become strangely swift, and never before has it been more imprudent and pointless even to make long-range forecasts. One thing that is certain, however, is that a weighty responsibility rests upon us. [...] The legacy that exists in 2018 will depend mostly on what the people of 1918, with whom the values of our times are held in trust, decide. Let us make sure that our children have no reason to hold us painfully to account, and that they receive a legacy of wisdom, energy and honour, enriched still further by our

virtues, our constancy, our loyalty and our self-sacrifice."

These words by Pierre de Coubertin ring as true today as they did 100 years ago, when he wrote them. What better time to reflect on his words than now, as we stand at the threshold of 2019. Looking back on the events that have shaped the Olympic year 2018, we can hear the echoes of Coubertin's times and we see that, in so many ways, they are still relevant in our day and age.

The year began with the Olympic Winter Games PyeongChang 2018, which were a success story in so many respects. From the sporting achievements and the athletes' experience to the excellent organisation and the financial success, these Games have opened up new horizons in more ways than anyone could have imagined only a few months ago.

The best expression of this was the joint march of the athletes of the NOCs of the Republic of Korea and the Democratic People's Republic of Korea at the Opening Ceremony. They entered the Olympic Stadium as one team, united behind one flag, the Korean unification flag.

This moment, of course, did not happen by chance. It was the result of a long process of negotiations and high-level government engagement by the International Olympic Committee that began back in 2014 and lasted until four hours before the Opening Ceremony.

With these powerful symbols and gestures in PyeongChang, we have seen how the Olympic Games can open the way to dialogue, how the Olympic values can open the way to a more peaceful future.

The success of PyeongChang was never a foregone conclusion. Only a few months before the Games, the thought of both Korean teams marching peacefully at the Olympic Games together seemed impossible: we were facing missile launches and nuclear tests on the Korean peninsula. But throughout even the most difficult times of political tensions, the IOC always kept the door open for the participation of North Korean athletes in PyeongChang.

Both leaders of both countries thanked the IOC afterwards for having opened the door for their peace talks through these actions. Speaking at the UN General Assembly in September 2018, President Moon Jae-in of South Korea highlighted once again the important role the IOC had played in opening the door for the current rapprochement. He said: "The IOC deserves a lot of credit for surprising changes of late by helping North Korea participate in the PyeongChang Winter Olympics."

During my visit to North Korea in March 2018, the country's leader Kim Jong-un said that the Olympic Winter Games had shifted the momentum in North-South Korean relations and that this was "totally attributable to the efforts of the IOC". He also committed that athletes from his country would participate in the Olympic Games Tokyo 2020, the Olympic Winter Games Beijing 2022 and the next editions of the Youth Olympic Games.

Both leaders asked the IOC to continue to support the ongoing political peace talks on the Korean peninsula through sport. The IOC is committed to doing this.

In PyeongChang, we sanctioned the systematic manipulation of the anti-doping system in Russia during the Olympic Winter Games Sochi 2014. The IOC sanctioned those entities involved, proportional to their levels of responsibility. At the same time, we upheld the principle of individual justice to which every human being is entitled. This is why we created a pathway for clean, individual Russian athletes to compete in PyeongChang, but only under the strictest conditions. In this way, we did justice to all athletes, regardless of their passport. With its suspension from the Olympic Winter Games PyeongChang 2018, the Russian Olympic Committee has served its sanction, while in other organisations procedures are still ongoing.

Another key event this past Olympic year was the Olympism in Action Forum, which took place in Buenos Aires just ahead of the Youth Olympic Games. Bringing together thought leaders from all walks of life to discuss emerging trends affecting the future of sport, the Olympism in Action Forum was an opportunity for the Olympic Movement to open its windows, let in fresh ideas and hear about new perspectives from a variety of voices. The Forum also benefited from the participation of many youth representatives and Young Change-Makers, who brought the views and voices of young people to the discussions. To allow for direct dialogue, critical voices were also invited to the Forum, engaging them in a frank exchange of views with representatives from the Olympic Movement. The Forum provided an overview of the vast number of activities and initiatives of the IOC and the Olympic Movement, ranging from gender equality and empowering women in and through sport to governance, sustainability and the future of the Olympic Games.

The Youth Olympic Games Buenos Aires 2018 were truly the Youth Olympic Games of a new era. Starting with the Opening Ceremony in the heart of the city – attended by hundreds of thousands of people in the streets – to the full venues, it was innovation from start to finish, bringing sport to where the people are. These Youth Olympic Games were more urban, more female and more inclusive than ever before. The urban parks concept was a great success, as demonstrated by the fact that over 1 million spectators filled the venues across the city with an amazing atmosphere. In an important milestone for gender equality in Olympic sport, Buenos Aires saw the first-ever Olympic sports programme with complete gender equality, with the same number of girls and boys taking part in the same number of sports events. New sports and disciplines brought additional youth appeal to the programme. The Argentinian people have every reason to be proud of this wonderful celebration of youth, sport and culture that they united behind with such great passion and enthusiasm. With this great success, Buenos Aires has shown the way for the Youth Olympic Games 2022 in Dakar, Senegal – the first-ever Olympic competition organised in Africa.

Reflecting on the words of Pierre de Coubertin, we see many of the themes he mentioned echoed in the events that shaped the Olympic year 2018. In many ways, we see that his great heritage is still very much alive and of more relevance than ever in our fragile world today. As present-day custodians of his great Olympic heritage, it is now our responsibility to carry the Olympic values to the future. In this Olympic spirit and building on the momentum from this past Olympic year 2018, we can look ahead with confidence and optimism to 2019.

## [Where we are going to]

The preparations for the Olympic Games Tokyo 2020 are in full swing and progressing in an excellent way. With 18 months before the opening of the Games, I have never seen an Olympic city that is as prepared as Tokyo, and we have every confidence that the preparations will continue as smoothly in the final stretch.

Looking ahead to 2019, a highlight of the 125th anniversary of the IOC's establishment by Pierre de Coubertin will be the much-anticipated opening of Olympic House, the new IOC headquarters. After a three-year renovation and reconstruction, the new building will bring together the IOC administration under one roof. Olympic House will become the new home for the entire Olympic Movement. Its design ensures that the building fits into its environmental and historic setting. The new headquarters is a bridge between the roots of the IOC in Lausanne and our vision for the future.

In 2019, we will have an important decision to select the host of the Olympic Winter Games 2026. The strong candidatures are embracing the Olympic Agenda 2020 reforms, as demonstrated by the fact that they plan to use 80 per cent of existing or temporary venues and facilities. We have made it clear that, in 2026, we want to return to a traditional winter sports country, and I am sure that we will have an excellent host city for the Olympic Winter Games 2026.

This upcoming year will also be important to reinforce the message that, when it comes to good governance, what affects one of us in the Olympic Movement affects all of us. This means that rules of good governance and ethics have to apply to the entire Olympic Movement. Everyone has a responsibility to uphold the standards of good governance in everything we do, because at the end of the day, we are only as strong as the weakest link. The IOC has already implemented all good governance measures called for under Olympic Agenda 2020. We have reformed, and we have changed. But we know that even the best rules will not make us immune to misconduct. No organisation in the world can be immune in this respect. It is an unfortunate fact that some of the challenges we are facing today originate from the time before our reforms came into effect. However, with the Olympic Agenda 2020 reforms in place, we are now able to handle wrongdoing in a better way than before the reforms. As recent events have shown, whenever such cases of wrongdoing arise, we take action and the necessary measures, because we know that it is in our own highest interest to protect the integrity of sport.

2019 will also be an important year to further strengthen the role of the International Testing Agency (ITA) to make testing and sanctioning independent from sports organisations and national interests. Much progress has been made already with 40 partners having joined the ITA, thereby avoiding even the perception of a conflict of interest and increasing the credibility of the anti-doping system of IFs and any major sports events organiser.

In our fragile world, which is full of uncertainty and confrontation, the IOC enjoys great stability against all the odds. The future of the Games is secured with the Olympic Winter Games Beijing 2022, the Olympic Games

Paris 2024 and the Olympic Games Los Angeles 2028 in place. We already have interest from numerous cities and NOCs for the Olympic Winter Games 2030 and even for the Olympic Games 2032, 13 years in advance. In these volatile times, the Olympic Games are more important than ever to bring the entire world together in peaceful competition. Our Worldwide TOP Partners and Rights-Holding Broadcasters, after a rigorous and diligent analysis, are demonstrating their confidence and trust in the Olympic Games and the IOC through long-term agreements, some until 2032.

We also see this expression of confidence through the success of the Olympic Channel – making the magic of Olympic sport and the Olympic athletes available throughout the year to everybody around the globe. The Olympic Channel's content resonates well, in particular with the young generation, as demonstrated by the 2 billion video views since it began operating two years ago. Attracting young people to the Olympic Games and the values of sport will continue with the increased localisation of Olympic Channel content in 2019.

Everything taken together – the growing relevance of the Olympic Games, the long-term financial security, and making Olympic sport attractive for young people – is what gives the entire Olympic Movement this great stability. In our fragile world, this stability is perhaps the strongest currency that you can have. Not many other organisations can claim to have this strong currency in our volatile times.

The athletes are at the heart of everything we do. With the adoption of the Athletes' Rights and Responsibilities Declaration, we have taken a historic step to strengthen the role of the athletes in our Olympic Movement. This Declaration also represents an emotional milestone for me personally.

As a former member of the first IOC Athletes' Commission, set up after the Baden-Baden Olympic Congress 1981, I was fighting for athletes' representation and athletes' rights. Ever since then, this topic has been close to my heart. Seeing this long process come to fruition is therefore of great personal satisfaction. The participation of more than 4,200 athletes in the preparation of the Declaration was a milestone with regard to the legitimacy of athlete representation because of its universality and diversity. Therefore, the IOC Athletes' Commission and its Steering Committee, like nobody else, can truly speak on behalf of the athletes of the world.

2019 will be a crucial year to roll out and implement this Declaration. Also for this reason, the IOC will hold the biggest-ever Athletes' Forum in April 2019. Many NOCs, Continental Associations and IFs are already supporting the Declaration, and I hope that many more will follow in 2019. I encourage all athletes to make their voices heard through their elected athlete representatives who will be present at this Athletes' Forum. It will mark a major step deepening and strengthening athletes' participation at the heart of the Olympic Movement.

For all these reasons, 2019 promises to be a year that will set the course for the future of the Olympic Movement in many different ways.

As Coubertin reminded us 100 years ago, we are only temporary trustees of his great heritage. Then as now, let us ensure that we continue to carry this responsibility with dignity so that we can pass on his Olympic legacy to the next generation "enriched still further by our virtues, our constancy, our loyalty and our self-sacrifice". We have every reason to look to the future with confidence and optimism. In this Olympic spirit to constantly strive further, I wish you a happy and prosperous New Year.

Thomas Bach

IOC President

## 17. New Year's Message for 2023 by IOC President Thomas Bach

The Winter Olympics took place in Beijing from February 4 to 20, making the Chinese capital the first city to stage the summer and winter editions of the Games.

However, Beijing 2022 took place against a backdrop of human rights concerns, with hosts China's treatment of Uyghur Muslims in Xinjiang and its record in Tibet and Hong Kong coming under scrutiny.

This sparked a diplomatic boycott from Western nations including the United States, Australia, Britain and Canada.

Beijing consistently denied the charges laid against it, and dismissed a United Nations (UN) report in August that found "serious human rights violations" against Uyghur Muslims and other ethnic minorities in Xinjiang as a "politicised document that ignores the facts".

The IOC's handling of these concerns was criticised by human rights groups, although earlier this year it introduced a Strategic Framework on Human Rights and launched an Advisory Committee on Human Rights.

Bach maintained an upbeat tone in his reflections on Beijing 2022, pointing to viewing figures of more than two billion and describing the event as "the most appealing sports and entertainment event in the world".

"These Olympic Winter Games faced unprecedented challenges against the backdrop of political tensions and a global pandemic," the IOC President said.

"Despite this, these Games offered the most outstanding conditions for the athletes in an absolutely safe and secure environment.

"The athletes expressed their gratitude by stepping up and amazing the world with their response to all the challenges and adversity.

"They showed all of us the best that humankind can be, if we come together in peace and solidarity."

Bach then turned to Russia's invasion of Ukraine, assisted by Belarus, in the days following the end of the Winter Olympics.

He reiterated the IOC's stance in response to the war, distinguishing between sanctions - including a ban on national symbols of both countries - and protective measures in recommending the non-participation of Russian and Belarusian athletes in international sport.

The German official said that sanctions "must and will remain firmly in place", but again blamed "political pressure and interference" for the introduction of measures against athletes which he claimed were "against our mission to unify the entire world in peaceful competition".

He referenced the UN General Assembly's resolution on "sport as an enabler of sustainable development", as he did after the IOC Executive Board meeting earlier this month, among the "encouraging statements and declarations".

"Such encouraging signs of support give us all the more reason to promote our unifying mission with our full determination - and it gives us hope that it will bring us closer to being able to once again fully live up to the mission of sport to unite the entire world in peaceful competition," Bach said.

"In this spirit, we can look ahead to 2023 with hope and optimism.

"All the support from all walks of life for our peace-mission shows: the power of sport as a force for good in the world is widely acknowledged - and it is needed more than ever.

"Especially in a time when division and conflict is gaining ground over dialogue and cooperation - in a time, when, tragically, it is not people but the guns of war that are doing the talking."

The IOC entertained a proposal at the Olympic Summit to allow Russian and Belarusian athletes to compete as neutrals at Olympic Council of Asia qualifying events earlier this month, which drew criticism from Ukraine including from the country's President Volodymyr Zelenskyy.

Bach pledged his support for Ukrainian athletes and the Olympic community in his New Year message, expressing a desire for a "strong team" to feature at Paris 2024 and Milan Cortina 2026.

Looking to the "pre-Olympic year" of 2023, Bach claimed that the Olympic Qualifier Series for Paris 2024 helped to promote athletes and sports "in new and exciting ways" and the inaugural Olympic Esports Week in Singapore in June would be "the next major step for us to engage even deeper with the young generation".

He promised that Paris 2024 will be "more inclusive, more youthful, more urban, more sustainable - and they will be the very first Olympic Games with full gender parity".

The IOC President concluded by offering best wishes for 2023.

"Our values, our solidarity, our unity, our peace-mission - all this makes our beloved Olympic Movement so unique," Bach said.

"This is the solid foundation on which we can build our future - on which we can build a better and more peaceful world through sport.

"So let us join hands to go faster, aim higher, become stronger - together.

"In this true Olympic spirit, I wish you all a happy, healthy and successful pre-Olympic year 2023."

## 18. New Year's Message for 2024(Year of Blue Dragon) by IOC President Thomas Bach

Dear Olympic friends,

At the start of this very special Olympic year, there is so much to be grateful for and so much to look forward to.

Kicking off this Olympic year will be the Winter Youth Olympic Games Gangwon 2024. Building on the great legacy of the Olympic Winter Games PyeongChang 2018, we will celebrate a new generation of athletes in Gangwon – "Growing Together and Shining Forever" is the slogan.

© IOC/Greg Martin

With the Olympic and Paralympic Games Paris 2024 only months away, the athletes, the fans, the entire Olympic community – all of us – are looking forward to a new era of Olympic Games: younger, more inclusive, more urban, more sustainable. The very first Olympic Games with full gender parity. The very first Olympic Games aligned with Olympic Agenda from start to finish.

It is inspiring to see everyone in the Olympic Movement making this new era of Olympic Games a reality. Therefore, we can look forward with great confidence to the Olympic Games Paris 2024 as a symbol of global unity and peace.

Our expectations for these Olympic Games are shared by billions of people. In these difficult times we are living through, people everywhere are exhausted and tired of all the antagonism, the hostility, the hate they are confronted with in every area of their lives.

Deep in our hearts, we are all longing for something unifying. Something that brings us together, despite the differences we have. Something that gives us hope. Something that inspires us to address problems in a peaceful way. Something that brings out the best in us. We are longing for the Olympic Games Paris 2024 to unite the entire world in peaceful competition.

These feelings are also shared by the international community. The United Nations General Assembly approved the Olympic Truce Resolution for Paris by an overwhelming majority and with no votes against – a remarkable display of unity in these divisive times.

We are very grateful for this strong global support. At the same time, all the great expectations for Paris mean a great responsibility for all of us – the responsibility to live up to these expectations.

We can only achieve this if we in the Olympic Movement stand together. Therefore, we need to stand against efforts to fragment world sport along political lines – and we need to stand together for the unifying power of sport.

Beyond the Olympic Games Paris 2024, we are standing united for our mission to make the world a better place through sport. With our Olympic Agenda 2020+5, we are strengthening the role of sport in society; promoting Olympic values in communities everywhere; improving lives with the power of sport; and in this way, contributing to achieving the UN Sustainable Development Goals in areas such as health, education, gender equality, climate action, peace and many more.

With Olympic Agenda, we are also driving forward the digitalisation of the Olympic Movement. The digital revolution, and in particular artificial intelligence and esports, offer us huge opportunities. We need to seize them now. This is why the IOC Esports Commission is studying the creation of Olympic Esports Games. This new endeavour has been received with enthusiasm by the esports community. We are truly breaking new ground. The strong momentum confirms the great potential that this exciting digital project represents for us. Whatever shape the Olympic Esports Games will take, our parameters and conditions are set. We will stay true to our values – the Olympic values of peace, respect, non-discrimination and solidarity.

When it comes to AI, our "change or be changed" imperative takes on new meaning. We want to use the transformative power of AI to support athletes and to drive the development of sport. This is about identifying talent; creating individualised training methods; making judging more objective; customising the individual viewing experience of billions of Olympic fans. The opportunities are boundless, and we will have to mitigate the risks.

Building on this momentum and energy, we can look to the future of our Olympic community with great confidence. United in all our diversity, we live our Olympic motto: we are going even faster, we are aiming even higher, we are getting even stronger – because we stand together. Faster, Higher, Stronger – Together.

What better place than Paris to celebrate this true Olympic spirit?

Paris: the birthplace of our founder, Pierre de Coubertin.

Paris: the City of Light.

Paris: the City of Love.

Paris: the city of a new era of Olympic Games.

In this Olympic spirit, I wish you all the very best for this Olympic year, 2024, and I look forward to seeing you soon in Paris for an unforgettable celebration of the joy of sport, for a celebration of our shared humanity.

# 19. IOC President Bach's Writing to Olympic Movement: Olympism and Corona (29 April 2020)

## OLYMPISM AND CORONA

With the global COVID-19 pandemic, we are all living in much uncertainty. At this point in time, this uncertainty is far from subsiding. We are all only beginning to understand the far-reaching consequences of the coronavirus crisis around the world. What is certain, however, is that this pandemic has affected and will affect all areas of society, including all of us in the world of sport, significantly. The global spread of the virus has meant that the Olympic Games Tokyo 2020 have had to be postponed to 2021, a historic decision that was taken in order to safeguard the health of the athletes and the hundreds of thousands of people involved in the Games. In this respect, please accept my sincere thanks and appreciation to each and every one of you for your strong support of the decision by the IOC Executive Board to postpone the Olympic Games Tokyo 2020, which we took together with our Japanese partners and friends. Given the difficult circumstances we are all currently facing, the very broad and overarching support for this decision was not a foregone conclusion. This is why the support of all 206 National Olympic Committees (NOCs), all Summer Olympic International Federations (IFs) plus the IOC Athletes' Commission and the continental athletes' commissions for this historic postponement is a great demonstration of the unity of the Olympic Movement under these unprecedented circumstances.

### 1) Coronavirus crisis management

Now we have another unprecedented challenge ahead of us – organising the postponed Olympic Games. This is a first in our long Olympic history, and it is an immense task for the IOC, our Japanese partners and friends, and all the members of our Olympic community. This new situation will need all our solidarity, creativity, determination and flexibility. We shall all need to make sacrifices and compromises. Extraordinary circumstances call for extraordinary measures. This situation requires every one of us to do our part, and this applies to all of us, including the IOC. For our part, we have made it clear that the IOC will continue to be responsible for its share of the operational burden and its share of the costs for these postponed Games, under the terms of the existing agreement for 2020 that we have with our Japanese partners and friends. Although it is too early to give an exact figure, we already know that we have to shoulder several hundred million US dollars of postponement costs. This is why we also need to look into and review all the services that we provide for these postponed Games. With regard to supporting the Olympic community that is affected by this crisis, we are already in fruitful discussions with the athletes, the NOCs and the IFs, as well as our commercial partners and sponsors. As immediate measures, we have already extended all Olympic grants to the NOCs to cover their preparations for the Games. This also applies to the grants for 1,600 Olympic Scholarship athletes worldwide and the IOC Refugee Team. The joint Task Force with the symbolic name "Here we Go" is already working at full speed in a highly professional way. It has established the priorities and management strategies to make these postponed Olympic Games feasible and successful. These priorities include first of all to create a safe environment with regard to health for all participants. Here, we can continue to rely on the advice of the World Health Organisation (WHO) concerning potential adaptations to the organisation of mass gatherings. With regard to feasibility, the IOC has provided a wide-ranging catalogue of cost-saving measures to the joint Task Force. By following this strategy, we have the unique opportunity to turn the celebration of the postponed Olympic Games Tokyo 2020 into a festival of unity for humankind, and a symbol of human resilience to overcome this coronavirus crisis. Imagine what a powerful signal of hope these Olympic Games will be for the world during these unprecedented times. The Olympic flame can be the light at the end of the dark tunnel that humankind currently finds itself in.

### 1) The post-coronavirus world

At this moment, nobody knows what the realities of the post-coronavirus world will look like. What is clear, however, is that probably none of us will be able to sustain every single initiative or event that we were planning before this crisis hit. We will all need to take a close look at the scope of some of our activities and make the necessary adjustments to the new realities. In this context, the IOC administration is reviewing the IOC's budget and priorities. This review will shortly be presented to the IOC Executive Board for discussion and approval. The motto when we launched Olympic Agenda 2020, and which is written on the wall at Olympic House: "Change or be changed", is in this crisis-time more relevant than ever. As challenging and difficult as the circumstances may appear right now, if we draw the right lessons from the current situation, we can shape our future to even strengthen the relevance of our Olympic Movement in the world. Therefore, we should drive further the reforms of Olympic Agenda 2020, in particular with regard to sustainability, in order to address this crisis. To accomplish this, as a responsible organization we should dare to look into the future of the world after this crisis. History tells us that significant crises or systemic shocks, like the coronavirus pandemic, have profound and far-reaching impacts on society at large. Therefore, we have to imagine in what kind of post-coronavirus world sport, the Olympic values and the Olympic Games will find themselves in. At this moment in time, nobody can truly predict the realities of this post-coronavirus world. But if we want to be prepared, we need to try to look further ahead. To this discussion I would like to contribute some food for thought: One could imagine three broad scenarios, while bearing in mind that these are by no means exhaustive, nor likely to become reality in their pure form, but will differ according to their national, regional and cultural background. In the first scenario, society will try to continue much like before the crisis. With this scenario, the current crisis would most likely exacerbate already existing social and economic inequalities. Too many inequalities and inefficiencies in too many societies have been laid bare in this crisis. The world will not be able to overcome these by blindly following computer algorithms based on data stemming from the past, like from the financial crisis in 2008. This crisis is very different. To overcome this crisis will require human excellence, experience and creativity. The second scenario is largely characterized by society and nations driven even more by egoism and self-interest. This scenario could lead to even more divided societies, to more inequalities, with all the social risks this entails for the political systems. It would lead to a dramatic worsening of international relations, protectionism and political confrontation in all aspects of human life: the economy, sport, culture, humanitarian aid, everything would become a political tool in this political confrontation. The main features of the third scenario are more solidarity and international cooperation. This scenario would mean that we have understood that we cannot predict or shape the future state of the world by relying solely on technology, and that no individual, no government, no nation can solve the big problems of humanity on their own. This would lead to efforts to share the hardship of the crisis in a fair way among people and nations, and to strengthen a fair and cooperative world order. Whichever elements of these scenarios are dominant, there will be a fundamental effect on sport and society at large. Being united by our Olympic values of peace, solidarity, respect and unity in all our diversity, we can make an important contribution to this post-coronavirus world. We can do so from a strong basis. Thanks to the many reforms of Olympic Agenda 2020 we are enjoying long-term stability. This allows us to shoulder not only our share of the postponement costs of the Olympic Games Tokyo 2020 but at the same time keep assisting the athletes and the Olympic stakeholders. Yet there is no reason to be complacent. This post-coronavirus world will confront us with more challenges, in particular social, economic and political ones. Therefore, we have to drive Olympic Agenda 2020 forward and adapt it.

### 1) Social impact

We can fairly assume that, in the post-coronavirus society, public health will play a much more important role. Sport and physical activity make a great contribution to health. While studies by the WHO had already demonstrated this with stunning results concerning non-communicable diseases, the coronavirus crisis teaches us how much a sound general health situation helps to overcome communicable diseases as well. Sport and physical activity are therefore the perhaps most low-cost tool for a healthy society. To make this even more evident too, the IOC is about to conclude a new Memorandum of Understanding with the WHO. We can highlight the significance of sport for inclusivity and integration. Sometimes, sport is the only activity that unites people regardless of their social, political, religious or cultural background. Sport is the glue bonding a society together. Such inclusivity is even more important in otherwise deeply divided societies. We shall also have to consider what social distancing may mean for our relations with e-sports. Whilst maintaining our principles by respecting the "red line" with regard to the Olympic values, we encourage all our stakeholders even more urgently to "consider how to govern electronic and virtual forms of their sport and explore opportunities with game publishers" (Declaration of the 8th Olympic Summit, 7 December 2019). Some IFs have already been very creative by organizing remote competitions. We should further strengthen these moves and encourage our joint working group to address this new challenge and opportunity.

### 1) Economic impact

Without any doubt, the current health crisis will lead to a long and deep economic crisis, the effect of which on sport may differ from country to country. This will depend greatly on the importance governments will give to the enormous social capital represented by sport when it comes to the allocation of the financial assistance provided by them for the recovery of economy. Therefore, we should strongly request governments to appreciate and honor the immense contribution of sport to public health, its importance for inclusion, social life and culture, and its important role for their national economies. In Europe, for example, a recent study showed that sport contributes more than two percent to GDP, a contribution which makes sport economically more important than a number of more traditional economic sectors. The same study found that nearly three per cent of all jobs in Europe are sport-related. Sport is therefore a big employer. This study, like many others, demonstrates that sport can play not just a positive social role but also an economic one in helping the world to recover from the crisis. We are not part of the problem. We can be part of the solution. To achieve this, governments must include sport in their economic support programmes. However, for most sports events, as for all sectors of society, things will not be as they were before. This is why the IOC should further strengthen the sustainability and feasibility reforms of Olympic Agenda 2020 with a new phase of the "New Norm" to make even more savings possible for the Organizing Committees of the Olympic Games. These new measures should lead to an even more restricted footprint for all the stakeholders at the Olympic Games. The IOC will also study whether and how we can accelerate our response to climate change. The IOC as an organization is already carbon neutral, as the Olympic Games Tokyo 2020 should also be. Our new aim could be to make them both climate positive even before 2030, which is the year targeted by the international community to achieve their climate goals. For the Olympic Movement as a whole, we may also have to look more closely into the proliferation of sports events, as we already discussed at previous Olympic Summits. The financial pressure on all the stakeholders, including NOCs, IFs and Organizing Committees, may require more consolidation in this respect.

### 2) Political impact

At least in some parts of the world, we may see more nationalism, more protectionism and, as a result, more political confrontation. Here, our Olympic values of solidarity, peace, respect for each other and for the global rules of sport need to be emphasized. By living in and strengthening solidarity we can show that respectful international cooperation produces better and fairer results than isolationism. We all have to make every effort to ensure that the Olympic Games are supported by the entire international community as the demonstration of the "Unity of humankind in all our diversity"; that the Olympic Games are building bridges for everybody without any kind of discrimination; and that therefore the Olympic Games as this unique sports, cultural and social event should be beyond any political or other divisive considerations.

### 2) The way forward

I hope that with these ideas I can contribute to a comprehensive discussion. Therefore, I propose a wide-ranging consultation among all of us under the guidance of the IOC Executive Board and the IOC Session, as we did for Olympic Agenda 2020. Already the Ancient Greeks, to whom we owe the Olympic Games, knew that with every crisis comes an opportunity. Let us take this opportunity in a way of unity and creativity to emerge from this crisis even stronger than before. The post-coronavirus world will need sport, and we are ready to contribute to shaping it with our Olympic values.

Lausanne, 29 April 2020

Thomas Bach

## 20. Strategic Framework on Human Rights to Realize Best Practices in the Selection of Future Olympic Games Hosts at the IOC Executive Board on 9 September 2022

1) *"This Framework will fundamentally shape the working practices of the IOC, the Olympic Games, and the entire Olympic Movement, ensuring that human rights are respected within our own respective remit"*
2) *"The overarching mission of the Olympic Movement, as you know, is for sport to contribute to a better world ... It will address selection of future Olympic Games hosts and the delivery of the Olympic Games."*
3) *"What is clear ... is the [host city selection] procedure, and there, you*

*can see from this Human Rights Framework that the Future Host Commission, which is leading this process, will be guided by the U.N. [Guiding Principles])"*

(1)Equality and non-discrimination

(2) Safety and well-being

(3)Livelihood and decent work

(4)Voice

(5)Privacy

***Four related Goal Targets:**

(1)Athletes

(2) IOC/IF/NOC and organizing committee workforce

(3)Workers in supply and value chains

(4)Olympic-related communities

*4) "We have, of course, taken note of this report.*

*5) With regards to the Olympic Winter Games*

*Beijing 2022, which fall within our remit, the IOC worked together with the organizing committee to ensure that all the obligations in the Host City Contract were met, and if you read the report by the U.N. High Commissioner and you look into the recommendations which are directed to the wider society, there is the call, therefore, for respect of the U.N. [Guiding Principles], and this is what we are doing*

## 21. IOC President Thomas Bach's Position on Russia's Participation in the Paris 2024 Games (IOC EB in March 2023)

1) "It is deplorable to see that some Governments do not want to respect the majority within the Olympic Movement and all stakeholders, nor the autonomy of sport which they are appraising and requesting from other countries in countless speeches, UN resolutions, European Union declarations and at every other opportunity."
2) "It is deplorable that these Governments do not address the question of double standards with which we have been confronted in our consultations."
3) "We have not seen a single comment on their attitude on the participation of athletes whose countries are involved in the other 70 wars and armed conflict in the world."
4) "It is even more deplorable that they grossly neglect the very clear

statement of the two special rapporteurs from the UN Human Rights Council, while in other issues they are always highlighting their firm requests for the respect of human rights."

5) "That both sides in this confrontation are not satisfied to say it diplomatically might indicate that we found some middle ground on which we all can move forward to make a contribution to understanding and peace through sport"

6) "Today after all the responses we got, I can only reaffirm that the entire Olympic Movement strongly stands by its values and by its mission to unite the world in a peaceful competition."

## 22. IOC President Thomas Bach's Message at Mumbai IOC Session (15 October 2023) about the Petitions by some IOC Members for the Extension of IOC President's Term of Office

1) "First of all, say thank you very much for your kind words of support, because I think these words of support are not only directed to me, they are directed to all of us"
2) "What made us overcome the challenges we had was exactly this unity, this support which you expressed with regard to many items overall at the time, and we can only be credible if we are appealing to all these divisive forces in the world, if we are appealing to respect the unifying of sport if we ourselves are unified."
3) "Otherwise, we have no credibility. If we are divided, how can we teach others about unity and our unifying power."
4) "You also know I am very loyal to the Olympic Charter"
5) "Being a core author of this Olympic Charter drives me to be more loyal to this Olympic Charter."
6) "You have heard the explanation of the chair of our Legal Commission in this direction"
7) "Thank you very much again, I am very touched by your support and friendship."

## 23. Midway Report about Olympic Agenda 2020+5 by IOC President Thomas Bach at Mumbai 2023 IOC Session on 10 October (What we can achieve together)

1) "Our world has changed in fundamental ways in recent years."
2) "As we anticipated at the beginning of the COVID-19 crisis, we are now facing its far-reaching social, financial, economic and political

consequences, which are exacerbated by the ongoing conflicts, wars and natural catastrophes that we must address."

3) "Olympic Agenda 2020+5 is our roadmap to prepare ourselves for this new world, and we can be proud of the progress that has been made across all 15 recommendations since it was adopted in March 2021."
4) "The accomplishments described in this Report are great examples of what we can achieve together, and are testament to the tremendous amount of work that has been carried out in partnership with our stakeholders."
5) "There is still more to be done, but we can already look forward to the Olympic Games Paris 2024 as the Games of a new era, inspired by Olympic Agenda 2020 and Olympic Agenda 2020+5 from start to finish."

## 24. Thomas Bach IOC President as Chair of IOC Refugee Foundation (14 December 2023)

1) "Sport is about so much more than physical activity.
2) Sport is empowerment.
3) Sport is health.
4) Sport is inclusion.
5) Sport is respect.
6) Sport is solidarity.
7) Sport is belonging.
8) Sport is peace.

## 25. IOC President Thomas Bach's Message of Condolences in Memory of the late Henry Kissinger (IOC Honor Member)

1) "When I was elected IOC President in 2013, I approached him and asked whether he would be ready to advise the IOC and me, as he had

done through the IOC 2000 Commission. "

2) "He immediately said yes. Since then, we spoke regularly and became friends."

3) "He gave me invaluable advice in all the many geopolitical issues the world and sport had to face in recent years."

4) "I will greatly miss a brilliant man and a warm-hearted friend. My thoughts are with his beloved wife Nancy and all his family."

**I would also like to pay my homage and personal respect to the late Henry Kissinger, the last IOC Honor member, who recently passed away. And I send my deepest sympathy and condolences to his bereaved family and the entire Olympic Movement. He kindly sent to me his message about my book publication as follows:*

*"Dear Professor Yoon,*

*Thank you for sending me a copy of your book, "When Sport meets the World Over Five Rings"*

*It gives me a very interesting and complete picture of the vast amount of planning and work that goes into hosting a successful Olympics.*

*Your enthusiasm, knowledge and experiences are a valuable resource and I appreciate your graciousness in thinking of me.*

*Warm regards,*

*Henry A. Kissinger"*

Mr Henry KISSINGER

USA

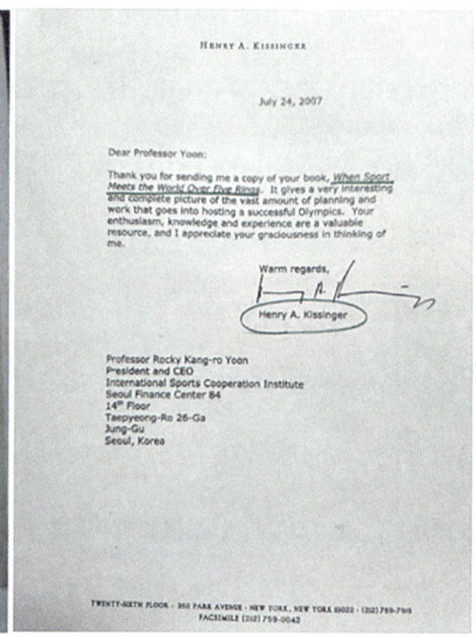

HENRY A. KISSINGER

July 24, 2007

Dear Professor Yoon:

Thank you for sending me a copy of your book, *When Sport Meets the World Over Five Rings*. It gives a very interesting and complete picture of the vast amount of planning and work that goes into hosting a successful Olympics. Your enthusiasm, knowledge and experience are a valuable resource, and I appreciate your graciousness in thinking of me.

Warm regards,

Henry A. Kissinger

Professor Rocky Kang-ro Yoon
President and CEO
International Sports Cooperation Institute
Seoul Finance Center 84
14th Floor
Taepyeong-Ro 26-Ga
Jung-Gu
Seoul, Korea

TWENTY-SIXTH FLOOR · 350 PARK AVENUE · NEW YORK, NEW YORK 10022 · (212) 759-7919
FACSIMILE (212) 759-0042

## 26. IOC President Thomas Bach's Brilliant Brain Child and a New Strategic Roadmap for the Future Olympic Movement, Olympic Agenda 2020+5 (Ref.: IOC website)

The 15 recommendations are based on key trends that have been identified as likely to be decisive in the post-coronavirus world. They are also areas where sport and the values of Olympism can play a key role in turning challenges into opportunities.

The key trends include:

1) The need for greater solidarity within and among societies;

*The growth in digitalization, while keeping in mind the need to expand

## 2032/2036년 포함 향후 올림픽개최도시 IOC 요구사항 및 주안점 5가지(지속가능 올림픽)

* Five "Flexible requirements to ensure sustainable Games" :

● Maximum use of existing venues(기존 경기장 최대 사용)
● Only existing mono-functional venues for Winter Games(동계올림픽, 기존 단 기능성 경기장 활용)
● Robust legacy plan for any new construction(신설경기장의 경우, 반드시 건실한 레거시플랜필수)
● No minimum capacity(경기장최소확보 좌석수제한철폐)
● Sharing opportunities(제반기회공유)

digital capability to the currently digitally underserved;

-The urgency of achieving sustainable development;

-The growing demand for credibility, both of organizations and institutions; and

-The need to build resilience in the face of the financial and economic consequences that will result from the COVID-19 pandemic and which will influence priority-setting among governments and enterprises.

2) The 15 recommendations, which have been inspired by these trends, call upon the IOC and the Olympic Movement to:

(1) Strengthen the uniqueness and the universality of the Olympic Games
(2) Foster sustainable Olympic Games
(3) Reinforce athletes' rights and responsibilities
(4) Continue to attract best athletes
(5) Further strengthen safe sport and the protection of clean athletes
(6) Enhance and promote the Road to the Olympic Games
(7) Coordinate the harmonization of the sports calendar
(8) Grow digital engagement with people
(9) Encourage the development of virtual sports and further engage with video gaming communities
(10) Strengthen the role of sport as an important enabler for the UN Sustainable Development Goals
(11) Strengthen the support to refugees and populations affected by displacement
(12) Reach out beyond the Olympic community
(13) Continue to lead by example in corporate citizenship
(14) Strengthen the Olympic Movement through good governance
(15) Innovate revenue generation models.

Mr Thomas BACH
GER

*(A handover ceremony of the keys to the IOC)*

**THOMAS BACH**
FRG

*(Thomas Bach as an Olympic Champion Montreal 1976)*

*(Gangneung Olympic Museum)*

*(IOC President Thomas Bach's Visit to Gangneung City for his Honorary Citizenship in March 2018)*

# 27. IOC President Thomas Bach's Official Visit to Gangneung Olympic Museum and Hand-Over of his Letter of Nomination for Membership of the IOC Culture and Olympic Heritage Commission to Prof, Rocky Kang-Ro YOON on 31 January 2024

Professor Rocky Yoon Kang-Ro

President

International Sport Diplomacy Institute

"Dear Friend,

It is a great pleasure for me to appoint you as a member of the:

Culture and Olympic Heritage Commission

Please find enclosed the composition of the Commission, which is chaired by IOC Member Mrs. Khunying Patama Leeswadtrakul.

Thanking you in advance for the valuable contribution you will provide to the work of this Commission, I remain,

Yours sincerely,

Thomas Bach
IOC President"

**More**
**Vividly, Impressively, Precisely**

Dr Thomas Bach

President

International Olympic Committee

<u>Subj.: Nomination</u>

Dear Honourable IOC President Bach,

I trust that you have returned home safely after another successful YOG, Gangwon2024 Winter Youth Olympic Games.

First of all, I appreciate very much your kind and thankful letter of nomination for me to be appointed as a Member of the IOC Culture and Olympic Heritage Commission chaired by Mme. Khunying Patama LEESWADTRAKUL, IOC Member in Thailand.

During the 42 years in the Olympic Movement both at home and abroad, I have been grateful to the IOC and the Olympic Movement, in general and the IOC President Thomas Bach, in particular.

I always think about you and the future of the Olympic Movement as a true sense of joy of my life.

During my entire Olympic life, I was amazingly crowned by your warm consideration for me, including but not limited to IOC Pierre de Coubertin Medal and the recent appointment for the positon as Member of the IOC Culture and Olympic Heritage.

I consider the above honors to be a true encouragement for me to continue to move forward to "Go faster, Aim Higher, Become Stronger, Together with the Olympic Movement".

In the meantime, may I take this opportunity to thank you so much for your kind and affectionate consideration toward me.

With my highest personal respect and profound gratitude for your great leadership,

Sincerely/Faithfully yours,

Prof. Rocky Kang-Ro YOON

President

International Sport Diplomacy Institute

Member of IOC Culture and Olympic Heritage Commission

## 28. IOC President Thomas Bach's Position on Russia through his Online Interview on 6 March 2024

1) *"The Russian government apparently is ignoring the fact they have forced us to action. It is their invasion and in particular it is their annexation of parts of Ukraine."*
2) *"What is also remarkable is that this aggressivity is coming from the very same government that was behind the scandalous manipulation of the anti-doping system before and during and even after [the 2014 Winter Games] in Sochi."*
3) *Now, she (Kamila Valieva) was misused for political purposes on top of that, by having to stand next to the president, Putin, at the opening ceremony of the so-called Future Games. In this way showing the disrespect for all the worldwide anti-doping rules.*
4) As for security concerns around the Israeli team, given past Muslim

extremism in France, *"Since the heinous attack on the Israeli team [at Munich 1972], there were always special measures being taken with Israeli athletes." "The authorities feel comfortable that the same will be true of course also for Paris, Marseille or wherever there will be Israeli representation."*

## 29. IOC President Thomas Bach, Recipient of the Inaugural 2024 WADA Play True Award in March 2024

He was selected as one of the recipients of the inaugural 2024 Play True Awards, which recognize individuals, groups and organizations that have contributed to the fight against doping at the WADA 2024 Annual Symposium Gala.

IOC President Thomas Bach gave a speech after accepting the above award:

"Protecting clean athletes is the ultimate goal. Tough sanctions and strong deterrence are extremely important, but they are not the goal. They are essential to protect clean athletes. That's what it's all about: Clean athletes."

## 30. IOC President Celebrated 100 years of Olympic Winter Games on 18 March 2024

1) "This first edition of the Winter Games was a real success among the people, and the media for its time, thanks to the determination, commitment and enthusiasm of the organisers and the people of Chamonix. The beauty of your mountains and the magic of winter sports won over the whole world," said IOC President Thomas Bach, addressing the local population gathered at the event."
2) "One hundred years on, the Chamonix Games are continuing to inspire people in the best possible way, through the staging of an event that left a sustainable legacy to future generations"
3) "I would like to warmly thank the town of Chamonix-Mont-Blanc, the people of Chamonix, and its Mayor, Mr Fournier. Thank you for

perpetuating this 100-year-old legacy, and for bringing together so many of your citizens to bring the Olympic spirit to life."

## 31. IOC President Thomas Bach's Remarks at the time of News Conference after the IOC Executive Board meeting on 19~20 March 2024

1) *"The preparations are going extremely well. ..."*

   *"Altogether, Paris is on track to welcome the world and to deliver exceptional*

2) *Olympic Games, in line – and fully in line, from the start to the finish – with Olympic Agenda 2020."*
3) *"So these Olympic Games Paris 2024 will be younger, they will be more urban, they will be more inclusive, they will be more sustainable and, as you know, the IOC has allocated the same number of quota places for male athletes and for female athletes, so they will be the first Olympic Games with full gender parity."*
4) *"We talked also about what has to be on everybody's mind and what unfortunately you know has to be a major concern for every organizer of a big event in world, and this is security."*
5) *"There, we received another very comprehensive report by the [French] Inter-ministerial Delegate [for Sport], Mr. Michel Cadot, and as a result, I can inform you that we have full confidence in the French authorities, and the French authorities, [in] their turn they can also benefit from a very close cooperation with their international*

*partners."*

6) *"The people around the globe are fed up with all the hate, the aggression, the extremely negative news, wars, conflicts they are facing day in and day out. And you really get the feeling that they, as we, in our hearts, they are longing for a positive message. They are looking for something what is unifying them in all these divisions and aggression. And they are looking for something what gives us hope in these otherwise so dark times."*
7) *"We don't have the power to make peace and to convince people not to hate each other, not to be so aggressive. Our mission is to send a signal, to set a symbol that despite all of these what is happening in the world, it is still possible to come together. And this is what we feel and ... that this is a feeling of many, many millions or even billions of people around the globe."*

## 32. IOC President Thomas Bach's Remarks at the 2024 ONOC General Assembly in Fiji on 26 March 2024

He highlighted two particular work streams: e-sports and e-games; and artificial intelligence along with the Olympic Games Paris 2024.

1) "With regard to e-sports and e-games, we cannot ignore the 3 billion people who are familiar with these games and are often not familiar anymore with sport and physical activity. We want to make an effort in this respect, whilst always adhering to our values of non-violence, non-discrimination, respect and tolerance. We have to approach this

community and win them over"

"AI has the potential to change sport in every respect; from the training of athletes, to judging and refereeing, to the fight against doping, to the experience of spectators and solidarity in sport. There

1) is huge potential, along with risks which have to be addressed. The Olympic Movement has to harness its benefits and understand its risks"
2) "They (Paris 2024) will be great Games because, from the beginning, Paris has done what you are doing – it has embraced the message and the method and tools of Olympic Agenda: planning from the beginning in a sustainable way, in an inclusive way, in an urban way. And on top of this, the IOC has ensured that there will be an equal number of quota places for male and female athletes at the Olympic Games for the first time in our history."

A new formula for engagement between sport and politics as intertwined and essential was described last week by International Olympic Committee President Thomas Bach in an important, 48-minute keynote address to the General Assembly of the Oceania National Olympic Committees, meeting in Fiji.

3) *"When speaking about good governance and promoting the relevance of sport in our society, then it's also about respecting the different roles of the actors in society.*
4) *"And that is, in particular, true for politics. We will, hopefully, always have issues with politics.*
5) *"Because if we don't have issues with politics any more, it means we are not relevant any more.*

6) *"Politicians are only interested in successful organizations. If we are not successful, if they don't have the feeling that we have access to so many people in society, that we can contribute something, they will not be interested.*

7) *"So, I hope we will always have issues with politics, but what we need to do is that we can address these challenges in the right way and that means that we have to deal with politics in mutual respect.*

8) *"It means for us, in the world of sport, we have to respect that the world is run by politicians, and not by us. Unfortunately. But we also have to make politics understanding, in politicians understanding that we can only contribute to society, if they respect our autonomy.*

9) *"If they want to politicize us, if they want us to use as political tools, we cannot contribute any more, because then we are losing our values.*

10) *"Politics is always divisive. You always have different opinions, you also always have confrontation, you always have a clash of interests. Sport is unifying. Sport is the contrary of being divisive. Sport is the glue which holds our societies together.*

"To mention only one example, for the differences between sport and politics. So we have to defend by all means our autonomy. And I say it here – I don't know for how many times I've said it

1) *already, but it needs, apparently, to be repeated – that does not mean that we are apolitical, that we behave as if we would live on an island of the Saints, and that we would not acknowledge that also our actions have a political impact, and should have a political impact.*

2) *"Because otherwise, again, we would not be relevant. But, and that's the difference, we have to be politically neutral. That means, for you*

*as an NOC, whoever is in government, always realize that tomorrow they can be in opposition. And the ones who are in opposition can be in government tomorrow.*

3) *"And that they have, by nature, different interests than we have and must have in sport. So, keep your neutrality, work closely with them, as long and as much they respect your autonomy. But draw the line when you feel they want to take you over and they want to absorb you into their political field.*
4) *"And what is true on a national level is also true in an international level. This is why the IOC Executive Board just last week, together with [IOC Vice President] John Coates [AUS] and [ONOC President] Robin Mitchell [FIJ], we passed a declaration against the politicalization of sport, which is about the international level, where we can see such kind of efforts by or the other governments trying to start organizing purely politically-motivated games and sports events without any respect for our values and for our rules."*

So we can say that, as of 25 March 2024, any further discussion of sport being separate from politics must be dismissed. Bach has worked tirelessly – and to the distress of many observers – to further embed the IOC in United Nations projects, which he also spoke to during his ONOC address.

By following this path, Bach believes that it is better, in today's ultra-connected world, to be engaged than apart. So far, he is pulling it off, but it is an open question how well any concept of comity amidst a deeply divided and increasingly hostile world can survive, let alone thrive, now, or for his successor

*Bach IOC President: digitalization "will determine the future of sport"*

5) IOC President Bach, now in his 12th year at the helm of the Olympic Movement, also spoke passionately and in deep detail about staying current and getting ahead of the digital future, and promised a new initiative from the IOC:

*6) "I would like to encourage you to stay ahead of the curve in particular with regard to the one topic that will determine the future of our lives, of our personal lives, that will determine the future of our societies, and which will also determine the future of sport and this is digitalization.*

*2) "The ever-accelerating development of digitalization will, within a couple of years, change our world. And this, when it comes to sport, true, in particular with regard to two work streams.*

*3) "The one is with regard to eSports and eGames, where we cannot ignore that about three billion people on this planet are familiar with these games, and are not necessarily familiar any more in the young age with sport and physical activity. Therefore, we have to look into this area. We cannot ignore it; if we just ignore it, we will lose with we have, with hard work, got back in the last couple of years and what we can see from the numbers and figures in [social-media] followership for games and for sports [by] the young generation. ...*

*4) "We have gained them back. But we will not maintain it, again, if we do not change, if we do not address their areas of society, if we do not address their lifestyle, if we do not address their interests, and there, eSports and eGames is a very important factor. This is why I've asked, there at the latest IOC Session in Mumbai last November our Esports Comission to study the establishment of Olympic*

*Esports Games, where we want to make an effort in this respect, while, of course, always respecting our values, our values of nonviolence, of non-discrimination, of respect and tolerance. These will not be given up, but we have to go, we have to approach this community, to win them over for us, and to keep them interested in us.*

5) *"And the other, even more overwhelming development is artificial intelligence, which has the potential to start to change sports in every respect, from the training of the athletes to judging and refereeing and the fight against doping, to the experience of spectators, be [it] live – where it will be more immersive – be [it] on the screen, where everybody can be there own director in the future and has not to rely on the directors of the broadcasts and so on.*

6) *"There is a huge potential, related also with an imminent risk, like every new technology has risks, which have to be addressed, but there again, sport is different. Not from all other areas of society, but from most of the other areas of society, because there they discuss whether AI will take over their areas. Whether AI will take over human beings, whether AI will replace human beings, and there, for not being alleged of something, let's take our profession, John [Coates, IOC Vice President], we remember that once we have been lawyers, where many people are saying in 10 years you don't need lawyers any more, maybe already in five years.*

7) *"This is different in sport. The 100 meters will always have to be run by an athlete. They will be run by a robot, it's not sport any more.*

8) *"So in sports, this principal question is answered: there in sports, AI can help , can assist, can support, but cannot replace the athlete.*

9) *"And it can help all of us organize sport in a more efficient, in a more sustainable, in a better way.*

10) *"There, you will see next month [in April], already in a couple of weeks – mid of next month – an initiative of the IOC where we will present such a project which brings together a vision of artificial intelligence in sport, and I can only encourage you maybe at your conference preceding your general assembly next year, maybe to dedicate to this topic of AI, in follow-up and implementation of this vision of AI in sport because, again, this will be the main challenge, and, you know me, I'm not so much worried about challenges. I always like to look at the bright side of life, to look at the opportunities AI is offering for us and to do it at the right time, again, before others are taking us over in this respect."*

## 33. IOC President Thomas Bach's Remarks on the occasion of the Olympic Torch Lighting Ceremony at Ancient Olympia on 15 April 2024

1) *"This power of sport will make the Olympic Games Paris 2024 a great symbol of human excellence and unity of all humankind in all our diversity. These expectations are shared by billions of people around the world.*

2) *"In these difficult times we are living through, with wars and conflicts on the rise, people are fed up with all the hate, the aggression and negative news they are facing day in and day out. In their hearts – in all our hearts – we are longing for something which brings us together. We are longing for something that is unifying. We are longing for*

*something that gives us hope."*

## 34. Olympic AI Agenda Launching Ceremony in London on 19 April 2024

Introducing the topic to a global online audience and more than 100 journalists on site, President Bach explained:

1) "When we launched Olympic Agenda, our comprehensive reform programme, in 2014, we did so under the slogan 'change or be changed' – for some of you here in Great Britain this may sound familiar, it's about 'To be, or not to be? That is the question'. Today we are making another step to ensure the uniqueness of the Olympic Games and the relevance of sport, and to do this, we have to be leaders of change, not the object of change. Today, with the ever- accelerating development of digital technology, and in particular AI, we are again at such a crossroads."
2) *"At the centre of the Olympic AI Agenda are human beings. This means: the athletes. Because the athletes are the heart of the Olympic Movement. Unlike other sectors of society, we in sport are not confronted with the existential question of whether AI will replace human beings. In sport, the performances will always have to be delivered by the athletes. The 100 metres will always have to be run by an athlete – a human being. Therefore, we can concentrate on the potential of AI to support the athletes.*
3) *"AI can help to identify athletes and talent in every corner of the world. AI can provide more athletes with access to personalised train-*

*ing methods, superior sports equipment and more individualised programmes to stay fit and healthy. Beyond sporting performance, AI can revolutionise judging and refereeing, thereby strengthening fairness in sport. AI can improve safeguarding in sport. AI will make organising sporting events extremely efficient, transform sports broadcasting and make the spectator experience much more individualised and immersive."*

## 35. IOC President Thomas Bach's Position on the Prize Money(US$50,000) Distribution Plan by World Athletics (through Interview with AFP on 27 April 2024)

1) *The international federations have to treat all their member federations and their athletes on an equal basis and to try to balance this gap between the privileged and the less or under-privileged.*
2) *Each pillar of the Olympic movement has its role to play. It's very clear what the responsibility of an international federation is and what the responsibility of a national Olympic committee is.*

## 36. IOC President Thomas Bach's Speech at 77th World Health Assembly Geneva, 27 May 2024

Your Excellencies,

The power of the collaboration between WHO and the IOC is best illustrated by our different "Let's Move" campaigns.

Already last year's campaign exceeded our expectations.

When our next "Let's Move" campaign kicks-off on Olympic Day, the 23rd of June, we will once again inspire people to move for health, getting millions of people around the globe to warm-up for the Olympic Games and celebrate the joy of sport.

This is why I invite also you to move, because sport keeps our mind and our body strong and healthy.

In this spirit, I would like to thank in particular the Director-General of the WHO, my dear friend Dr. Tedros Ghebreyesus, for the kind invitation to address you, the 77th World Health Assembly.

It is indeed a great honour to be here with you today.

Our meeting allows me to express my appreciation to everyone at the World Health Organization for your guidance, reassurance and support during the dark days of the pandemic.

The pandemic made it crystal clear how important sport is for our physical and mental health.

Sport can save lives.

Obesity, cardiovascular predispositions and other non-communicable diseases were the reasons for the vast majority of mortality during the pandemic.

For all these diseases and predispositions, sport is an excellent tool for prevention.

This is precisely what WHO and the IOC addressed through our joint campaigns like "HealthyTogether" or "Let's Move" – getting millions of people to stay strong and active when life as we knew it ground to a halt.

Countless athletes stepped up to the fight against the virus, joining the pro-vaccination campaigns, working in hospitals, helping and comforting people, encouraging us to stay active and healthy – showing us that sport gives us hope.

A highlight of this athlete's engagement was our digital Olympic workout, which in one single day introduced 500 million people around the globe to our joint campaign.

We took our cooperation to a new level when it came to organising two editions of Olympic Games during the pandemic.

It is no exaggeration to say that without the WHO, and in particular without our great friend Dr. Tedros, the Olympic Games Tokyo 2020 and the Olympic Winter Games Beijing 2022 would not have taken place in a safe way.

Thanks to the comprehensive countermeasures and vaccination programmes that we developed together with the WHO, we could make these Olympic Games safe for everyone – and without a single recorded transmission from the participants to host communities.

This is why it is also a great pleasure to see Professor Katalin Kariko here, who was at the origin of the vaccine development that we could all benefit from and I would like to thank her for this great contribution to humankind and in particular to the Olympic Games.

And I am very happy to have learned this morning that it was not your only contribution to the Olympic Movement – your daughter as a double Olympic champion is a great example of a healthy mind in a healthy body.

In Tokyo and Beijing, the athletes amazed us with their response to all the challenges, showing all of us the best that humankind can be, if we come together in peace, solidarity and unity of purpose.

This reaction of the athletes touched the hearts of billions of people around the world. If these Olympic Games would not have taken place, we would have a lost an entire generation of athletes.

This is why, in the name of all these Olympic athletes, and may I under the supervision of my dear friend, IPC President Andrew Parsons, also say the Paralympic athletes, I would like to thank you for standing by our side in these extremely difficult times.

Since then our partnership continues to go from strength to strength.

We continue to make sport available as the low-cost high-impact tool par excellence for public health.

As part of this effort, IOC and WHO are pioneering new ways of cooperating at the grassroots level, bringing together the expertise of both local health authorities and sport organisations.

Our aim is to facilitate access to community sport activities for over one million people. As part of this joint initiative, we are training coaches, teachers and community health workers of 500 different organisations.

We are doing so through innovative partnerships between National Olympic Committees, local health authorities and sports organisations at the community level.

This is why I would like to encourage you, for not to say, to urge you, to replicate this model of cooperation in your countries. Engage with your National Olympic Committee and your local sport organisations to integrate the low-cost high-impact tool of sport in your healthcare and education systems.

Looking further ahead, we see a great need for future cooperation with

WHO to promote the health of refugees. It was encouraging to see the WHO including health of refugees and migrants in your most recent Global Action Plan.

For the IOC, our work to support refugees through sport is led by our Olympic Refuge Foundation.

The ambitious goal of the Foundation is to give access to safe sport to one million young people affected by displacement by the end of this year.

Probably the most emblematic symbol of our commitment to refugees is the IOC Refugee Olympic Team, which we created for the first time at the Olympic Games Rio 2016, and which will participate with a record number of refugee athletes at the forthcoming Olympic Games Paris 2024.

Through this extensive refugee work together with UNHCR, we are noticing that specialist organisations are realising the importance of sport to address mental health issues.

Just to give you one example: a recent independent study of our sport for mental health programme for refugees in Uganda showed that severe depression from participants who engaged in sport dropped from 57 per cent at the beginning to just 6 per cent at the completion of the programme.

The control group, which did not engage in sport, showed only a very modest drop in depression symptoms.

Seeing this, we extend our hand to you, the WHO and public health authorities, to work closely together for and with refugees.

Your Excellencies, the theme of this World Health Assembly "All for Health, Health for All" is a timely call for collective action. Addressing global health challenges is a team effort.

The world of sport is ready to be a part of this team to build healthy and resilient communities everywhere.

Therefore, speaking under the control of my friend Dr. Tedros, I for once will dare to suggest a humble addition to your well-selected theme today: "All for Health, Health for All… Sport for All".

From our longstanding experience to put sport at the service of society, we know that we have to bring the health benefits of sport to where the people are – this means at the grassroots level, in local communities everywhere.

The Olympic Games Paris 2024 will demonstrate this in a spectacular way.

A programme introducing 30 minutes of daily exercise in primary school throughout France is on track to reach more than four million children.

Paris 2024 is promoting sport and physical activity in over 4,000 municipalities across France. All these efforts to bring sport to where the people are will culminate with the Marathon Pour Tous, the Marathon For All, when over 40,000 people will run the same marathon route just hours before the Olympic athletes.

But Paris is only the most visible aspect of our mission to make the world a better place through sport.

Through our partnership with the WHO, we are going to communities everywhere around the globe, bringing sport to all.

We all share the same objective: All for Health. Health for All. Sport for All.

To build healthy and resilient communities we have to act faster, aim higher, be stronger – and we have to join hands.

In this spirit, I invite all of you to truly live our Olympic motto: Faster, Higher, Stronger – Together.

## 37. IOC President Thomas Bach's Remarks on Paris 2024 at IOC EB Meeting on 13 June 2024

*"Paris is not only on track to deliver the first-ever Olympic Games aligned with our Olympic Agenda reforms, but they are ready. They are set.*

*"You can feel this in the discussions with everybody, but also in the city. So I had a pretty emotional moment there on Saturday afternoon, it was unbelievable. They had put up, over the night, the [Olympic] Rings at the Eiffel Tower, and then on Saturday, we went there. I wanted to see it first-hand; photos are nice, so we went to the Trocadero – full of people, everybody in awe – looking at the Rings and the Eiffel Tower.*

*"Then it was about sunset, then the Eiffel Tower turned first into bronze, then into gold, in the background, you had the cupola of the dome of the Invalides, shining in gold, it was really breathtaking.*

*"Then we were waiting for a couple of minutes, and then the sun set, and the Rings were illuminated. It's really unbelievable and you can feel this in the city."*

## 38. IOC President Thomas Bach's Remarks on Olympic Day Celebration at Olympic House on 21 June 2024

"Olympic Day is of particular importance for the Olympic Movement, and for Lausanne, which is celebrating its 30th anniversary as the Olympic Capital."

"The world is looking forward to these Olympic Games as a moment of togetherness. A moment of joy. A moment of hope. A moment of solidarity. A moment of peace."

## 39. IOC President Thomas Bach's Remarks on Baron Pierre de Coubertin on 23 June 2024 at Sorbonne University

"The Olympic Games and the sports system he created have stood the test of time"

"For this reason, France can be proud of Coubertin and his legacy"

"Every human being has the right to be judged only in the context of his or her time".

"I'd like our visionary founder to be judged more often in the same way. Coubertin was what we would call today a peace activist."

## 40. IOC President Thomas Bach's Opening Statement in a Panel Discussion of the 56th Session of the UN Human Rights Council in Geneva on 6 July 2024.

"In just 25 days from today, we can celebrate the Opening Ceremony of the Olympic Games Paris 2024,"

"As it stands now, we are confident to count on the presence of athletes from the territories of all 206 National Olympic Committees and the IOC Refugee Olympic Team on this occasion, to embody this unifying mission and this unifying power of the Olympic Games. In these times of divisions, wars and conflict, this is a very important and powerful signal for unity and for peace [...] Our mission goes hand-in-hand with human rights, especially the most fundamental of human rights: peace."

## 41. IOC President Thomas Bach's Remarks on 13 July 2024

On his way to the Olympic Games Paris 2024, IOC President Thomas Bach welcomed the Olympic Flame 'en route' to Paris. The ceremony took place at the Clos de Vougeot Chateau near Dijon, with a number of French Olympians. At the same time, the President became a Grand Officier of the Confrérie des Chevaliers du Tastevin (Fraternity of Knights of the Wine-tasters' Cup), the highest distinction of the Confrérie. Speaking on this occasion, President Bach emphasised that

"on many points, the world of wine and the world of sport are close. [...] The winemaker, like the athlete, must demonstrate patience, rigour and resilience. Both have the same quest: perfection." He added: "To get to the Olympic heights of wine or sport, you need unwavering dedication and a creative spirit. Only those who have tireless passion and decisive commitment can succeed in their art."

## 42. IOC President Thomas Bach's Speech at the Opening Ceremonies of Paris2024 Olympic Games

Good evening Paris! Good evening France!

Dear athletes,

Dear President of the French Republic, Mr. Emmanuel Macron,

Dear President of the Paris 2024 Organising Committee, my fellow Olympian and dear friend, Tony Estanguet,

Dear Mayor of Paris, Mrs. Anne Hidalgo,

Your Excellencies,

Dear Olympic friends,

Finally, the moment has arrived: welcome to the Olympic Games Paris 2024!

My heartfelt thanks go to our gracious French hosts. Thank you for welcoming us in such a spectacular way. The Olympic flame will make Paris and all of France shine even brighter.

We are deeply grateful to all our French friends. First and foremost to the President of the French Republic. All our gratitude also goes to the public authorities at all levels as well as the Paris 2024 Organising Committee, under the excellent leadership of my fellow Olympian, Tony Estanguet. You are bringing our Olympic Agenda reforms to life by making these Games wide open. All of us will experience Olympic Games that are more inclusive, more urban, younger and more sustainable – the first Olympic Games with full gender parity on the field of play.

A special thanks goes to the thousands of volunteers. Thank you for your commitment. Your smiles make us fall in love even more with Paris and France.

Our thanks also go to whole team of the Organising Committee, of the public services and to everyone who is contributing to make these Olympic Games an unforgettable experience.

What better place than Paris, to share this magic of the Olympic Games with the whole world.

Paris, the birthplace of our founder, Pierre de Coubertin, to whom we owe everything.

Paris, City of Light, where he created the modern Olympic Games.

Paris, City of Love.

Thank you, France, for this magical welcome.

Dear fellow athletes,

This is the pinnacle of your Olympic journey. You have come to Paris as athletes. Now you are Olympians.

Stepping into the Olympic Village, you realise like generations of Olympians before: now I am part of something bigger than myself. Now we are part of an event that unites the world in peace.

In our Olympic world, there is no "global south" or "global north". We all respect the same rules and each other. In our Olympic world, we all belong.

As Olympians, we care for each other. We do not only respect each other, we live in solidarity with each other. All of you have experienced this and benefitted from our Olympic solidarity on your long journey to finally becoming Olympians. This solidarity is made possible through the generous support of all our Media Rights Holders and TOP Partners. All together, we thank them and everyone who supported you on your Olympic journey.

In a world torn apart by wars and conflicts, it is thanks to this solidarity that we can all come together tonight, uniting the athletes from the territories of all 206 National Olympic Committees and the IOC Refugee Olympic Team.

Welcome to the best athletes of the world – welcome, Olympians!

Some may say, we in the Olympic world, we are dreamers.

But we are not the only ones.

And our dream is coming true tonight: a reality for everyone to see. Olympians from all around the globe, showing us what greatness we humans are capable of.

So I invite everybody: dream with us. Like the Olympic athletes, be inspired with the joy that only sport can give us. Let us celebrate this Olympic spirit of living life in peace, as the one and only humankind, united in all our diversity.

This is why tonight, with my heart full of emotions, I invite the whole world: let us celebrate this joy of sport together with all the athletes. Have faith in the future. Together, let us celebrate the best of our shared humanity.

Long live the Olympic Games! Long live France!

Now I have the great honour of inviting the President of the French Republic, Mr. Emmanuel Macron, to declare open the Games of the 33rd Olympiad Paris 2024.

# 43. IOC President Thomas Bach's Comments on the First Week of Paris 2024 and on the Women Boxers

*"I think what we can say so far and what has become clear to everybody, France and the French people have welcomed the world with open arms and open hearts and have given the world a glimpse of France and a glimpse of the passion of the French people for sport.)*

*"This is France completely in love with the Olympic Games, in the city of love, Paris, not only in Paris, but overall in France."*

That's International Olympic Committee Thomas Bach (GER) praising the first week of the Paris Olympic Games, adding that he was especially impressed by the passion not only of the athletes, but the spectators:

*"All this creates a magic that inspires the world."*

As a former fencer, he also noted that *"You have never seen fencing until you have seen fencing in the Grand Palais,"* and tried a not-so-successful quip about the triathlons:

*"The triathlon was sensational, or should I say, Seine-sational. I don't know if it works, but I gave it a try, you know. At least, say it was a good try."*

Noting the strong television and digital engagement in many countries, he noted that *"We are on track for more than half of the world's population to follow the Olympic Games Paris 2024."*

Then it was on to boxing, of course, and the continuing fracas over boxers Yu-ting Lin (TPE: 57 kg) and Imane Khelif (ALG: 66 kg) in the women's division. Nine of the 15 questions were about this and Bach's reply to the first inquiry – what can the IOC do to stop this – was the most insightful:

*"To put an end to it is more up to you than up to us."*

Then this:

*"Let's be very clear here. We are talking about women's boxing. We have two boxers who were born as a woman. They have been raised as a woman. Who have a passport as a woman. And who have competed for many years as woman. And this is the clear definition of a woman.*

*"There was never any doubt about them being a woman. What we see now is that some want to own the definition of who is a woman. And there I can only invite them to come up with a scientific-based new definition of who is a woman, and how can somebody being born, raised, competed and having a passport as a woman, cannot be considered a woman.*

*"If they are coming up with something, we are ready to listen, we are ready to look into it, but we will not take part in a politically-motivated, sometimes politically-motivated, cultural war.*

*"And allow me to say that what is going on in this context in the social media, with all this hate speech, with all this aggression and accuse, and fueled by this agenda, is totally unacceptable."*

He also noted the comments of Angela Carini, who retired after 46 seconds of her bout with Khelif:

*"I would also like to quote here, the Italian boxer, who was competing against the Algerian female boxer, she said: "You know, these controversies have definitely made me sad and I feel sorry for my opponent, who is also only here to fight. I have nothing against Khelif. If I met her again, I would hug her."*

*"I think this explains it all, and this is what the Olympic spirit is about.*

*The respect for your opponent, whether you win or whether you lose, and by the way, both of these women have lost a number of fights.*

*"Imane alone has lost nine in international competitions in the recent years, and there was never an issue about this. She has even been invited by the Italian boxing federation to train with her Italian fellow athletes in Italy, and there was no issue about this."*

Bach was asked if the noise on this issue was perhaps part of a Russian-backed disinformation campaign to try and hurt the Paris Games:

*"I cannot make this precise, but what we have seen from the Russian side, in particular, from the international federation from which we had to withdraw the recognition for many reasons [IBA], that they have undertaken, already way before these Games with a defamation campaign against France, against the Games, against the IOC, and they have made a number of comments in this respect which I do not want to repeat, to give them too much honor.*

*"So if you want to have an idea about the credibility of information coming from this not-anymore-recognized international federation, I can only suggest to you, look into the comments they and the leaders of this federation have made recently, and then make your own judgement."*

German investigative reporter Jens Weinreich, writing in The Inquisitor, pointed to when the IBA pivoted to disqualify Khelif:

*"Imane Khelif, who has been boxing internationally since 2018, was listed and tolerated as a woman in the realm of the IBA until she won in the [round of 16] against Russia's Azalia Amineva at the 2023 World Championships in New Delhi."*

Khelif's wins in the quarters and semis were taken away and the semifinal loser was promoted to the final. Wrote Weinreich: *"This is where the Kremlin speaks."*

Bach, for his part, made the IOC's position on boxing and the Olympic Games clear:

*"We want boxing in the program of the Olympic Games. This is the target. But the boxing can only be in the Olympic Games in L.A. if we have a reliable partner. So now the national boxing federations, they have to make their choice. It's up to them.*

*"If they want their athletes to win medals in Olympic Games, in a fair competition, with an international federation with a good reputation, with a good governance, with a clear anti-doping policy, with financial transparency, then they must found an international federation as a partner for the IOC. It is in their hands and for their athletes to win medals, if they want them to win medals."*

## 44. News Conference by IOC President Thomas Bach on 10 August 2024: Giving High Praise to the Paris 2024 Games and Underscoring the Reforms he brought to the Olympic Movement in 2014

*"These Olympic Games, Paris 2024, a love story."*

*"The athletes, the French people and the fans all around the world are in love with the Games, and with each other. In the venues, in the streets of Parisat the Olympic Village, you can feel and experience and see the enthusiasm, which is shared by everyone.*

*"We have all seen the way that France and the French people have taken these Games really to their hearts. It was not just a sober organization, it was a celebration coming from the heart, with all the friendliness, the hospitality, the curiosity, the interest was really heart-warming to see, and you could see hundreds of thousands, millions of the French people on the streets of Paris and full stadia everywhere."*

(That's International Olympic Committee President Thomas Bach (GER) at his Friday news conference, giving high praise to the Paris 2024 Games and underscoring the reforms he brought to the Olympic Movement in 2014):

*"These are exactly the Games we envisaged with Olympic Agenda: more sustainable, more urban, younger, more inclusive, first Olympic Games with full gender parity. That was the vision of Olympic Agenda. And all of this with the athlete at the center of all the efforts."*

Bach remarked on the remarkable connection between the athletes and what was missing – due to Covid – in Tokyo, the fans:

*"The athletes inspired the audience and the audiences giving this inspiration back to the athletes, so you can see, really, a spiral of excitement growing."*

(He was also grateful to the excellent work of the Paris 2024 organizers and the support of the local, regional and national governments, especially in a time when there is no majority party in the National Assembly and all of the ministers were holdovers):

*"All these achievements would not have been possible without an organizing committee as a partner who fully shares, and shared from the very beginning of their planning, all our values, our mission and our values. And therefore, I cannot thank enough the organizing committee under the great*

*leadership of my fellow Olympian Tony Estanguet for the great work. ...*

*"In this sense, I would like to include all the members of the organizing committee, all the workforces of the different kinds, the security teams, of course, the volunteers, whose smiles and friendliness I think we all benefitted from, and everyone else involved. It was also, from them, an Olympic-quality performance.*

*"This is also true for the public authorities, the public services here at all levels here in France starting from the President of the Republic, to the many municipal authorities and services, all over France."*

Asked about the future of the Games and what to expect from Los Angeles in 2028, Bach emphasized:

*"It's up to each organizing committee to adapt the relevant measures in their way. ... When it comes to more urban, then L.A. must, because of the structure of the city, take a different approach. You don't have city centers in L.A. with iconic landmarks as you have here in Paris ...*

*"Each edition of the Games has to be different. If L.A. would like to copy the Eiffel Tower, it would be a recipe for disaster. Each Olympic Games have to be authentic and have to be creative and have to show the culture of the host country, the host city and to be open to share this with the world."*

Bach was asked about all the pre-Games worries, and noted, *"It is human that before such an event is taking place, that there are many people who have many concerns and they think about kind of risks here and risks there. But the proof is in the pudding."*

He was also asked about what Paris 2024 could have done better. His response:

*"This is not a serious question."*

# 45. Thomas Bach IOC President's Prepared Address on 10 August 2024 to Decline a Request to Extend his Mandate beyond the Term Limits

*"Many of you have asked me to have my mandate extended and to agree with a change to the Olympic Charter for this purpose. ...*

*"As a result of deep deliberations and extensive discussions, also with my family, present in the room, I have come to the conclusion that I should not have my mandate extended beyond the term limits enumerated by the Olympic Charter."*

*"In order to safeguard the credibility of the IOC, we all, and in particular, I, as your President, have to respect the highest standards of good governance which we have set for ourselves."*

*"I was one of the promoters and authors of such a term limit at the time of the review of the revision of the Olympic Charter. Until today, I strongly believe that after 12 years in the office as IOC President, our organization is best served with a change in leadership."*

Speaking about his watch-phrase of "change or be changed," Bach, now 70, said, *"This mantra also applies to me."*

Bach referred to the IOC's excellent standing, with Olympic Games already awarded for 2028 and 2032 and Winter Games awarded for 2026-30-34, and $13.5 billion in committed revenues through 2032. But also spoke directly about his concerns for the future, especially the IOC's new Esports Games and its artificial intelligence initiative:

*"To implement effectively all these projects, to address the technological*

*tsunami of converging sciences like A.I., biochemistry and neuroscience, you need to be immersed in this digital world. You need to participate in this digital world. You need to have a deep understanding of these new ways of thinking and communicating. Otherwise, you cannot safely navigate our Olympic Movement ship through the high waves of this tsunami.*

*"For this new way of living, I, with my age, I am not the best captain. New times are calling for new leaders. I know, with this decision, I am disappointing many of you. I can only plead to you to respect that I am deeply convinced this to be in the best interest of our beloved Olympic Movement."*

So:

*"I want to insure a smooth transition and hand over the steering wheel of our ship to my best possible successor, whom you will choose. To facilitate this, I will ask the Executive Board to schedule the election for March 2025, and the beginning of the mandate of the President for June 24, 2025."*

## 46. IOC President Thomas Bach's Speech at the Closing Ceremonies of Paris 2024 Games

Dear President of the French Republic, Mr. Emmanuel Macron,

Dear President of the Paris 2024 Organising Committee, my fellow Olympian and dear friend, Tony Estanguet,

Dear Mayor of Paris, Mrs. Anne Hidalgo,

Dear Olympic friends,

Dear fellow Olympians,

Despite all the tensions in our world, you came here from all the 206 National Olympic Committees and the IOC Refugee Olympic Team, to make the City of Light shine brighter than ever before.

Your performances were amazing. You competed fiercely against each other. Every contest on the edge of perfection. Every performance sparking excitement around the world. You showed us what greatness we humans are capable of.

During all this time, you lived peacefully together under one roof in the Olympic Village. You embraced each other. You respected each other, even if your countries are divided by war and conflict. You created a culture of peace.

This inspired all of us and billions of people around the globe. Thank you for making us dream. Thank you for making us believe in a better world for everyone.

We know that the Olympic Games cannot create peace. But the Olympic Games can create a culture of peace that inspires the world. This is why I call on everyone who shares this Olympic spirit: let us live this culture of peace every single day.

These Olympic Games could only inspire the world, because our French friends have prepared the stage. And what an amazing stage it was!

Millions of people celebrating the athletes in the streets of Paris and all across France. Millions of spectators in iconic venues creating an overwhelming atmosphere. More than half of the world's population sharing this spectacular celebration of the unity of humankind in all our diversity.

The Olympic Games Paris 2024 were a celebration of the athletes and sport at its best. The first Olympic Games delivered fully under our Olympic Agenda reforms: younger, more urban, more inclusive, more sustainable. The first ever Olympic Games with full gender parity.

These were sensational Olympic Games from start to finish – or dare I say: SEINE-sational Games.

The Olympic Games Paris 2024 were Olympic Games of a new era.

That is why I would like to thank all our French friends. First and foremost, my warmest thanks go to the President of the Republic, Emmanuel Macron, for his tireless support. My heartfelt thanks goes to the Organising Committee, under the excellent leadership of my fellow Olympian, Tony Estanguet, for making these Games wide open. All my gratitude goes to the public authorities at all levels and to the public services, for their essential contribution.

All our thanks and recognition go to our Olympic community – the National Olympic Committees, the International Federations, our TOP partners and the Media Rights- Holders. Together, you have contributed to Olympic Games of a new era in every respect. And for this you can be proud forever.

A special thank you to all the wonderful volunteers. You will be forever in our hearts.

Dear French friends, you have fallen in love with the Olympic Games.

And we have fallen in love with all of you.

Thank you Paris, thank you France!

Long live the Olympic Games! Long live France!

[Flame extinguishing]

And now, with my heart full of emotions, I have to perform one more task: I declare the Games of the XXXIII Olympiad Paris 2024 closed.

In accordance with tradition, I call upon the youth of the world to assemble four years from now in Los Angeles, United States of America, to celebrate with all of us the Games of the XXXIV Olympiad

## 47. Author's Letter to IOC President Thomas Bach on 18 August 2024 on his Determination not to extend his term as IOC President and His Ten Commandments

As always, I hope this message finds you in good spirits, following the successful Paris 2024 Games under your charismatic, yet. flexible leadership.

First of all, I feel I must pay my highest respect to you for your unwavering determination not to agree to an extended term as IOC President for the sake of safeguarding the spirit of good governance.

It was an act of implementation of good governance well-preserved in your "Unprecedented Masterpiece of Olympic Agenda 2020+5" in the history of the Olympic Movement.

I still vividly remember, like I smell the fresh paint, your acceptance speech of the Election of the 9th IOC President in the 125th IOC Session in

Buenos Aires on 10 September 2013, as follows:

"I will also work for and with you in the coming years and want to win your confidence, too."

"I know about the great responsibility of an IOC President."

"This makes me humble.

"I want to lead the IOC according to my motto": "**Unity in Diversity**"

"I want to be a President for all of you."

"This means I will do my very best to balance well all the different interests of the stakeholders of the Olympic Movement."

"This is why I want to listen to you and to enter into an ongoing dialogue with all of you."

"You should know that my door, my ears, and my heart are always open for you."

**My First Four-Line Poem** (IOC President Thomas Bach)

Your achievements, accomplishments, contributions, reforms, devotions, services over a wide spectrum with humbleness for the advancement of the global Olympic Movement as IOC President are phenomenal, marvelous, incomparable, impeccable, unprecedented, insightful, outstanding, prominent, innovative, incredible, amazing, adorable, awesome, just to say the least to describe what you have done so far.

You are indeed by far the most respected, reliable, and robust leader that inspires not only the global Olympic Movement but also the global citizens beyond generations, thus redeeming humanity in history.

You are really one-in-a-million human-being in this selfish, greed-driven, present mixed-up world.

In particular, you have genuinely created your own unique words that many people have been inspired and motivated with some of them which I would also like to enumerate as attached.

"Change or be changed"

(Presentation of IOC Pierre de Coubertin Medal to me in Seoul, October 2022)

What impressed me most was your philosophy well-epitomized as **"Thomas Bach's Ten Commandments for the Olympic Movement"** on the occasion of your 10-year anniversary as IOC President as follows:

1) Bidding for Olympic Games should not create losers, who waste millions for absolutely no return.
   (The IOC now selects its hosts through a mostly-private discussion process.)

2) An Olympic Games must conform to the city, region or country where it is held, and not require unnecessary expenditures.

3) It is considered best if no new venues or permanent constructions are undertaken for a Games, unless as part of an otherwise useful local development plan.

4) Sport must go to where the people are, not require people to come to it.

(This was successfully demonstrated at the 2018 Youth Olympic Games in Buenos Aires at the free, open-air opening ceremony at the iconic Obelisk, and transferred to Paris 2024 with its opening on the Seine.)

5) Sport must appeal to youth, or in Olympic-speak, "be more urban" and "youth-oriented."
(Thus the inclusion to the permanent program of skateboarding, sport climbing and surfing from 2028 and the IOC moving toward its own "e-sport Olympics.)-----> the recent creation of OEG(Olympic Esports Games) starting from 2025 in Saudi Arabia
6) Sport governance through the "solidarity model," in which money is distributed through National Olympic Committees for development projects and athlete support, rather than simply paying athletes directly through prize money.
7) Strict requirements for gender equality in terms of the number of men's and women's athletes competing, which will be reached at Paris 2024.
8) Strenuous anti-doping measures, preferably handled by an independent agency; the IOC created the International testing Agency in 2018, which has quickly absorbed most of the anti-doping programming for Olympic-sport federations.
9) Athletes are not responsible for the actions of their government, so long as they are not affiliated with their government.
10) The IOC should respect, follow and implement the directives and regulations of the United Nations.

Mr. President, I am because of you!!!

# 48. Personal Thinking & Possible Solution about Cricket into LA 2028 Games (From Author's Letter to IOC President Thomas Bach on 17 September 2023)

While I read the news and reports on the Cricket as one of the potential additional team sport for the LA2028 Olympic Games, I thought about how to smoothly incorporate Cricket into the official sports program without conflict of interest.

Given the fact that Cricket has gained overall global popularity in general, and its explosive and exclusive status as an essential sport in the Commonwealth Games countries comprising about 75 member-nations+ plus, in particular, I thought it would be an excellent idea for the global Olympic Movement to also share, at first hand, such popularity together with global blessings in the upcoming Los Angeles 2028 Games.

No one will dispute the fact that Cricket is the most popular sport in the world's most populous country, India.

According to some global media report, Cricket "would bolster dwindling broadcast revenue for the IOC and raise the popularity of the Olympic Games in the world's most populous nation."

Only stumbling block for Cricket, I presume, is the size of the participating team athletes as LA2028 Games organizers must adhere to the overall quota of 10,500 athletes as stipulated in the Olympic Charter – down from the 11,400 that participated in Tokyo 2020 Games. Those numbers, I heard, work against the inclusion of team sports

Cricket is "seen as a huge opportunity for the Olympics and the International Cricket Council (ICC) has developed an Olympic-sized T20 format that is gaining traction."

My thinking and solutions for Cricket to be safely on the official sports program of the LA 2028 Games are as follows:

1) No matter how many athletes would have to be added, the number of those additional athletes to be invited should be defined and calculated in the realm of the responsibilities of the Organizers as it would correspond to the desired additional sports to be showcased together with other potential sports in the Games
2) Therefore, the IOC would remain safe and sound in maintaining its original quota of 10,500 athletes for the existing 28 sports in principle.
3) As I understand, there would be no limit on how many options LA 2028 can name. This is the point of generous benefit exclusively given to the organizers, I guess.
4) Should there be a huge opportunity to generate a considerable amount of extra revenues and global popularity for the benefit of the LA 2028 as well as the IOC in the long run, it would be just fitting and proper that Cricket should be added to the options by LA 2028 without concerns from the IOC side, overrunning the number of athletes of 10,500 already set in the Olympic Charter.
5) In conclusion, the number of 10,500 athletes is to be untouched, and the increased number of athletes from additional sports beyond is to be in the hands of the organizers in a close cooperation with the IOC and the relevant IFs, which the IOC accordingly would only need to add or revise some conditional phrases likewise in the bylaws of its Olympic Charter in the near future.

International Olympic Committee
Sports Department

Unclassified

Prof. Rocky Yoon Kang-Ro
President
International Sports Diplomacy Institute

Lausanne, 26 September 2023
Ref. 2023 KML/sbn
By e-mail

Dear Prof. Yoon, dear Rocky,

I hope this letter finds you well. We thank you for your letter of 17 September addressed to the IOC President regarding the Olympic Games Los Angeles 2028 (LA28) Sports Programme and the potential inclusion of Cricket.

Regarding the inclusion of Cricket in the Olympic Games LA28, as you know, the opportunity to propose to the IOC additional events from new sports (i.e. outside the initial sport programme) is granted to each Organising Committee of the Olympic Games (OCOG) in line with the new flexibility introduced by Olympic Agenda 2020 and ultimately reflected in Rule 45 of the Olympic Charter. The LA28 OCOG may, at its sole discretion, propose to the IOC the inclusion of one or more additional events governed by IOC recognised International Federations (IF).

The LA28 OCOG has yet to make a proposal for new additional sports to the Olympic Programme Commission (OPC). Once received, the OPC will review the proposal and then make its recommendations to the IOC Executive Board and report to the IOC Session.

The OPC will reconvene separately, following the Olympic Games Paris 2024 to review the athlete quota and event programme for the Olympic Games 2028. As part of this assessment, careful consideration will be given to the total number of athletes involved.

Maison Olympique, 1007 Lausanne, Switzerland | Tel. +41 21 621 6111 | Fax +41 21 621 6216 | www.IOC.org

Regarding the athlete quota, thank you for your proposal and points of consideration in your letter it is indeed of value.

Once again, your feedback is appreciated. Thank you and very best regards,

Kit McConnell
IOC Sports Director

*(Reply from IOC Sport Director Kit McConnell)*

# 49. Age-Algorithm of Human Life-Span and New Age-Calculation Model (From my letter to IOC President Thomas Bach on 24 May 2021)

### 1) Age-Algorithm of Human Life-Span and New Age-Calculation Model

In accordance with some of the UN data in 2015, there are about 500,000 people who have lived over 100 years globally. This figure showed 4 times more in comparison of that of 20 years ago. It is also expected that the relevant figure would be increased at a much faster speed.

It is, recently, reported that the global IT enterprise, Google, has embarked upon a Life-Extension Project with enormous amount of investment, whose objective is to extend human life-expectancy as long as 500 years.

I do not know whether we could live that long as Google's Life Extension Project, but I think the era of 120 years of average life-span could come into being realized much faster than we might think.

Average human life-span used to be below 50 years in 1900, but current average life-span of Koreans has already surpassed 80 years.

In particular, during the past 200 years, with the state of nutrition and hygiene having been improved, and medical technology including medical treatment and health care also developed by leaps and bounds, human life-span has been extended gradually as long as 3 months per year on a continued basis.

With this phenomenon in mind, the new age-calculation method was once popular in Japan, a nation considered as a leading longevity country. This method is simply to multiply each individual age by 0.7. This theory is based on the current life style benefitting contemporary people with improved life patterns, thus living far much younger than previous generations. The newly calculated age is practically reflecting the gradual decrease of age in physical and mental aspects.

According to this new age-calculation method, 50 years old man is 35 years old, 60 years old woman is 42 years of age, and 70 years old man is 49 years of age, thus 120 years old human becoming just 84 years of age!

In our mindset, our way of thinking still seems preoccupied with the notion in the era of 60 year-long life span. In general, 20~30 years old people are considered as young generation, 40~50 years old as middle-aged generation, 60 years and above as the elderly, and those whose age are over sixties are implicitly programmed as senile, impotent, and declining age group.

On the basis of the concept of this preoccupation, the retirement age, in general, is set to be 65 years old in most countries, and to be categorized as old and senior group. It is known that 65 years old as retirement age stemmed from the German system having implemented pension payments for those having reached 65years of age in 1889. It is worth taking note that in those days, the average life-span was less than 50 years of age. Gerontological scholars mentioned that current 70years of age live lives similar to those of 50 years old.

### 1) Age-Algorithm of the Olympic Movement in the New Era

When applying to the above new age-calculation system, the current age (70) for retirement of IOC members elected after 1999 is just 49years old. Then it is about time to reconsider the retirement age limit of IOC members as stipulated in 1999 IOC Reforms. As you well recall, the 1999 reforms inclusive of 12 radical decisions were adopted and approved in a very short space of time by the extraordinary IOC Session. Some were good, but some others need to be restructured and reconsidered as time goes by, I believe.

The No. 6 item of the 1999 Reforms limited the term of IOC President for 8 years and allowed to be reelected only for further 4 years.

The No. 8 item referred to the IOC members' age limit lowered to 70.

My suggestions consist of two points as follows:

1) IOC members' retirement age would have to be pragmatically upgraded to 80 years old, which could be calculated as 56 years of age in consideration of current trend of human life style as mentioned-above.
2) The term of IOC President would have to be continued at least up to 16 years (8+8) instead of 12 years (8+4) in order to guarantee the good governance processing your accumulated knowledge, experiences and insightful wisdom for the global Olympic Movement in the midst of current Coronavirus Pandemic and the Post Coronavirus Era in the Earth Village.

## 50. Creation of New Organization "WAVA" (World Anti-Violence Agency in Sport) by IOC (From my Letter to IOC President Thomas Bach on 23 march 2024)

It would be one of the aims to upgrade and best optimize the "Sustainable Culture:" of the global Olympic Movement including but not limited to "art, history, focus on values, academic research and patrimonial collection" as defined in the mission of our Commission as it is.

In the mixed-up and complicated world today, it is my firm conviction that the IOC is reputed and well-recognized as the sole trust-worthy organization to uphold and recover the human values through Olympic principles and Olympic Spirt that requires mutual understanding, mutual respect, and mutual trust.

In this context, the violence-ridden world, especially in the global sport movement, it is my sincere belief that we would need to establish, disseminate, and propagate the spirt of the "Culture for Non-Violence in Sport (Sexual Abuse, Beating-up during Athletes Training, Bullying, Power-Abusing just name a few in cooperation with the WAVA in Sport(World Anti-Violence Agency) hopefully to be created under your outstanding leadership sooner than later, pending approval of the IOC EB and the IOC Session. It would recover, repair and re-generate the true sense of the sportsmanship not only in the field of sport but also out of the competition sites in our daily life.

## 51. Game Changer for the "Olympic Games of a New Era" (From my letter to IOC President Thomas Bach on 12 December 2024)

Extending to you my personal Season's Greetings, I am writing this letter to share with you about the epoch-making project of an unprecedented, spectacular Game Changer for the future "Olympic Games of a New Era" as you mentioned in the recently held Olympic Summit in Lausanne.

The name of the "Game Changer" would be referred to as "**Crusi-**

um Project" (Ubiquitous Mobile Cruise +Stadium on the Seas) which would showcase a remarkable action-plan for the future Olympic Games by providing the future Olympic Games Hosts, wherever available and applicable, with sustainable, cost-efficient, environment-friendly, legacy-guaranteed, recyclable, reusable, reproducible, portable-removable-detachable, specially prefabricated, built-in cruise facilities originally created and designed mainly and initially for the use of detachable and tailor-made football stadium(s) whose elaborately viable designs and technologies belong to the Chairman of the global Korean Ship-Building Enterprise since a decade. Recently I talked about the possible launching this grand project, including but not limited to the Olympic Games with Chairman Kang who, used to be Chairman of the STX Group, initiated and propelled this grand practical idea to be put into actual service when and where available.

For your perusal, I would like to introduce the basic details on the applications of the above "Crusium(Cruise +Stadium)" ship-building as follows:

1) The size and shape of the "Crusium" can be flexibly built during the decision- making process according to the specific use as per such requests.
2) The examples of the strategic usage of "Crusium" are as follows:
   (1) Stadium for Football, Hockey, Baseball, Cricket, etc.
   (2) Opera House, Pop Recital, etc. following the Sporting Events
   (3) Cruise Separation available as the Crusium consists of 3 Cruise-Fleet Units
   (4) Enormous Diversity for Support of International Event, Convention, Exhibition including Accommodation services available as

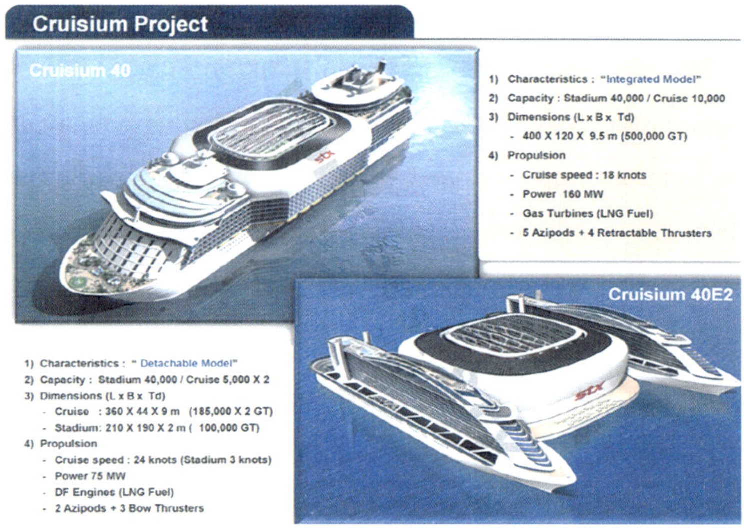


the "Crusium" is movable. travelable anywhere with integrated cruise fleet.

(5) Crusium's seating capacity would be estimated around 40,000~50,000.

3) Period of "Crusium" ship-building would need 3 years after completion of specific shipbuilding design as per respective use.

The Crusium Project would perfectly serve the purpose of a revolutionary, multifunctional-design ship-building implementation process to be utilized and applied to multi-sports events running the gamut from the Olympic Games, through individual sporting events, to MICE (Meeting-Incentive-Convention-Events & Exhibition) industry according to the need and demands to be specified in the future.

In this context, I am confident that this "Crusium Project" would serve as a "Game Changer" to be able to contribute to the New Revolutionary

Method to benefit the Olympic Movement in terms of climate change, CO-2gas emission reduction, white-elephant facilities disposal, especially legacy issues, all at once, sustainably, effectively, efficiently, and economically.

As you mentioned recently, "Olympic Games are more urban, more youthful, more sustainable, more inclusive", "Olympic Agenda 2020 built on the three pillars of Credibility, Sustainability and Youth." and "The Games met the expectations of the world." "People were longing for something that gives them hope." "They were longing for something that gives them joy." In the above contextual vision and concept, the Crusium Project would perfectly fit all your philosophy values in the future.

As you continue to lead the global Olympic Movement until 23 June 2025 as IOC President, let me reiterate that it would be just fitting and proper that you should also continue to serve as a "**Life-Time Honorary IOC President even afterward** in order for your successors to be able to learn from your impeccable wisdom, insightful experiences, and sustainable guidance based on the spirit of Good Governance under your brain child, the **Olympic Agenda 2020+5.**

Therefore, I believe that it would be about right and perfect timing for you to launch a new, historic, differentiated, and sustainable project for the Olympic Games of a New Era, thereby opening up a New Horizons with "Crusium Project" that I humbly and gladly propose to you today.

Partnership is sharing, and sharing is gathering, and gathering together is the essence of the Olympic values and philosophy of yourself as well as Baron Pierre de Coubertin who emphasized the importance of **Education through Sport** while enjoying **Sport, Art, and Technologies working together**.

In the meantime, may I take this opportunity to ask for your thoughtful consideration of the “Crusium Project”.

Should there be an interest in further studying this project, I am ready to serve your purpose by providing further detailed feasibility through due elaborate and professional presentation by a potential team in the near future.

## 52. Bach and His Honorary Citizenship of Gangneung (Ice Venue City of PyeongChang 2018 OWG)

“As a token of my appreciation for your exquisite and insightful contribution to the greatest success of PyeongChang2018, I would like to pay tribute to you with a 4-line poem I wrote right this morning.”

IOC President Thomas Bach had no reason to refuse my goodwill gift of 4-line poem as a tribute to him with his last name spelling of “BACH”.

I started to pronounce my 4-line poem present dedicated to IOC President Thomas Bach as follows:

B—Brilliant

A—Amazing and

C—Charismatic

H—Hero of Heroes

Upon departure at the end of his visit of Gangneung City Hall, I handed over to him the 4-line poem I hand-wrote on that morning.

IOC President seemed pleased, and he appreciated my gesture, saying “I will keep it to my heart” with 4-line poem paper note put in his dress shirt pocket near his heart

## 53. Article on IOC President Thomas Bach on 24 June 2025 by The Sports Examiner

At 71 years, five months and 26 days, Thomas Bach (GER) is now the Honorary President of the International Olympic Committee, having completed his 12 years as the leader of the Olympic Movement on Monday.

His two terms saw plenty of controversy, upheaval and success, and while his legacy will still be shaped by future events, it's not too soon to consider what he achieved and where he stands among the nine leaders of the Olympic Movement.

Bach came in at a time of turmoil, but also with money in the bank. At the end of the Jacques Rogge (BEL) tenure, in 2013, the IOC showed $3.448 billion in assets and $1.745 billion in reserves, designed to allow the organization to survive even with the cancellation of an Olympic Games or Winter Games.

But there was discontent, and disunity, as Rogge had been a fairly weak leader, especially compared to his predecessor, Spain's Juan Antonio Samaranch, who had modernized the IOC dramatically over 20 years, but who had also been in charge as corruption had followed the expansion of the Olympic Games into a desirable political achievement.

So Bach sought to change things. And he did:

#### ▪ Host City selection

The 1999 corruption reforms implemented in the wake of the selection of Salt Lake City as the host for the 2002 Winter Games had not ended the problem. Questions were raised about the 2009 selection of Rio de Janeiro (BRA) for the 2016 Olympic Games and possibly Tokyo in 2013 for the 2020 Olympic Games.

Further, the demands of the bid process required host cities and countries to spend millions chasing IOC members and creating ever more lavish spectacles to try and impress them.

Bach ended this with his signature reform, Olympic Agenda 2020, passed in December 2014. First among the 40 recommendations was to limit and simplify the process and where and how candidate cities could spend money. In 2019, public campaigning was essentially ended with the creation of Future Host Commissions for the Olympic Games and Winter Games, with which interested parties could enter "continuous dialogue" on possible candidatures.

After the 2015 election for the 2022 Winter Games in which four European candidates withdrew and Beijing (CHN) won over Almaty (KAZ) by 44-40, Bach saw the interest in bidding for the Games at an all-time low.

With Paris (FRA) and Los Angeles (USA) both interested in 2024, Bach arranged for a double award – the first time in a century for the IOC – for 2024 and 2028 and gave him time for more reforms. The last host election with competitive voting by IOC members was in 2019, as Milan Cortina (ITA) defeated Stockholm (SWE), 47-34, to host the 2026 Winter Games, with hosts set for 2028-2030 Winter-2032-2034 Winter.

Now, bidding costs are a tiny fraction of what they were previously, and losing bidders are not publicly humiliated by standing in a room watching some other city/region/country delegation celebrate.

The IOC membership does not like having this decision, in effect, removed from their hands, and there are changes being discussed. But Bach's vision produced a healthy interest in hosting the Games that works, albeit with a lot less drama.

### ▪ Hosting of the Games

With the passage of Olympic Agenda 2020 and a series of smaller reforms packaged as "The New Norm" in 2018, the IOC completely changed its view of how the Olympic and Winter Games should be hosted.

New stadiums just for the Games were out and use of existing facilities was suddenly not only preferred, but required wherever possible. The IOC's new approach was summarized as:

*"The Games should adapt to the host, not the host to the Games*

*"The project must be aligned with local long-term socio-economic development plans. Existing venues should be used as much as possible, even if they are outside the main host region. New venues should be built only if there is a solid legacy and business case, in line with the needs of the population."*

If no existing venue was available, a temporary solution was now preferred, saving billions in expenditures on facilities that were not really needed. Moreover, the IOC's new view allowed potential hosts to spread a Games more widely and take advantage of regional facilities, not just ones within a city.

### ▪ Russia and doping

A December 2014 documentary on the German ARD channel – "Secret Doping – How Russia Makes Its Winners" – exposed a massive Russian state-sponsored doping program that exploded in 2015.

A World Anti-Doping Agency inquiry report released in November 2015, led by the highly-respected IOC member Dick *Pound* (CAN), confirmed the scheme and led to a suspension of the Russian Anti-Doping Agency.

The IOC was caught in the middle, with the Rio Games coming quickly, and Bach eventually announced that the International Federations could decide at what level Russian athletes could participate. From 436 athletes in London in 2012, Russia had 282 in Rio and just one in track & field, long jumper *Darya Klishina*, who lived and trained in the U.S.

The Russian Olympic Committee was suspended for three months over the doping scandal in late 2017, allowing only "neutral" athletes for the 2018 Winter Games in South Korea. By mid-2018, the IOC had helped to found the independent International Testing Agency, to actually carrying our doping programs at major events so that no accusations of bias could be alleged.

A 2017 IOC review commission head by IOC member Denis Oswald (RUS) disqualified 43 Russian athletes from the 2014 Sochi Winter Games, although 30 findings were reversed by the Court of Arbitration for Sport. But Bach and Russia would be at odds from here on.

### ▪ Russia and war

Russia's place at the Olympic Games was impacted by the doping scandal for years and only the "Russian Olympic Committee" was allowed to compete at Tokyo 2020 in 2021. Then, just after the closing of the 2022 Winter Games in Beijing (CHN), Russia invaded Ukraine and began an aggression which continues to this day.

The IOC led the response, recommending that athletes from Russia and its ally Belarus, be removed from international competitions for their own safety, and banning all teams. This was complied with almost immediately.

As the Russian invasion dragged on and degenerated into stalemate thanks to Ukrainian resistance, Bach quietly oversaw a movement to allow athletes from Russia and Belarus who had not supported the war to be able to compete as "independent neutral athletes" in individual events. Eventually, just 17 Belarusian and 15 Russian athletes were allowed to compete at the Paris 2024 Games, across 10 sports.

In response to the takeover by the invading Russians of regional sports organizations that had been under the control of the Ukrainian National Olympic Committee, the IOC suspended the Russian Olympic Committee in October 2023. That ban still stands.

### ▪ Tokyo 2020 and Covid-19

Bach's biggest challenge came with the arrival of the unexpected Covid-19 pandemic that forced the first-ever postponement of an Olympic Games, from 2020 to 2021.

There was a widespread belief that these Tokyo Games would never happen. But they did, without spectators and with unpleasant, antiseptic conditions that strained everyone's patience. But they happened, and the Japanese government announced just 163 positives among 676,789 tests (0.02%).

Essentially the same playbook was used for the 2022 Beijing Winter Games, with just 172 Covid-19 positives reported out of 2,022,170 tests (0.01%).

Both Games came off, meaning Rogge's rainy-day reserves did not have to be tested, although the IOC made loans to International Federations which could not wait until 2021 for the television revenue dividend they were expecting at the end of 2020.

If this sounds like a lot, these are just the most impactful highlights of the Bach Era. He was a decisive leader, but also encouraged discussion and consultation, even if he already had an idea of what the end result would be.

And he had a lot of other things going on:

- Under Bach's leadership, the first IOC Refugee Olympic Team appeared in Rio in 2016 and the project continues to grow.
- Bach undertook a first-ever liaison with the electronic gaming community, eventually resulting in an agreement to create the first Olympic Esports Games in Saudi Arabia. Originally slated for 2025, the first edition is now expected to be held in 2027.
- Given its financial resources and the growth of a professional staff beyond 500, Bach's IOC built Olympic House in Lausanne to house its entire workforce and create an architectural statement on the size and power of the Olympic Movement.

He also championed much closer relationships with international organizations, especially those related to the United Nations, and other non-governmental organizations worldwide.

Bach also oversaw a continuing expansion of the IOC's financial power, with broadcast rights increasing and also The Olympic Partner (TOP) program, which had 15 companies signed up for the 2021-2024 quadrennial ending with the Paris Games.

So Bach passed the torch to new IOC President Kirsty Coventry (ZIM) with $6.120 billion in total assets, with reserves of $4.880 billion.

So where should Bach be ranked among the nine IOC chiefs? **TSX looked at the rankings question previously in 2020**, asking whether Samaranch was the greatest IOC President ever.

My answer then was no, that Samaranch who brought the IOC from carbon paper to computers during his time – must be ranked second, to French founder Pierre de Coubertin, the inspiration and driving force that brought the Games back from memory to reality.

Samaranch created the modern IOC, and Bach re-engineered it to fit 21st Century needs for economy, involvement and values. As he reminded audiences relentlessly, today's Olympic Games must be "*fully aligned with our Olympic Agenda reforms; Games that are younger, more urban, more inclusive and sustainable.*"

So, for me, Bach ranks third, and well ahead of the other six:

(4) Sigfrid Edstrom (SWE: 1942-52)

(5) Jacques Rogge (BEL: 2001-2013)

(6) Henri de Baillet-Latour (BEL: 1925-42)

(7) Demetrios Vikelas (GRE: 1894-96)

(8) Avery Brundage (USA: 1952-72)

(9) Lord Killanin (IRL: 1972-80)

And what about Coventry? At 41, she is the youngest IOC chief since de Coubertin, the first woman, first African and with seven Olympic medals, the most decorated athlete ever to serve as the IOC's leader.

She inherits an immensely powerful IOC, that dominates all of the Olympic Movement with the exception of football and FIFA, but that still has issues with Russia, the desire by top athletes for more money from their sports, and a rambunctious, talented membership that wants a lot more say in what happens than they had under Bach.

Rich Perelman

Editor/The Sports Examiner

# 54. Author's Last Official Letter addressed to Dr. Thomas Bach as Incumbent IOC President (on 20 June 2025)

As recently as 20 June, I wrote a letter, with a copy to IOC President-elect Kirsty Coventry, to IOC President Thomas Bach saying that the letter would most probably the last one as in 3 days' time on 23 June 2025 on the Olympic Day, there would be a key-handover ceremony from outgoing 9th IOC President Thomas Bach to incoming 19th IOC President Kirsty Coventry at the Olympic House, Lausanne.

"Dear Most Distinguished and Peace-loving IOC President Thomas Bach,

First of all, I would like to take this opportunity to extend to you my warmest personal greetings.

I presume that this letter would most probably be the last one sending to you as IOC President, as there will be a key-handover ceremony scheduled in 3 days on 23 June, the Olympic Day.

Briefly, I feel I must tell you how much I was truly indebted to you for what you have done for me during your tenure as IOC President mostly since PyeongChang2018, including but not limited to awarding to me the prestigious IOC Pierre de Coubertin Medal in 2022, and nomination as member IOC Culture and Olympic Heritage Commission in the early part of 2024 as well as your personal applications for me as IOC Member to the IOC Members

Election Committee in the latter part of 2024.

Thanks to your valued nomination for me, I was able to play a role not only in our Commission meeting online last November, but also in the International Seminar, related to Cultural Olympiad of Milan Cortina 2026

OWG, to play a part as key-note speaker for FICTS - Fédération Internationale Cinéma Télévision Sportifs, founded on 1983, with its headquarters in Milan (Italy) - Via De Amicis, 17 (in the Roman amphitheatre), joined by 130 Countries as recently as 4-7 June in Treviso-Verona-Venice, Italy.

At the end of the above event, FICTS President Prof. Franco Casani proposed to me to become a **FICTS Ambassador**, and as of 17 June, I received his letter of nomination as FICTS Ambassador as attached_

Considering your multidisciplinary and impactful contributions to the global Olympic Movement, I am convinced that you would continue to serve not only as an Honorary IOC President for life, but as a God Father of the global Olympic Movement for many and many years to come.

Should there be any services in the future that I can do to help disseminate the Olympic Ideals, I will be more than happy to be at your disposal at anytime.

"Sustainability is Reminiscence of the Past."

"Sustainability is Introspect of the Present."

"Sustainability is Hope for the Future."

Thanking you again and looking forward to the pleasure of meeting with you again in the future, I remain,"

## 55. Very Last Letter addressed to me by 9th IOC President Thomas Bach as Incumbent IOC President on 23 June 2025 and Author's Reply

Immediately after I received the above letter from IOC President

International Olympic Committee
The President

Professor Rocky Yoon Kang-Ro
President
International Sport Diplomacy Institute

Lausanne, 7 September 2023

Dear Professor Yoon,

Thank you very much for your letter of 25 August and for the impressive list of recommendations and references to your many book publications.

This illustrates everything that you enjoy about the Olympic Movement and your great sense of commitment over the past 40 years.

Thank you again for your continued commitment, and I hope that you will continue to serve and contribute to the Olympic Movement in the same spirit for many years to come.

Wishing you all the best, I remain,

Yours sincerely,

Lausanne, 23 June 2025

Dear Friend,

Thank you very much for your recent letter and your kind words, which are greatly appreciated.

It has been a privilege to serve the Olympic Movement and to have friends like you at my side.

Hoping our paths will cross again in the future and wishing you all the best in your endeavours, I remain,

With kind regards

Thomas Bach's last official letter as incumbent IOC President, I sent to him my last official letter to him as follows:

"Thank you very much for your reply which I received with special emotions today. And I have mixed feelings about what the future would hold without your best optimized and timely implementation flow from your experiences, knowledge, and wisdom as top-most leader of the global Olympic Movement so far, while I also strongly trust the brilliant and refined leadership to be showcased by 10th IOC President Kirsty Coventry.

While I convincingly believe, with her track records, that your successor, the 10th IOC President Kirsty Coventry, would highly respect and value your leadership footprints, including but not limited to your historic brainchild "Olympic Agenda 2020+5", I am convinced and persuaded with absolute certainty that you would also willingly render your well-deserved advice and insights in order for her to keep the future Olympic Movement solidly on the right track and desirable directions. As you mentioned, "We can move Faster, we can aim higher, and we can stay stronger, together!"

As this letter would serve as my very first letter to you as Honorary IOC President for Life from today after the IOC Presidential Key-Handover Ceremony, I would like to take this opportunity to pay my highest respect and tribute to you for what you have achieved so far for the entire global Olympic Movement and what you would definitely contribute to the advancement of the future Olympic Movement from now.

Olympic HIGHLIGHTS

The President with Rocky Kang-Ro Yoon. © IOC / Greg Martin

The President met Rocky Kang-Ro Yoon, President of the International Sport Diplomacy Institute and Standing Advisor to the Korea Sports Promotion Foundation (KSPO), who is also a member of the IOC Culture and Olympic Heritage Commission.

Reminiscing our good old yet fresh memories and extraordinary friendship shared with you when in office as IOC President, I would still do my utmost to serve and make the global Olympic Movement in the future a continued resounding success modelling after your tangible and intangible great Olympic legacy accumulated, if such opportunity allowed.

In addition, it is my firm belief and conviction that you will continue to remain as global Olympic God Father taking care of not only the current Olympic Movement but also the Olympic Refuge Foundation as its President in the same spirit and manner as in the past.

In the meantime, may I take this opportunity to reiterate my most profound gratitude to you for your thoughtful and benevolent consideration and encouragement for me to be able to find resilience and vitality in the Olympic Movement, I remain, "

# 56. Very First Letter addressed to Author by 10th IOC President Kirsty Coventry on 21 June 2025 and Author's Reply

The following day on 21 June 2005, I received a letter from IOC President-elect Kirsty Coventry as a reply to my earlier letter of congratulations for her overwhelming victory in the IOC Presidential election in March as follows:

Immediately after reading her letter, I wrote back to her as follows:

"Dear IOC President-elect Mme Kirsty COVENTRY,

I trust that this letter finds you in good spirits and in good health.

First of all, I appreciate very much your kind and friendly words in your letter dated 17 June 2025

Since I worked for the global Olympic Movement starting from the Korean Olympic Committee in 1982 one year after Seoul 1988 was elected as Host City of the Games of the 24th Olympiad at the IOC Session in Baden-Baden West Germany on 30 September 1981, I participated in each and every Olympic edition (Summer and Winter) since LA 1984 Games until Salt Lake City 2002 OWG all along as Acting Chef-de-Mission of the Korean Olympic Delegation. After SLC 2002, I also took part in the Games in my other capacity, such as Secretary General of the PyeongChang Olympic Winter Games Bid Committees (for 2010-2014) and Special Advisor (for 2018).

During my first Olympic Games in Los Angeles 1984, I encountered Mme. Anita DeFrantz, in the Olympic Village, while she, walking with

International
Olympic
Committee
**President-elect**

Professor Rocky Yoon Kang-Ro
President
International Sport
Diplomacy Institute

Lausanne, 17 June 2025

Dear Professor Yoon,

Thank you for your kind and thoughtful congratulations on my election as the 10th President of the International Olympic Committee. Your words of encouragement and warm wishes mean a great deal to me as I step into this important role, and they remind me of the incredible community that makes the Olympic Movement so special.

With the continued support and dedication of friends of the Olympic Movement like you, I am confident that we can further strengthen the values of excellence, friendship, and respect that the Olympic Games represent.

Thank you as well for your kind proposal to meet. Regrettably, I was not in Lausanne at the time of your meeting with the IOC President, Thomas Bach. I trust it was a valuable and meaningful discussion.

Once again, thank you for your message

Yours sincerely,

Maison Olympique, 1007 Lausanne, Switzerland | Tel. +41 21 621 6111 | Fax +41 21 621 6216 | www.IOC.org

her walkie-talkie, was playing her role as part of LAOOC1984 in the USC Olympic Village.

My personal Olympic highlights include but not limited to the experiences at the SLOOC (Seoul 1988 Olympic Organizing Committee) as a

first-hand witness of the signing ceremony of the Olympic TV rights deal with NBC covering the Unites States territories held at the Westbury hotel in New York City, accompanying then-Sport Minister and Executive President of SLOOC in 1985. After that, the IOC EB kindly allowed me the opportunity to cherish the valuable memories and experiences when I was selected at the IOC EB by 7th IOC President Juan Antonio Samaranch with the recommendation by the late Un-Yong Kim(KOR), IOC EB member, as one of the members of the IOC Evaluation Commission for 2008 Olympics under the Chairmanship of the late Hein Verbruggen(NED) as IOC member and UCI President, having visited 5 finalist candidate cities of Beijing-Osaka-Toronto-Istanbul-Paris). What a precious series of on-site Olympic knowledge accumulation chance of the Candidate Cities!

In 2008, ANOC Founder-President Mario Vazquez Rana also honored me with the ANOC Merit Award at the opening ceremony of the ANOC General Assembly held in Beijing.

And next highlights were the 10-year long experiences with the PyeongChang OWG Bid Committees (2010-2014-2018) and its Organizing Committee(PyeongChang2018) named as POCOG as Special Advisor to POCOG President, whose Games was spot-lighted worldwide as a "Peace Olympics", thanks to the outstanding leadership and diplomatic skills showcased by 9th IOC President Thomas Bach. And now here I stand as IOC Member of the Culture and Olympic Heritage Commission and IOC Pierre de Coubertin Medalist (2022), all of which are absolute thanks to 9th IOC President Thomas Bach, to make a long story short. I would better stop elaborating my Olympic footprints and stories for today.

In addition, I was also delighted and honoured enough to have had a good and continued working relationship with 7th IOC President Juan Antonio Samaranch, 8th IOC President Jacques Rogge, and likewise 9th IOC President Thomas Bach who has been not only myself, but also for the absolute majority, most respected and distinguished Olympic God Father in the history of the Olympic Movement.

More
Vividly, Impressively, Precisely

In 2 days' time on 23 June 2025, you will start your long and heart-throbbing Olympic leadership journey as 10th IOC President, and it is my ardent wish and aspiration that my personal Olympic tradition to serve you, the IOC President, would also be continued for the furtherance of the Olympic values and advancement of the global Olympic Movement, utilizing my 43 year-long experiences and knowledge, so far, to be shared to achieve the ESG-oriented SGDs of the Olympic Movement. Olympic life goes on...

In the meantime, may I take this opportunity to be able dedicate my 6 and 8-line Poem for you as follows:

- Kirsty 6-Line Poem : A Legacy of Unity

- K-Kindred spirit guiding nations with grace,
- I-Inspired by sport, where dreams find their place.
- R-Resilience shines in every stride she takes,
- S-Sharing hope, the bond that never breaks.
- T-Torchbearer of vision, her leadership so bright,
- Y-Yearning for peace, under the Olympic light., celebrating change, as she takes flight.

- Coventry 8-Line Poem : A Legacy in Motion

- C-Cherished Leader, with Courage So Bright,
- O-Opening doors to Light of Unity in Diversity.
- V-Valor and Grace in Every Stride,
- E-Empowering Hearts Worldwide.
- N-Nations Inspired by your Steady Hand,
- T-Torchbearer of Dreams, across the Land.
- R-Resilience Defines your Journey So True,
- Y-You Lead us Forward with a Vision Anew.

In conclusion, may I also take this opportunity to reiterate my personal congratulations to you on 23 June, the Olympic Day, and look forward to the pleasure of meeting and working with you and the Honorary IOC President for Life Thomas Bach from 24 June onward together for the advancement of the global Olympic Movement in the near future, I remain,

"Together, we can raise the bar even much higher!"

"Together, we can go much Faster,

"Together, we can jump much Higher,

"Together, we can become much Stronger. "

With my warmest congratulations and best wishes,"

## 57. The 9th IOC President Dr. Thomas Bach's 12-Year Long Leadership & Contribution together with Highlights of his Famous Analects and Speeches (2013-2025)

The 9th IOC President Thomas Bach is often characterized by his simple but long-lasting magic words penetrating and appealing to the global sport people, especially in the Olympic Movement.

Even myself have continuously been intrigued and touched by his pithy epigram that stings the people to the quick even into our heart and memory.

**My First Four-Line Poem** (IOC President Thomas Bach)

As for me personally, the most universal and touching word is "**Unity in Diversity**", followed by many others, including but not limited to "**There is no one-size-fits-all solution**", "**without losing political neutrality**", "**Olympic legacy for sustainability, flexibility, practicality, good governance, gender equality**, "**Unifying Power of sport and Olympics to bring together people**", exquisitely melted in his brain child masterpiece, "**Olympic Agenda 2020+5**", which is a "Strategic Roadmap of the Future Olympic Movement" and updated Olympic motto of "Faster, Higher, Strong, **Together**" in the IOC's 130-year long history as of 23 June 2024 since its creation in 1894.

Dr. Thomas Bach as unprecedented performing designer and strategist of the destiny of the future Olympic Movement, more importantly for me, is one of my three most respected IOC Presidents along with the 2nd IOC President Baron Pierre de Coubertin, IOC Founder and Renovator of the modern Olympic Games and I was also awarded the IOC Pierre de Coubertin Medal in October 2022 and the 7th IOC President Juan Antonio

Samaranch who saved the Olympic Movement from several attempts of Olympic boycott, especially Seoul 1988 Games.

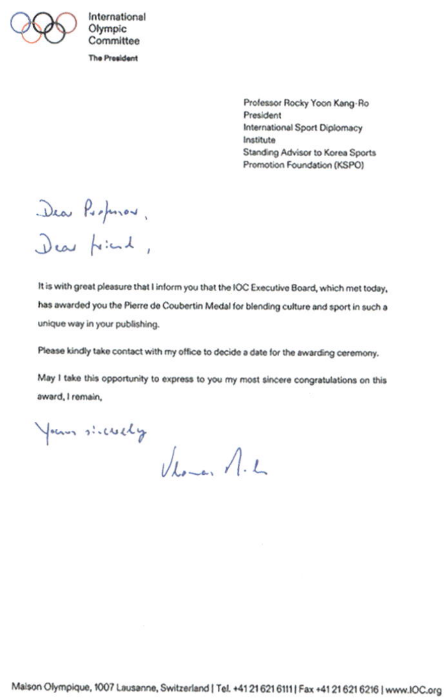

International Olympic Committee
The President

Professor Rocky Yoon Kang-Ro
President
International Sport Diplomacy Institute
Standing Advisor to Korea Sports Promotion Foundation (KSPO)

Dear Professor,
Dear friend,

It is with great pleasure that I inform you that the IOC Executive Board, which met today, has awarded you the Pierre de Coubertin Medal for blending culture and sport in such a unique way in your publishing.

Please kindly take contact with my office to decide a date for the awarding ceremony.

May I take this opportunity to express to you my most sincere congratulations on this award, I remain,

Yours sincerely

Maison Olympique, 1007 Lausanne, Switzerland | Tel. +41 21 621 6111 | Fax +41 21 621 6216 | www.IOC.org

My very first personal gift for him was a 4-line poem presented at the time his visit to Gangneung City for his honorary citizenship in mid-March 2018, during which he named it as an "Olympic City", actually Ice sports venue city of the PyeongChang2018 Winter Games.

The second and third versions of my 4-line poems dedicated to him were also presented in honor of and with my highest respect to his century-long global contribution to the successful organization of the PyeongChang2018 Winter Olympic Games, which is still remembered as "Peace Olympics" thanks to his unique and unprecedented diplomatic skills and leadership between two Koreas through the Olympic bridges. No one will dispute the fact that he well-deserves the Nobel Peace Prize recipient at an appropriate timing in the very near future, I believe.

**Four-Line Poem I For IOC President Thomas Bach**

1)B----Brilliant
2)A----Amazing
3)C----Charismatic
4)H----Hero of Heroes

**Four-Line Poem II For IOC President Thomas Bach**

1)B-----Because of you
2)A-----All the world
3)C-----Commemorates, Congratulates, and Celebrates
4)H-----Humanity and Hope
"Hope Lights Our Way"

**Four-Line Poem III For IOC President Thomas Bach**

1)B-----Bravo, Mr. President!
2)A-----Amazing, Awesome! Admire you from the bottom of my heart for
3)C-----Crowning the Olympic Movement under your outstanding leadership and chairmanship. Therefore, I say, and we say;
4)H-----Hallelujah ! God bless you !

**Dedicated by Rocky YOON Kang-Ro**

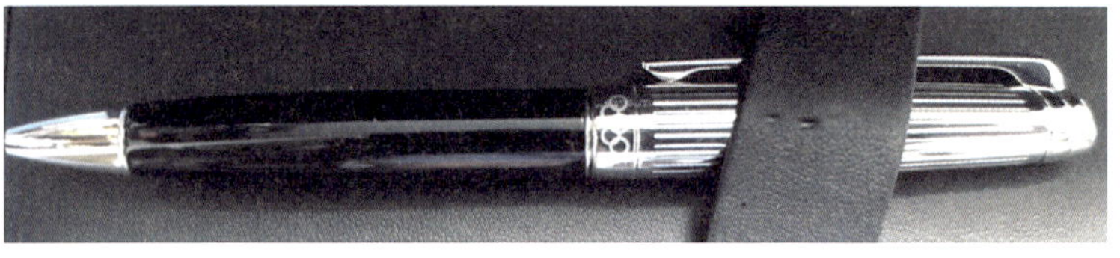

*(IOC President's First Gift for me after Signing Ceremony of MOU Between Olympic Museum and Gangneung Olympic Musuem, Lausanne/April 2018)*

Dear Honourable Honorary IOC President for Life Thomas Bach,

Thank you very much for your reply which I received with special emotions today. And I have mixed feelings about what the future would hold without your best optimized and timely implementation flow from your experiences, knowledge, and wisdom as top-most leader of the global Olympic Movement so far, while I also strongly trust the brilliant and refined leadership to be showcased by 10th IOC President Kirsty Coventry.

While I convincingly believe, with her track records, that your successor, the 10th IOC President Kirsty Coventry, would highly respect and value your leadership footprints, including but not limited to your historic brainchild "Olympic Agenda 2020+5", I am convinced and persuaded with absolute certainty that you would also willingly render your well-deserved advice and insights in order for her to keep the future Olympic Movement solidly on the right track and desirable directions. As you mentioned, "We can move Faster, we can aim higher, and we can stay stronger, together!"

As this letter would serve as my very first letter to you as Honorary IOC President for Life from today after the IOC Presidential Key-Handover Ceremony, I would like to take this opportunity to pay my highest respect and tribute to you for what you have achieved so far for the entire global Olympic Movement and what you would definitely contribute to the advancement of the future Olympic Movement from now.

Reminiscing our good old yet fresh memories and extraordinary friendship shared with you when in office as IOC President, I would still do my utmost to serve and make the global Olympic Movement in the future a continued resounding success modelling after your tangible and intangible great Olympic legacy accumulated, if such opportunity allowed.

In addition, it is my firm belief and conviction that you will continue to remain as global Olympic God Father taking care of not only the current Olympic Movement but also the Olympic Refuge Foundation as its President in the same spirit and manner as in the past.

In the meantime, may I take this opportunity to reiterate my most profound gratitude to you for your thoughtful and benevolent consideration and encouragement for me to be able to find resilience and vitality in the Olympic Movement, I remain,

As IOC President Bach once mentioned, "At this moment in time, no other event brings the entire world together in peace, like the Olympic Games.

The Olympic Games are the best expression of our values in action.

The Olympic Games must be beyond all the political tensions.

The Olympic Games must not be a tool for political maneuvering.

The Olympic Games must be seen as a stage for dialogue.

The Olympic Games are a symbol of hope and for peace.

This is the message the Olympic Movement promote.

In this way, the Olympic Games can play an important part to promote friendship, peace and solidarity through sport in the post-coronavirus world."

### 1) The way forward & Proposal

Having watched a series of current developments in the aftermath of the global COVID-19 pandemic impact on the Olympic Movement in general and the Tokyo2020 in particular, I have to come to think about how to best contribute to the solutions related to the preventive and precautionary countermeasures.

Many global entities are endeavouring to research over how to find suitable solutions such as developing some sorts of anti-corona virus vaccine, etc. However, according to some of various experts, similar or different kinds of pandemic virus outbreak phenomenon may take turns to show up every 3~4 years at intervals mainly due to influences from ecological instability.

At this juncture, I would like to propose that the Olympic Movement suggest its own vaccine to help protect and enhance the Olympic Games, including but not limited to (1) Sport-vaccine, (2) Eco-vaccine, (3) Behaviour-vaccine, and eventually (4) Olympic vaccine. Among them, I do believe the Olympic vaccine is just about what the humanity really needs for consolation.

Aristotle once said, "We are what we repeatedly do. Excellence, then, is not an act, but a habit."

"New Horizons, New Blessings; Sport is the Answer" in the post-coronavirus world.

## 58. Proposals III for the Post Corona Olympics (About How to Best Optimize the current Crisis for the Future Olympic Movement)

I think we need to find ways and means to address a specific soft-landing paradigm from conventional compactness-oriented Games to multi-functional and "Phono-Sapiens" Games with digital platform methods. In addition, it is about time for multi-faceted structures of current International sports organizations to be systematically and appropriately pruned in some ways.

It should be differentiated between "before corona"(B.C.) and "post corona"(P.C.) era. Corruption used to be another form of coronavirus. Some of the briefs of my Post-Corona Proposals are as follows:

1) We need now "Integrity-Vaccine" in addition to "Eco Vaccine" and "Behavior Vaccine" as first proposed "One-Strike-Out Integrity Rule" to be applied to the entire Olympic Movement with immediate effect.
2) Phono-Sapiens' digital platform
3) Post-Corona World: Homo-Symbiosis in place of Home-Sapiens
4) Platform=Network=Human Relations
5) Connectivity and Connected-Oriented marketing and business model, such as Air B&B and Uber Car Sharing, etc.
6) IOC's New Normal: Engagement--Inclusiveness--Connectivity
7) New Olympic Value Chain:
(1) On-Line Membership
(2) On-Line Olympic Movement
(3) On-Line IOC Session (Untact Conference Model)
(4) Value-Creating Olympic Marketing
8) Shift in approach as a result of corona pandemic
9) Virtual Coordination as a new model
10) Time for a new phase of the New Norm --New Normal—New Standards
11) "#Stay Strong, Stay Healthy, Stay Active" need to be incorporated into IOC's New Normal and New Motto of the Post Corona Era
12) "IOC and Olympic Movement 4.0" in line with Industry 4.0 in Germany
13) Harmonized Convergence of Fluid Intelligence(Youth) and Crystalized Intelligence(Aged)
14) Additional Requirements for Future Olympic Games Participants:
(1) Quarantine Passport

(2) Health Passport

15) Olympic Medal Plaza for both Winter and Summer Games

16) Each IP (Internet Protocol) Camera in the FOP including Main Stadium would cover at least 100 digital spectators anywhere, thus increasing virtual seating capacity with no need to secure obligatory stadium /venue seating requirements by IFs. IP cameras up to more than 100 units could be installed in and around the stadium and venues. Each IP Camera would serve as at least 100-spectators worth bundles of tickets which would increase the ticket sales revenue as well. Each IP Camera-Viewing Right would be on sale in addition to real tickets.

17) VR (Virtual Reality), AR (Augmented Reality) and MR (Mixed Reality) Rights need to be secured and protected by the IOC in the future Olympic Games

The Olympic Movement would have to create a new model to showcase "Fast to Follow" and "First to Move".

## 59. Dr. Thomas Bach's Resonating Words of Jewels (100)

The 9th IOC President Thomas Bach is often characterized by his simple but long-lasting magic words penetrating and appealing to the global sport people, especially in the Olympic Movement.

Even myself have continuously been intrigued and touched by his pithy epigram that stings the people to the quick even into our heart and memory.

As for me personally, the most universal and touching word is "**Unity in**

**Diversity**", followed by many others, including but not limited to "**There is no one-size-fits-all solution**", "**without losing political neutrality**", "**Olympic legacy for sustainability, flexibility, practicality, good governance, gender equality**, "**Unifying Power of sport and Olympics to bring together people**", exquisitely melted in his brain child masterpiece, "**Olympic Agenda 2020+5**", which is a "Strategic Roadmap of the Future Olympic Movement" and updated Olympic motto of "Faster, Higher, Strong, **Together**" in the IOC's 130-year long history as of 23 June 2024 since its creation in 1894.

Dr. Thomas Bach as unprecedented performing designer and strategist of the destiny of the future Olympic Movement, more importantly for me, is one of my three most respected IOC Presidents along with the 2nd IOC President Baron Pierre de Coubertin, IOC Founder and Renovator of the

International Olympic Committee
The President

Professor Rocky Yoon Kang-Ro
President
International Sport Diplomacy Institute
Standing Advisor to Korea Sports Promotion Foundation (KSPO)

Dear Professor,
Dear friend,

It is with great pleasure that I inform you that the IOC Executive Board, which met today, has awarded you the Pierre de Coubertin Medal for blending culture and sport in such a unique way in your publishing.

Please kindly take contact with my office to decide a date for the awarding ceremony.

May I take this opportunity to express to you my most sincere congratulations on this award, I remain,

Yours sincerely

Maison Olympique, 1007 Lausanne, Switzerland | Tel. +41 21 621 6111 | Fax +41 21 621 6216 | www.IOC.org

modern Olympic Games and I was also awarded the IOC Pierre de Coubertin Medal in October 2022 and the 7th IOC President Juan Antonio Samaranch who saved the Olympic Movement from several attempts of Olympic boycott, especially Seoul 1988 Games.

My very first personal gift for him was a 4-line poem presented at the time his visit to Gangneung City for his honorary citizenship in mid-March 2018, during which he named it as an "Olympic City", actually Ice sports venue city of the PyeongChang2018 Winter Games.

The second and third versions of my 4-line poems dedicated to him were also presented in honor of and with my highest respect to his century-long global contribution to the successful organization of the PyeongChang2018 Winter Olympic Games, which is still remembered as "Peace Olympics" thanks to his unique and unprecedented diplomatic skills and leadership between two Koreas through the Olympic bridges. No one will dispute the fact that he well-deserves the Nobel Peace Prize recipient at an appropriate timing in the very near future, I believe.

*His Life-time Contribution to **Olympic Movement (Unity in Diversity)**

*His Twelve Year-long Dedication to **World Peace (Give Peace a Chance!)**

**Four-Line Poem I For IOC President Thomas Bach**

1)B----Brilliant
2)A----Amazing
3)C----Charismatic
4)H----Hero of Heroes

**Four-Line Poem II For IOC President Thomas Bach**

1)B-----Because of you
2)A-----All the world
3)C-----Commemorates, Congratulates, and Celebrates
4)H-----Humanity and Hope
"Hope Lights Our Way"

**Four-Line Poem III For IOC President Thomas Bach**

1)B-----Bravo, Mr. President!
2)A-----Amazing, Awesome! Admire you from the bottom of my heart for
3)C-----Crowning the Olympic Movement under your outstanding leadership and chairmanship. Therefore, I say, and we say;
4)H-----Hallelujah ! God bless you !

**Dedicated by Rocky YOON Kang-Ro**

*His Humanitarian Aspirations towards **Olympic Refugees (Sympathy for Underprivileged)**

(1) Thank you from the bottom of my heart.

(2) This is really an overwhelming sign of trust and confidence.

(3) "I know about the great responsibility of an IOC President."

(4) "This makes me humble.

(5) "I want to lead the IOC according to my motto": 'unity in diversity.'

(6) "This means I will do my very best to balance well all the different interests of the stakeholders of the Olympic Movement."

(7) "This is why I want to listen to you and to enter into an ongoing dialogue with all of you."

(8) "You should know that my door, my ears, and my heart are always open for you

(9) He wants to keep the Olympic Games "**unique**" and not "**diluted by other events**," while ensuring the awarding of the Games is based on "the interest of the IOC in an in-depth review and risk analysis of a bid on the one hand, and the interest of a potential bidder in a social and promotional return on investment on the other

(10) "I want to be a **President for all of you**."

(11) The Olympic Games must be **beyond all the political tensions**.

(12) The Olympic Games must **not be a tool for political maneuvering**.

(13) The Olympic Games must be seen as **a stage for dialogue**.

(14) The Olympic Games are **a symbol of hope and for peace**.

(15) "In the Olympic Movement, everybody enjoys the same rights and the same obligations, and everyone deserves the right to a fair procedure."

(16) "We can **avoid even the perception of a conflict of interests**, and we can harmonize better and make **the fight against doping even stronger and more effective**."

(17) "Following **the reforms of Olympic Agenda 2020**, we are in a good position to address all these matters swiftly, even if they are from the past.

(18) Based on this new governance model we can move forward with confidence."

(19) "**What affects one of us affects all of us**."

(20) "The stage is set for the best athletes of the world to celebrate the Olympic Winter Games in PyeongChang.

(21) We **cannot ignore the political tension on the Korean peninsula**."

(22) "But in all the talks with leaders the Olympic Games were never put in doubt.

(23) The Games have to be **beyond any politicization**.

(24) All have to be equal and all welcome.

(25) The Games are **a stage for dialogue to build bridges**."

(26) "This world is **more fragile than ever**, and we can see in **many parts of the world crises, tensions, and financial and commercial instability**."

(27) "Enjoying 11 years of stability with two such outstanding Olympic cities and countries is really an achievement we can build on."

(28) "It gives us the opportunity to keep changing and to address all our challenges with a very solid foundation.

(29) It gives us time to think, time to breathe. But also to enjoy stability in this world is possibly the most valuable currency in the

world at this time,"

(30) There is '**No One-Size-Fits-All' Solution**.

(31) Sport is one of the few things with **the power to unite all people** in an increasingly fragile world

(32) Sport is **an anchor of stability** for so many people, regardless of background, nationality or belief.

(33) **This unique power of sport to unite all of humanity** is one of the most important things that the Olympic Games can give us in our troubled times.

(34) "Sport has **the power to change the world**" (These were the words of **Nelson Mandela**, the great humanist and leader)

(35) You can inspire others to change, only if you are ready to change yourself. We have all gathered here to lead this change in sport.

(36) **Success is the best reason for change.**

(37) The success of today gives you only the **opportunity to drive the change for tomorrow**

(38) If we do not address these challenges here and now we will be hit by them very soon.

(39) If we do not drive these changes ourselves others will drive us to them. We want to be the **leaders of change, not the object of change.**

(40) **To change or to be changed**, that is the question.

(41) We need to change because **sport today is too important in society to ignore the rest of society.**

(42) We are not living on an island, we are living in the middle of a modern, diverse, digital society

(43) If we want our **values of Olympism** - the values of **(1) Excellence, (2) Respect, (3) Friendship, (4) Dialogue, (5) Diversity, (6) Non-Discrimination, (7) Tolerance, (8) Fair-Play, (9) Solidarity, (10) Development and (11) Peace** - if we want these values to remain relevant in society, the time for change is now.

(44) We are living in a world more fragile than ever.

(45) We see **political crisis, financial crisis, health crisis, terrorism, war** and **civil war**.

(46) We are living in a society more fragmented, more individualized, you could even say more selfish than ever.

(47) We are living in a global society with more opportunities than ever.

(48) Opportunities **for communication, for dialogue, for global solidarity, for social development, and for peace**. We are living at a moment when we do not know which way the world will choose to go - or worse which way the world will let itself go.

(49) Our message of **dialogue**, of **respect for rules**, our message of **tolerance, solidarity and peace** – that this Olympic message is perhaps more relevant than ever.

(50) This modern world takes less for granted, has no place for complacency, questions even those with the highest reputation. This world takes much less on faith.

(51) In the **Olympic Agenda 2020** we are addressing these questions under the **three overarching topics** of **(1) sustainability, (2) credibility, (3) youth.**

(52) With a new philosophy in the bidding procedure we are encour-

aging potential candidate cities to present to us a holistic concept of respect for the **environment, feasibility and of development**, **to leave a lasting legacy**

(53) With these far reaching changes we respect that there is no "**one size fits all solution**" for the sustainability of Olympic Games.

(54) Host city candidates strive for very different development goals and start from very different points of development. We embrace this diversity.

(55) In fact, **this diversity is part of the magic of the Olympic Games.**

(56) With the Olympic Agenda 2020 we promote and support this diversity by **creating more flexibility**, more flexibility for the organization and the programme of the Olympic Games. At the same time, we safeguard the unity of the Olympic Movement by ensuring the respect of the host for our values and the respect for the athletes who are at the heart of the Olympic Games.

(57) With the Olympic Agenda 2020 we are addressing **the topic of credibility** - credibility for competitions as well as for organizations

(58) Therefore, we will strengthen our **good governance, transparency and ethics**.

(59) The Olympic Movement is all about the **clean athletes**. They are our **best ambassadors**, they are our **role-models**, they are **our treasure**. Therefore, we have first and foremost to **protect the clean athletes**.

(60) We have an interest and **a responsibility** to **get the couch potatoes off the couch**. Only children playing sport can be future athletes. Only children playing sport can enjoy the **educational and health**

**values of sport**.

(61) This **Olympic Agenda 2020** is like **a jig-saw puzzle**. Every piece, every recommendation, has the same importance. Only when you put all these 40 pieces together you see the whole picture. You see progress in ensuring the success of the Olympic Games, progress in safeguarding the Olympic Values and progress in strengthening sport in society.

(62) With the composition of the Working Groups we have opened up to society. We have opened our windows to let fresh air in. We have opened our minds to the **advice of high-ranking representatives from other NGO's, from politics, from culture, from business**

(63) All their most welcome input is reflected in this Olympic Agenda 2020. We do not want, and we cannot afford to leave this as a one-off event. If we want to turn these changes into progress, we need to continue this dialogue.

(64) Therefore, we do not only open our windows but also our doors for consultations with different NGO's, with political leaders, with the cultural community and with entrepreneurs.

(65) This diversity is an enrichment. This diversity is an even greater enrichment, because at the same time you strengthened the unity with regard to our vision and our values. So let us together use this momentum for progress through change. **Let us unite behind our Olympic Agenda 2020**. Let us demonstrate the true meaning of **Unity in Diversity**. Let us together shape an even brighter future for this magnificent, truly global Olympic Movement.

(66) In a world where mistrust and uncertainty are on the rise, sport is

a source of joy and inspiration for so many people, giving us hope that our shared humanity is stronger than the forces that want to divide us. An international survey has found that these Olympic Games are strongly associated with positive attributes such as **"excellence", "friendship" and "respect"**, among many others.

(67) With this global visibility comes responsibility for the world of sport.

(68) Because of the **unifying power of sport**, there are high hopes and even higher expectations for sports organizations from the general public – and rightly so.

(69) The role of sport in society is more relevant today than ever before

(70) In sport, the success of today means nothing for tomorrow. As an athlete, I learned that your performance will ultimately be judged by how you rise to the occasion.

(71) The success of today only gives you the strength to address the challenges of tomorrow.

(72) This is the same approach that the Olympic Movement will take to tackle the challenges that lie ahead in 2017.

(73) There are many challenges on our agenda, so we cannot afford to stand still.

(74) We need to rise to the occasion in the New Year.

(75) **International Day of Peace** is to be celebrated around the world today (21 Sept), with Bach discussing "the unifying power of sport" in a video message.

(76) **"Sport contributes to Peace by unifying people."**

(77) "The Olympic Games today are the only event in our world which manages to really bring the entire world together.

(78) "Athletes come to the Olympic Games respecting the same rules, all being equal, without any discrimination."

(79) Bach repeated this sentiment of Tokyo 2020 being **a beacon of hope** in his message.

(80) **"This post-coronavirus world** will be **very different from the one we used to live in."**

(81) "And I hope that we all have learned from this crisis that we need more solidarity, within societies and among societies.

(82) "Only in this joint effort can we overcome this crisis and prevent a new crisis.

(83) "The Olympic Games Tokyo 2020, which have been postponed to 2021, will send **a message of hope, of peace and unity of humanity."**

(84) **"Solidarity is not just about respecting each other, but also helping each other and being part of a community."**

(85) "And this is what these athletes and the National Olympic Committees are doing together with the IOC.

(86) "We are supporting this principle, not only by organizing the Olympic Games, but also by distributing 90 per cent of all our revenues to the development of sport worldwide in real Olympic solidarity."

(87) Bach also revealed his top three demonstrations of peace in sporting history.

(88) This included the **unified Korean team** at the Pyeongchang 2018 Olympic Games, **Nelson Mandela awarding South Africa the trophy at the 1995 Rugby World Cup** - the first major sporting event to take place in South Africa following the end of apartheid - and the **creation of the IOC Refugee Olympic Team.**

(89) “When I saw this team, marching behind the Olympic flag into the stadium and the way they were received by their fellow athletes and by the public, it still gives me goosebumps today.”

(90) **“This world is run by politics and not by sports organizations.”**

(91) “Therefore, to preserve the autonomy, we have to have a partnership and mutual respect.

(92) “On the one hand, our respect for the priorities of politics, and on the other hand, their respect of the politics for the autonomy of the IOC, making them aware that we can only accomplish our mission if we have this autonomy, if we are **politically strictly neutral**.

(93) “And what this means, you can see **from the Korean issues.**

(94) “If we would not have been **strictly politically neutral**, we could never have achieved the **joint march behind the one flag nor the joint women’s ice hockey team.”**

(95) “The idea of Olympic Agenda 2020 is to give more flexibility to cities and allow more creativity.

(96) “Every crisis comes an opportunity.”

(97) “Charge boldly through the clouds and do not be afraid. The future belongs to you.”

(98) “Let us show that sport is also always about ambition and optimism.”

(99) “Let us not rest on our current position of strength.”

(100) “Let us make sure that we can enjoy such stability also in the years to come.

# 60. Author's Life-long Contribution Records

## Rocky Yoon's Life-Long 10 Contribution Records Through Sport Diplomacy (42 Years)

(1)World First-Ever Korean Kimchi Proposed-Recognized-Accepted- Implemented-Enjoyed mostly by non-European Athletes as Global K-Food/Balanced Olympic Food(Strategic Growth of Korean Athletes Winning More Olympic Medals)

(2)Coordinated-Achieved Korea's First-Ever Signature between Two NOCs of South-North Korean NOCs of Sports Exchange Agreement during Busan2002 Asian Games

(3)Intervened eventually To Delete "Caffeine" From the IOC Prohibited Substance List sometime in 2003

(4)First-Ever Intervention(IOC EB-NOCs Joint Meeting) To Include Taekwondo as an Olympic Programme Sport(late 1980s)

(5)First-Ever Proposal for Olympic Motto To Be Readjusted & Reinforced & Upgraded as More V.I.P. In Line with Modern Sports Evolvement Since Athens1896 Games

(6)First-Ever Request & Realization of Substantial Increase (Double the Volume)of KOC Revenue Generation From Annual IOC Distribution Fund via then-Meridian/IOC Marketing Agency(1988~1989)/Samsung TOP Partnership Since 1987

(7)Negotiated & Realized First-Ever Savings of US$20 Million Deposited as Non-Performance Bond at HSBC From OCA Plus Gained Foreign Exchange Marginal Profit For Busan City As Part of Busan 2002 AG Bid Commitment to OCA(Power of Sport Diplomacy)

(8)Negotiated & Realized First-Ever Savings of US$3 Million+ US$ 2 Million For 1999 Gangwon Winter Asian Games Organizing Committee From OCA & AG Athletes' Village Operations (Power of Sport Diplomacy)

**9)Negotiated & Realized First-Ever Signature of MoU Between IOC President-Olympic Museum Director and Gangneung Olympic City Mayor-GOM at IOC HQs.(Apr. 2018)**

**10)Built & Operated First-Ever Private PyeongSan Sport Museum(2004) & First-Ever Pro Bono Donation of All Collection Items-Olympic and Sport Souvenirs-Memorabilia To Gangneung Olympic City For Exhibition & Display at Gangneung Olympic Museum in Progress For Olympic Education & Engagement For Youths both at Home and Abroad(Oct. 2015)**

# Chapter 19:

# *Tributes of Encouragement from Global Leaders including Thomas Bach for Rocky Kang-Ro YOON(Author)*

**Rocky Yoon & Three IOC Presidents Samaranch-Rogge-Bach (1982~2025)**

*(From left to right: the 7th IOC President Juan Antonio Samaranch, the 8th IOC President Jacques Rogge, the 9th Current IOC President Thomas Bach)*

## 1) Princess Royale

*Full Text:

“Dear Mr. Yoon, the princess Royale has asked me to thank you for your letter and book on Sport Diplomacy you kindly sent. Her Royal Highness has taken the book back to her private residence to read. It was very thoughtful of you to consider sending a copy. I do hope it has been a success. The Princess Royal sends you and your family her best wishes."

Yours Sincerely,

Miss Any Briggs/Assistant Private Secretary [HRH The Princess Royal]

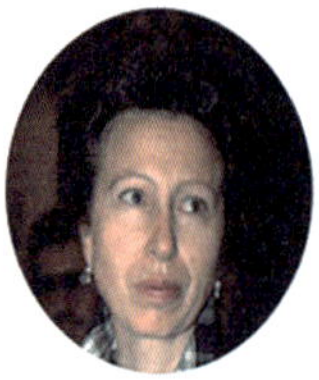

HRH the Princess ROYAL

GBR

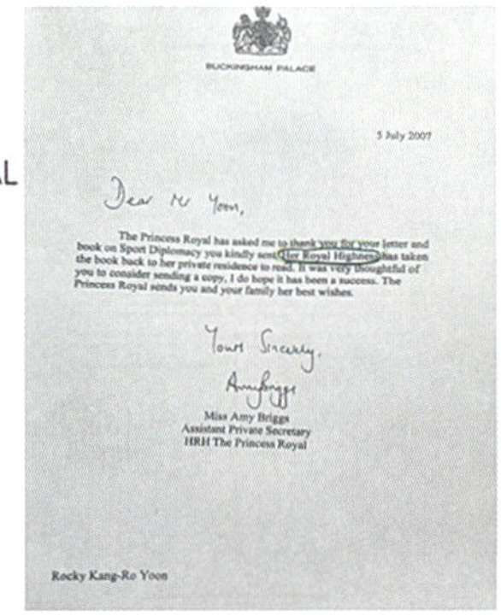

BUCKINGHAM PALACE

5 July 2007

Dear Mr Yoon,

The Princess Royal has asked me to thank you for your letter and book on Sport Diplomacy you kindly sent. Her Royal Highness has taken the book back to her private residence to read. It was very thoughtful of you to consider sending a copy. I do hope it has been a success. The Princess Royal sends you and your family her best wishes.

Yours Sincerely,

Amy Briggs

Miss Amy Briggs
Assistant Private Secretary
HRH The Princess Royal

Rocky Kang-Ro Yoon

## 2) IOC President Thomas Bach

*(With IOC President Thomas Bach: From Left at PyeongChang2018 Office Special Lecture-Gangnung City Hall for Honorary Citizenship in March 2018-IOC Pierre de Coubertin Medal Presentation Ceremony in 2022)*

## [Presentation Ceremony of the Pierre de Coubertin Medal to Prof. Rocky Kang-Ro YOON /Seoul, October 2022]

*"It is with great pleasure to inform you that the IOC Executive Board, which met today, has decided to award you the Pierre de Coubertin Medal for blending culture and sport in such a unique way in your publishing" (Letter by IOC President Thomas Bach about the decision by IOC Executive Board dated 9 September)*

Dear friends,

For our founder, Pierre de Coubertin, the Olympic Games were always much more than just a sporting event. He wanted to make the world a better place through sport and its values. This remains the overarching mission of the IOC and the entire Olympic Movement to this day.

Dear Rocky,

Having known you for such a long time, I can say from personal observation that during all these many years, your commitment to the Olympic Movement has always been a reflection of this vision of our founder.

Making the world a better and more peaceful place through sport has always been your guiding principle throughout your illustrious career.

At the Korean Olympic Committee, as the Korean Sport and Olympic Committee was formerly known, you were deeply involved in the successful organisation of the Olympic Games Seoul 1988. These Games left a remarkable sporting legacy to the people of Seoul and the Republic of Korea.

My personal connection to Seoul and Korea also began during these Games. At the time, I was the athletes' representative on the Games' steering committee. Ever since then, Seoul and its people have a very special place in my heart.

After the closing of the Olympic Games Seoul 1988, promoting the legacy of these Games has been the guiding theme of your career. As Standing Advisor to the Korea Sports Promotion Foundation, you have taken part in long-term projects including the Seoul Olympic Legacy Forum, which is taking place this week right here in Seoul.

You spent more than two decades as an official delegate for the NOC of the Republic of Korea, serving the development of sport and spreading the Olympic values throughout the country. During this time, your outstanding dedication to the athletes is reflected in the fact that you were a leading member of the South Korean delegation for an incredible ten editions of the Olympic Games.

Over the years, you have always shown a desire to share and pass on your extensive Olympic experience. Most recently you did so by providing guidance and counsel to the Organising Committee of the Olympic Winter Games PyeongChang 2018 in your capacity as senior advisor to the OCOG President. I am very grateful to say that the IOC, through its Evaluation Commission for the Olympic Games Beijing 2008, has also benefited your deep expertise.

Your belief in the power of sport has also guided you in your current role as President of the International Sport Diplomacy Institute. In this capacity, you are continuing to keep the legacy of Seoul 1988 alive, in particular through your active engagement with young people. With your lectures at renowned universities, you are inspiring the new generation with our shared Olympic values.

Perhaps nothing illustrates your passion for sport better than the creation of the Pyeongsan Sports Museum close to your home town, where thousands of Olympic artifacts and memorabilia are on display, many from your private collection.

Having just recently published the book "True Record and Stories of Korea Sports Diplomacy" you show no signs of slowing down. On the contrary, your unwavering commitment and enthusiasm for the Olympic Games continues to reach new heights. This is why today, we salute and honour your unique contribution and deep-rooted attachment to the Olympic values.

Dear Mr. Yoon Kang-Ro, dear Rocky,

In recognition of your outstanding achievements in supporting the cause of world sport and your faithfulness to the Olympic ideal as illustrated by Pierre de Coubertin, reviver of the Olympic Games, it is an honour and pleasure to present you with the Pierre de Coubertin Medal.

## [Foreword for my Book titled "True Records and Stories of Korea Sport Diplomacy "The New Horizons" By IOC President Thomas Bach]

It only seems like yesterday that we were celebrating a world united by sport in peaceful competition at the Olympic Winter Games PyeongChang 2018. The magic of Olympic sport on snow and ice, the unforgettable performances by the athletes and the wonderful hospitality of the Korean people and will live on in our hearts forever. The Olympic Winter Games PyeongChang 2018 also sent a powerful message of peace from the Korean Peninsula to the world. That moment came when the athletes from the National Olympic Committees of the Republic of Korea and the Democratic People's Republic of Korea entered the Olympic stadium as one team, behind one flag, the Korean Unification flag. This one moment demonstrated the unique power of sport to unite the whole world in peace. To me, this is the most powerful message of the Olympic Games. With these powerful symbols in PyeongChang, we have seen how the Olympic Games can open the way to dialogue. This moment did not happen by chance. It was the result of a long process of negotiations and high-level government engagement by the International Olympic Committeethat began back in 2014 and lasted until a few hours before this unforgettable Opening Ceremony. We know that sport alone cannot create peace. But as we saw in PyeongChang, the Olympic Games can open the way to a more peaceful future. This power of sport to unite the world in peaceful competition is a central theme in this insightful book that chronicles the history of the Olympic Movement in the Republic of Korea. My personal connection with the Korean people began during the Olympic Games Seoul 1988. At the time, I was the athletes' representative on the Games' steering committee. This early contact with the Koreans and the Korean culture left a lasting impression on me that continues to this day. It is in this context that I got to know and appreciate Rocky Kang-Ro Yoon as a leading figure in Korean sport. Building on his great knowledge on the Olympic Movement, he is ideally placed to share his many accounts of the rich Korean sporting history and the role that sport can play to make the world a better place. In order to shape the future, one needs to understand the past. This is why this book is a timely contribution to inspire the next generation of sport leaders with the lessons of the past, as they shape our way forward.

# [IOC President's Letters to Prof, Rocky Kang-Ro YOON]

## 9th IOC President Thomas Bach's Letters to Rocky YOON Kang-Ro(2018~2024)

## 3. Letter from 8th UN Secretary General Ki-Moon BAN

Dear Dr. YOON,

First of all, I would like to take this opportunity to wholeheartedly congratulate you on your nomination as Member of the IOC Culture and Olympic Heritage Commission Member.

In addition, please accept my warm congratulations again on your honor to be presented the IOC Pierre de Coubertin Medal in Seoul by IOC President Thomas Bach. I was sorry for not having been able to attend the above awarding ceremony due to my pre-engaged commitment at the same time.

In particular, I have been greatly impressed by your untiring efforts through your hard work of writings about the Olympic news and stories, thus disseminating the Olympic values in Korea and beyond.

More importantly, I realized that thanks to your great insight, enthusiasm and efforts, the Korean Kimchi has been included as an official menu item at the Olympic Village restaurant on a continued basis since 1992 Barcelona Olympics. On behalf of Korean people as well as sport people, my special thanks and tribute should go to yourself as a brilliant sport diplomat.

It is my ardent wish that we will continue to work together for the solemn goal, as set by IOC and the UN, of "Peace and Development through Sport"

What impressed me most while I served as UN Secretary General was the declaration by UN to designate the date of 6 April every year as "International Day of Sports for Development and Peace"

At that time, I used to share and consulted valued views with the late Jacques Rogge (the 8th IOC President) and IOC Vice President Thomas Bach.

One thing which was not well-known was that until 2009, the IOC had not been granted UN Observer Status. In my capacity as UN Secretary

General, I formally addressed this matter in order to get things done. As a result, the IOC President was able to enjoy the official status to have a seat attending at the UN General Assembly since then.

May I take this opportunity to ask you to continue to contribute not only to the Olympic Movement but also to the World Peace and SDGs through sport with enthusiasm

With my best wishes for your continued commitment and endeavors for the advancement of the Olympic Movement,

Sincerely,

Ki-Moon BAN

8th UN Secretary General

## 4) Letter from HM Willem-Alexander of the Netherlands, IOC Honorary Member

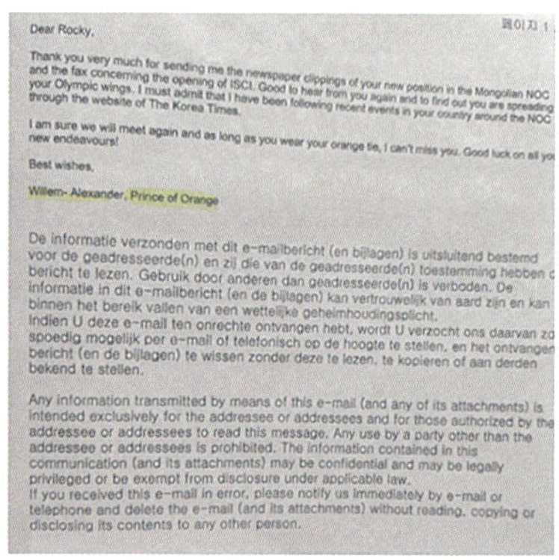

페이지 1

Dear Rocky,

Thank you very much for sending me the newspaper clippings of your new position in the Mongolian NOC and the fax concerning the opening of ISCI. Good to hear from you again and to find out you are spreading your Olympic wings. I must admit that I have been following recent events in your country around the NOC through the website of The Korea Times.

I am sure we will meet again and as long as you wear your orange tie, I can't miss you. Good luck on all yo[u] new endeavours!

Best wishes,

Willem- Alexander, Prince of Orange

De informatie verzonden met dit e-mailbericht (en bijlagen) is uitsluitend bestemd voor de geadresseerde(n) en zij die van de geadresseerde(n) toestemming hebben [d]it bericht te lezen. Gebruik door anderen dan geadresseerde(n) is verboden. De informatie in dit e-mailbericht (en de bijlagen) kan vertrouwelijk van aard zijn en kan binnen het bereik vallen van een wettelijke geheimhoudingsplicht.
Indien U deze e-mail ten onrechte ontvangen hebt, wordt U verzocht ons daarvan zo spoedig mogelijk per e-mail of telefonisch op de hoogte te stellen, en het ontvangen bericht (en de bijlagen) te wissen zonder deze te lezen, te kopieren of aan derden bekend te stellen.

Any information transmitted by means of this e-mail (and any of its attachments) is intended exclusively for the addressee or addressees and for those authorized by the addressee or addressees to read this message. Any use by a party other than the addressee or addressees is prohibited. The information contained in this communication (and its attachments) may be confidential and may be legally privileged or be exempt from disclosure under applicable law.
If you received this e-mail in error, please notify us immediately by e-mail or telephone and delete the e-mail (and its attachments) without reading, copying or disclosing its contents to any other person.

*Full Text:

"Dear Rocky,

Thank you very much for sending me the newspaper clipping of your new position in the Mongolian NOC and the fax concerning the opening of the ISDI (International Sport Diplomacy Institute). Good to hear from you again and to find out you are spreading your Olympic wings. I must admit that I have been following recent events in your country around the NOC through the website of The Korea Times.

I am sure we will meet again and as long as you wear orange tie, I can't miss you, Good luck on all your new endeavor!

Best wishes
Willem-Alexander, Prince of Orange

## 5) Letter from H.S.H. Prince Albert II of Monaco

HSH the Sovereign Prince ALBERT II

MON

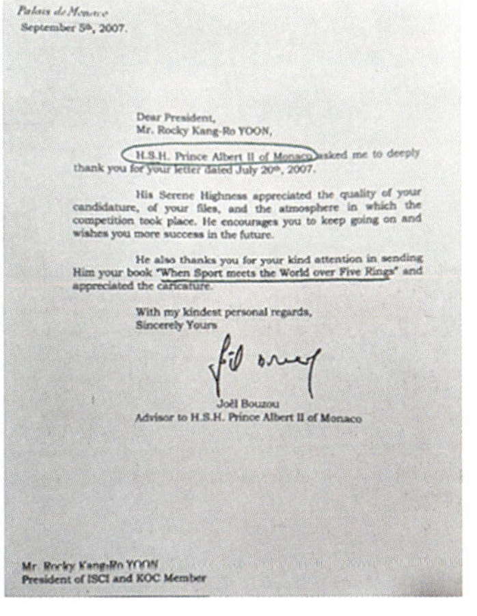

Palais de Monaco
September 5th, 2007.

Dear President,
Mr. Rocky Kang-Ro YOON,

H.S.H. Prince Albert II of Monaco asked me to deeply thank you for your letter dated July 20th, 2007.

His Serene Highness appreciated the quality of your candidature, of your files, and the atmosphere in which the competition took place. He encourages you to keep going on and wishes you more success in the future.

He also thanks you for your kind attention in sending Him your book "When Sport meets the World over Five Rings" and appreciated the caricature.

With my kindest personal regards,
Sincerely Yours

Joël Bouzou
Advisor to H.S.H. Prince Albert II of Monaco

Mr. Rocky Kang-Ro YOON
President of ISCI and KOC Member

*Full Text:

"Dear President, Mr. Rocky Kang-Ro YOON,

H.S.H. Prince Albert II of Monaco asked me to deeply thank you for your letter dated July 20th, 2007.

His Serene Highness appreciated the quality of your candidature, of your files, and the atmosphere in which the competition took place. He encourages you keep going on and wishes you more success in the future.

He also thanks you for your kind attention in sending Him your book, 'When Sport Meets the World Over Five Rings' and appreciated the candidature.

With my kindest personal regards,
Sincerely yours

Joel Bouzou
Advisor to H.S.H. Prince Albert II of Monaco

## 6) Letter from The Grand Duke of Luxembourg, IOC Member in Luxembourg

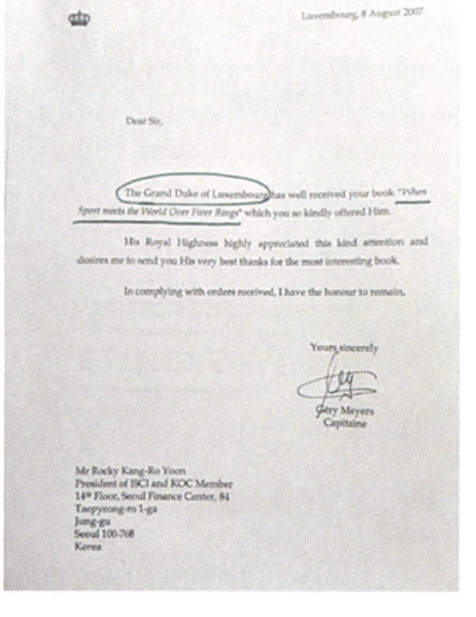

Luxembourg, 8 August 2007

Dear Sir,

The Grand Duke of Luxembourg has well received your book *"When Sport meets the World Over Fiver Rings"* which you so kindly offered Him.

His Royal Highness highly appreciated this kind attention and desires me to send you His very best thanks for the most interesting book.

In complying with orders received, I have the honour to remain,

Yours sincerely

Géry Meyers
Capitaine

Mr Rocky Kang-Ro Yoon
President of ISCI and KOC Member
14th Floor, Seoul Finance Center, 84
Taepyeong-ro 1-ga
Jung-gu
Seoul 100-768
Korea

*Full Text:

"Dear Sir,

The Grand Duke of Luxembourg has well received your book, *'When Sport Meets the World Over Five Rings'*, which you so kindly offered Him.

His Royal Highness highly appreciated this kind attention and desires me to send you His very best thanks for the most interesting book.

In complying with orders received, I have the honor to remain,

Yours sincerely,

Gery Meyers

Capitain

## 7) Letter from the late Mr. Henry A. Kissinger, IOC Honor Member in the United States

Mr Henry KISSINGER

USA

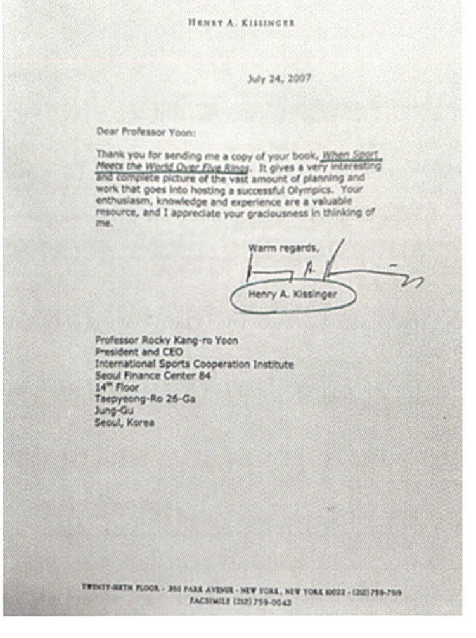

HENRY A. KISSINGER

July 24, 2007

Dear Professor Yoon:

Thank you for sending me a copy of your book, When Sport Meets the World Over Five Rings. It gives a very interesting and complete picture of the vast amount of planning and work that goes into hosting a successful Olympics. Your enthusiasm, knowledge and experience are a valuable resource, and I appreciate your graciousness in thinking of me.

Warm regards,

Henry A. Kissinger

Professor Rocky Kang-ro Yoon
President and CEO
International Sports Cooperation Institute
Seoul Finance Center 84
14th Floor
Taepyeong-Ro 26-Ga
Jung-Gu
Seoul, Korea

TWENTY-SIXTH FLOOR - 350 PARK AVENUE - NEW YORK, NEW YORK 10022 - (212) 759-7919
FACSIMILE (212) 759-0043

*Full Text:

"Dear Professor Yoon:

Thank you for sending me a copy of your book, *'When Sport Meets the World Over Five Rings'*, It gives a very interesting and complete picture of the vast amount of planning and work that goes into hosting a successful Olympics. Your enthusiasm, knowledge and experiences are a valuable resource, and I appreciate your graciousness in thinking of me.

Warm regards,

Henry A. Kissinger

## 8) A Tribute from Mme. Anita DeFrantz, IOC Member in the United States, Chair of the Women and Sport Commission (1995-2014), and Chair of the IOC Athletes' Commission Election Committee (1996-2014)

*Tribute for the Author:

"Secretary General Rocky YOON has played a leading role as long-standing regular member of all sport-related meetings, conferences, General Assemblies, Olympic Chefs-de-Mission meetings and others. Rocky YOON has positioned himself as an exemplary leading figure and valued indispensable member by faithfully digesting and implementing universal principles of the Olympic Games coupled with his sense of humor enough to please the people around him all along." (Retranslated from the

*(With Mme. Anita L. DeFrantz)*

Korean version once already translated from the original English version)

## 9) Letter from Prof. Dr. h.c. Berthold BEITZ, IOC Honorary Member in Germany

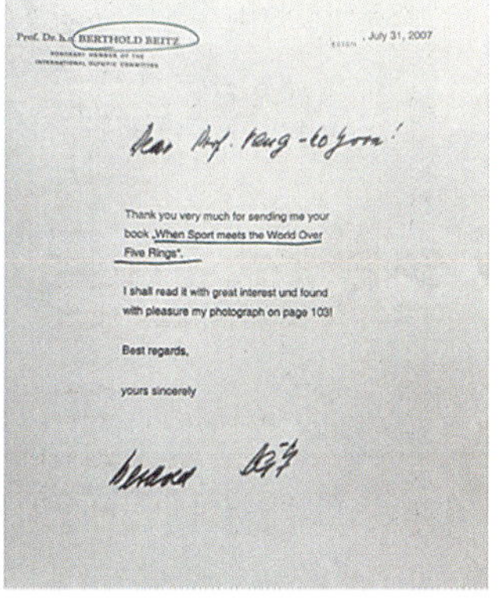

Prof. Dr. h.c. BERTHOLD BEITZ

, July 31, 2007

Thank you very much for sending me your book „When Sport meets the World Over Five Rings".

I shall read it with great interest und found with pleasure my photograph on page 103!

Best regards,

yours sincerely

*(Mr. Se-Jik PARK, SLOOC1988 President, Dr. Berthold BEITZ, Juan Antonio Samarmach)*

*Full Text:

"Dear Prof. Rocky Kang-Ro YOON,

Thank you very much for sending me your book, *'When Sport Meets the World Over Five Rings'*.

I shall read it with great interest und found with pleasure my photograph on page 103.

Best regards,

Yours sincerely,

Berthold BEITZ

## 10) A Tribute from the late Mr. Kun Hee LEE, IOC Member and Chairman of Sam Sung Group

***Summary**: "Congratulations on Rocky YOON's book publication containing his 20 plus years' vivid experiences on the international sport diplomacy field with his sense of humor and wits. He has participated in 10 editions of the Olympic Games and served as a first Asian IOC Evaluation Commission Member for the Olympic Games 2008, thus representing Asia as an Olympic Ambassador. He opened the International Sport Diplomacy Institute and PyeongSan Private Sport Museum which helped to greatly contribute to the sport development of Korea as well." (Translated and Summarized from original Korean version)

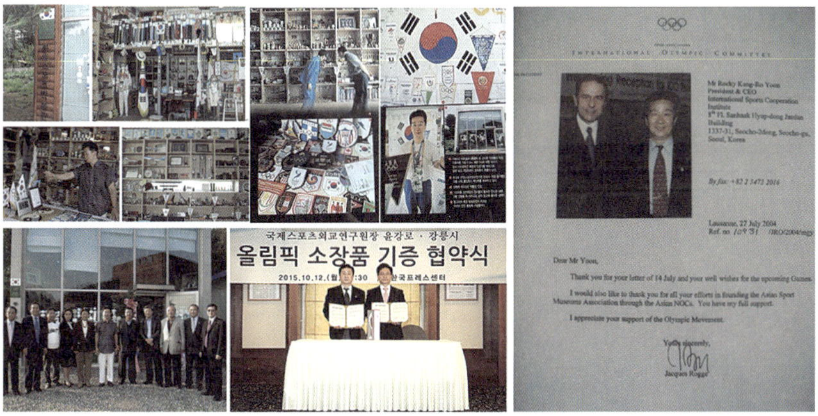


(Mr. Kun Hee LEE and Rocky YOON during TV Interview)

## 11) A Tribute from the late Dr. Un-Yong KIM, former IOC Vice President, GAISF & ARISF President, WTF President, KOC President, IOC TV Commission Chairman

(With Dr. Un-Yong KIM)

*Summary:

"Congratulations on a book publication. Rocky YOON is indeed a talented asset in the Korean sport history with skills in foreign languages, congenial affinity, and foresightedness with which he greatly contributed to the successful staging of many multi-international Games that Korea hosted. He actively and friendly demonstrated his outstanding skills all over the world, thus upgrading the status and image-making of Korea, I am confident that he will emerge as an exemplary sport diplomat and prominent leader in the global Olympic Movement sooner than later." (Translated and summarized from original Korean version)

## 12) A Tribute from Mr. Ung CHANG, IOC Member in DPR Korea and International Taekwondo Federation(ITF) President

*Summary:

As I hear that Prof. Rocky YOON Kang-Ro who is President of the In-

*(With Mr. Ung CHANG, IOC Member in DPR Korea/Now IOC Honorary member)*

ternational Sport Diplomacy Institute is publishing a book compiling the stories of the history of sport diplomacy and his own experiences despite the fact that there will be more opportunities, lessons and the road of experiences in the future, I feel how fast the time flies with no exception.

Over the past 30 years of the vicissitudes of powerful politics, historical environment, the sport diplomacy could be defined as inerasable records by Prof. Rocky YOON Kang-Ro who has immensely contributed to the advancement and pioneering of the North-South Korean sports relations with an aim to realize "One Korea" and its Unification through sport. Currently Rocky YOON Kang-Ro temporarily stepped aside from the front line of sport diplomacy due to unavoidable circumstances, but time will surely come for him to deploy his unmatched talents and skills accumulated through his experiences and friendly human interactions in the foreseeable future. At the very moment of such timing, I am awaiting his even better and more brilliant activities and remarkable contribution on a higher level in the sport diplomacy field in the same manner and spirit as in the past. I wish that his book would serve as a textbook providing the next generation with good lessons and life values of sport diplomacy, even though his valuable writings could not contain the real-time facts in a proper manner under some difficult circumstances. I am confident that this book will receive warm and sincere support from all walks of life including sportspeople who expect the leading role in realizing the national unification. (Translated from the original Korean version)

# 13) Letter from the late Mr. Mario Vazquez Rana, ANOC President and IOC Executive Board Member

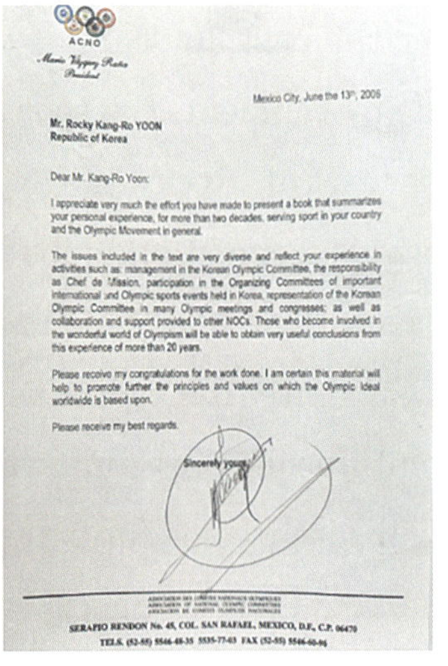

ACNO

Mario Vázquez Raña
President

Mexico City, June the 13th, 2006

**Mr. Rocky Kang-Ro YOON**
**Republic of Korea**

Dear Mr. Kang-Ro Yoon:

I appreciate very much the effort you have made to present a book that summarizes your personal experience, for more than two decades, serving sport in your country and the Olympic Movement in general.

The issues included in the text are very diverse and reflect your experience in activities such as: management in the Korean Olympic Committee, the responsibility as Chef de Mission, participation in the Organizing Committees of important international and Olympic sports events held in Korea, representation of the Korean Olympic Committee in many Olympic meetings and congresses; as well as collaboration and support provided to other NOCs. Those who become involved in the wonderful world of Olympism will be able to obtain very useful conclusions from this experience of more than 20 years.

Please receive my congratulations for the work done. I am certain this material will help to promote further the principles and values on which the Olympic Ideal worldwide is based upon.

Please receive my best regards.

Sincerely yours,

SERAPIO RENDON No. 45, COL. SAN RAFAEL, MEXICO, D.F., C.P. 06470
TELS. (52-55) 5546-48-35 5535-77-03 FAX (52-55) 5546-60-[illegible]

*(With Mr. Mario Vazquez Rana)*

***Summary:**

"Congratulations on your book publication. The issues included in the text are very diverse and reflect your experiences in activities such as management in the Korean Olympic Committee, the responsibility as Chef de Mission, participation in the Organizing Committees of important international and Olympic sports events held in Korea, representation of the Korean Olympic Committee in many other meetings and congresses, as well as collaboration and support provided to other NOCs, Those who become involved in the wonderful world of Olympism will be able to obtain very useful conclusions from this experience of more than 20 years Please receive my congratulations on the work done. I am certain this material will help to promote further the principles and values on which the Olympic ideal worldwide is based upon. Please receive my best regards." (Summarized from original English version once translated from Spanish)

## 14) Letter from Mr. Gerhard Heiberg, IOC EB member (Now IOC Honorary Member) in Norway, IOC Marketing Commission Chairman and IOC Evaluation Commission Chairman for 2010 OWG

"I congratulate you on your book and I could be quoted on the following:

I have known Mr. Rocky Kang-Ro YOON for many, many years. He is an absolute asset to international sports and especially to the international Olympic Movement. His experiences and knowledge of international sports are of great value and his sense of humor makes it always interesting to be with him. I would like to wish him good lucj with his book and with his many plans for the future.

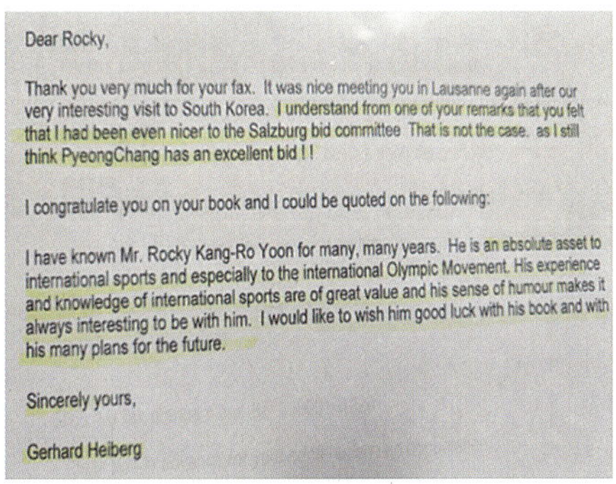

Dear Rocky,

Thank you very much for your fax. It was nice meeting you in Lausanne again after our very interesting visit to South Korea. I understand from one of your remarks that you felt that I had been even nicer to the Salzburg bid committee That is not the case. as I still think PyeongChang has an excellent bid ! !

I congratulate you on your book and I could be quoted on the following:

I have known Mr. Rocky Kang-Ro Yoon for many, many years. He is an absolute asset to international sports and especially to the international Olympic Movement. His experience and knowledge of international sports are of great value and his sense of humour makes it always interesting to be with him. I would like to wish him good luck with his book and with his many plans for the future.

Sincerely yours,

Gerhard Heiberg

*(With Mr. Gerhard Heiberg)*

Sincerely yours,

Gerhard Heiberg"

## 15) Letter from Mr. Sergey Bubka, IOC Member in Ukraine and former IOC Athletes Commission Chairman

"First of all, I wish to congratulate on your book publication. Book publishing is a great work of art, and I would like to read that book. I know you are an expert and specialist as far as sport is concerned. You have already served, contributing for such a long time to the advance-

*(With Mr. Sergey Bubka)*

ment and promotion of the Olympic Movement, and you deserve highest praise in terms of sport diplomacy in that you have served and devoted yourself to the development of the Olympic Movement through your National Olympic Committee. I consider it a great pride and joy to share with you such memorable and enjoyable experiences as IOC Evaluation Commission members together for the 2008 Olympics in which I admired your outstanding competence, profundity, expertise, and knowledge about the Olympic world. As for me, it was considerably effective and pleasant experiences to work with many consummate experts in the IOC Evaluation Commission like yourself. Through that international activities, we became mutual friends and I am proud of the fact that we still share goodwill friendship. I am certain that your book will enjoy high popularity and favorable reviews not only from sportspeople, but also world-wide general public." (Retranslated from Korean version once already translated from the original English version)

## 16) Letter from the late Mr. Hein Verbruggen, IOC Member in Netherlands, UCI and SportAccord President and Chairman of IOC Evaluation Commission for 2008 Olympics

*Full Text:

"Dear Rocky YOON,

It is with great pleasure that I write these lines as an introduction for a book that my close friend "Rocky YOON will publish very soon. I have

*(With Mr. Hein Verbruggen)*

understood that this book will serve Koreans to get acquainted with useful and applicable English expressions for daily life. Few people would be better qualified than Rocky YOON to write such a book as he indeed has great language skills. I have been more than once in a position to admire his linguistic capacities and not only in Shakespeare's language. Serving together on the IOC Evaluation Commission for the Candidate Cities for the 2008 Summer Olympics, I remember very well an audience we had with the French President, Mr. Jacques Chirac. Asking questions to various members, the President also turned to "Rocky", he was answered not only

in impeccable French, but also with extraordinary vocabulary-a "delicate choice of words"-as The President put it. I am therefore convinced that the uality of his book will be outstanding. Good luck, "Rocky"

Hein Verbruggen"

## 17) A Tribute from Mme. Els Van Breda Vriesman, Former IOC Member in Netherlands and FIH President

***Summary:**

[About Rocky YOON] "Rocky YOON who has been indisputably recognized as a remarkable contributor to the Olympic Movement nearing 30 years (as of 2006) is a true friend for all of us and trustworthy colleague with the greatest of pleasure. It was not until I noticed his well-rounded and outstanding skills and talents while we worked together as members of the IOC Evaluation Commission for 2008 Olympics that I recognized his real values. Rocky's merits demonstrating his devoted sincerity and passion as well as his firm conviction to realize the Olympic ideals were part of

*(First from Left: Els Van Breda Vriesman)*

core elements to come to admire and respect him toward his hidden qualities. Rocky YOON who covered almost every position and task related to sport in Korea was enough to impress all people by proving his capabilities through his immediate understanding of whatever issues arisen anytime and timely insightfulness acquired from his well-preserved experiences. It was what he always moved my heart about. It is with all my joyful heart to deliver my message of congratulations for his remarkable merits and values as an outstanding Olympic Ambassador, utilizing and mobilizing all my vocabularies." (Retranslated from the Korean version once already translated from the original English version)

## 18) A Tribute from Mr. Keven Gosper, Former IOC member in Australia, IOC Press Commission Chairman and ONOC President

***Summary:**

"I have known Rocky YOON for quite a long time. Rocky is an enthusiastic and optimistic friend with overall skills and qualities who can achieve anything. He deserves my respect. He is a man of devotion and responsibilities to do the job running the gamut from PR, international relations, through smoothly organizing international sports events, to useful advices, you name it. I am sure that Rocky, therefore, must be one of the best known sport Ambassador in Korea.

I can trust him as a colleague with his challenging spirts and his devoted attitudes which always made things well achieved. What impressed me most was his far-reaching knowledge and insightfulness about the International Federations, NOCs, Olympic Games, and overall Olympic Movement to say the least. Rocky is indeed a globally recognized person in the sport world." (Retranslated from Korean version which was once translated from the English version)

*(With Mr. Keven GOSPER/Dr. Robin Mitchell, Rocky YOON and Mme. Gunilla Lindberg)*

## 19) Letter from Mr. Joao HAVELANGE, Lifetime IOC Member in Brazil and (Former)FIFA President

*Full Text: "Dr. Mr. President, Rocky Kang-Ro YOON,

I received your kind letter, dated June 27, 2007 with a copy of a book entitled 'When Sport Meets the World Over Five Rings', which I immediately read carefully and I want to congratulates you for this episodes and stories and experiences by you.

Thanking you again for the admirable book. I send you very best regards.

Joao HAVELANGE

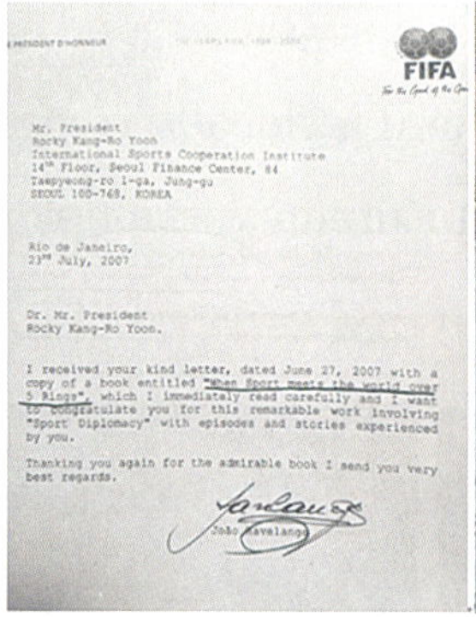

FIFA

Mr. President
Rocky Kang-Ro Yoon
International Sports Cooperation Institute
14th Floor, Seoul Finance Center, 84
Taepyeong-ro 1-ga, Jung-gu
SEOUL 100-768, KOREA

Rio de Janeiro,
23rd July, 2007

Dr. Mr. President
Rocky Kang-Ro Yoon.

I received your kind letter, dated June 27, 2007 with a copy of a book entitled "When Sport meets the world over 5 Rings", which I immediately read carefully and I want to congratulate you for this remarkable work involving "Sport Diplomacy" with episodes and stories experienced by you.

Thanking you again for the admirable book I send you very best regards.

João Havelange

(With Hon. Joao HAVELANGE and Football Emperor Pele)

## 20) A Tribute from Mr. Sh. Magvan, IOC Honorary Member in Mongolia

***Summary:**

"I was very glad to be given an opportunity to visit the Sport Museum built by Dr. Rocky YOON who is may long-time friend. In addition,

(First from right is Mr. Sh. Magvan)

I would like pay my respect to him for his contribution to the promotion of the Olympic Movement and his enthusiasm to have created his "PyeongSan Private Sport Museum" which was the first one in Asia. He has received the Honorary Doctor's Degree at the Mongolian National Sport Academy in Ulaanbaatar. He deserved more than that. He is a person who has truly devoted himself to the advancement of the Olympic Movement. In addition, I wish a great success in his book."

## 21) Letter from Mr. Tommy Sithole, (Former) IOC member in Zimbabwe, Secretary general of the ANOCA and IOC Director of International Cooperation

***Summary**: "Dear Rocky, I can't wait for your book with much expectations. If the contents of your book would be of interesting and pleasant rewarding with which you presented us during the IOC Evaluation Commission visits as the same members for the 2008 Summer Olympics, I have no doubt that your book would surely hit the jackpot. Please continue to make your hope and dream progressed as we all draw it. Then you will feel your

*(With Mr. Tommy Sithole during the visit to Candidate Cities for the 2008 Olympics as IOC Evaluation Commission Members at the IOC EB meeting room for the Final Report Drafting of the IOC Evaluation Visits)*

life very fruitful and rewarding." Retranslated from the Korean version once already translated from the original English version)

## 22) A Tribute from H.E. Seung-Soo HAN (Former President of UN General Assembly, and Former Prime Minister/Bid Committee President-PyeongChang2014)

***Summary:**

"Rocky YOON's knowledge, data and experiences are not simply his own individual asset, but an invaluable asset for entire Korean sport circles in a professional spirit and manner. His book is providing vivid stories to many of us that we never experienced. I am confident that he will continue to play a bigger role so that Korea would be better showcased in many

*(Second from Right: Hon. Seung-Soo HAN)*

other areas through sport in general and the success of the PyeongChang Olympic Winter Games in particular." (Translated and Summarized from original Korean version)

## 23) A Tribute from Mr. Yong-Sung PARK, Former IOC Member and IJF & KOC President

***Summary:**

"Secretary General Rocky YOON has been a sustainable human landmark from Korea having represented the Olympic Movement across the world. He is ubiquitous and no one will dispute the fact that Rocky de-

*(With Mr. Yong-Sung PARK)*

serves to be defined as International Friendship Ambassador in the international sport world. Secretary General YOON has a strong and influential grip over the global map, and advanced the rights and benefits of the Olympic Movement with corresponding influences above and beyond the cultures, thus referring to as Mr. Invincible in the working group level. What is more important is that he has achieved such results with the unprecedented degree of passion and intensity.

Having started his challenges while getting involved with the organization of the Seoul 1986 Asian Games as well as Seoul1988 Olympic Games, Rocky has accumulated his power with pride, honor, and ethical reputation transcending the differences of generations of the entire sportspeople around the globe. There have been a number of globally prosperous sports figures from Korea in the Olympic Movement, the case of Rocky YOON is particularly unique in that he has smoothly expanded his capabilities and the fruitful results of influence as an individual. Memories about sport in Korea for those who once visited must have been formed through the human warmth, intelligence and generosity experienced at first hand with Rocky YOON. Most parts of the Korean history, culture, and reputation have been disseminated through Rocky YOON. Rocky YOON is Korea's beating 'Heart and Soul'. (Translated from original Korea version)"

## 24) A Tribute from Ms. Barbara Kendall, (Former) IOC Member in New Zealand

***Summary:**

"Rocky belongs to the most splendid, colorful, and passionate group

(With Ms. Barbara Kendall)

among the global Olympic Movement family members. I ask you to continue to keep up your good work and services."

## 25) A Tribute from Dr. Chung-won Choue, President of World Taekwondo

***Summary:**

"I congratulate Rocky YOON Kang-Ro who has constantly served for the Olympic Movement, currently working as President of International Sport Diplomacy Institute on his book publication. He has published a book titled 'War without Gunfire' based on his vivid experiences in the international sport scenes. He has greatly contributed to the promotion of

Korea's prestige in the international sport stages through his participation in the Summer and Winter Olympic Games since 1982 as acting Chef de Mission of the Korean Delegations in charge of overall administrative matters with the various Organizing Committees. As he was born on the Olympic Day of 23 June, I think that he is destined to work his lifetime for the Olympic Movement, and I am confident that he will further contribute to the advancement of the Olympic Movement both at home and abroad. Rocky YOON's various pioneering activities as well-showcased in the field of sport diplomacy will indeed play an exemplary role model for many young people who would like to work as future sport diplomats. This book would serve a very valuable references for those who wish to accurately understand the Olympic Movement and aspire to become sport diplomats in the future." (Translated from the original Korean version)

*(With Dr. Chungwon Choue)*

## 26) A Tribute from Mme. Francoise ZWEIFEL, (Former)IOC Secretary General and Olympic Museum Director

***Summary:**

"For many years, I have known Rocky YOON very well in the Olympic Movement. He also demonstrated his unique passion, devotion and well-deserved merits of motivation while proceeding his job in a sustainable and flexible manner for which I always felt grateful to him toward his

*(With Mme. Francoise Zweifel at my Private PyeongSan Sport Museum)*

excellent individual qualities. Rocky has played a very important role in promoting the sport development and the advancement of the Olympic Movement not only in Korea and Asia but also in the whole world. Rocky has been a core partner for the IOC, in particular. Without thinking that we are core people, we worked hard together with open and amicable mind. Truly grateful Rocky, Please make your all-out efforts for Olympism and sport, and I wish you all the best for many years to come!" (Retranslated from the Korean version once already translated from the original English version)

## 27) A Tribute from Mr. Gilbert Felli, (Former) IOC Executive Director of Olympic Games

***Summary:**

"I am proud and pleased to learn that my friend Rocky YOON is pub-

(With Mr. Gilbert FELLI)

lishing his book about sport diplomacy and the Olympic Movement based on the stories about his experiences on the spot. I think his book must have reflected as real as his brilliant activities performed in the sport world. I believe that his book will serve as valuable references to all Korean people who are interested in sport and the Olympic Movement. This new pioneering project is his completed crystal of Rocky YOON's erudite and comprehensive knowledge and ideas. So many people in the Olympic Movement have already benefited from Rocky YOON's immeasurable and diverse ideas for such a long time. We are much grateful to Rocky YOON, and I hope all the readers should recognize the important values of this book" (Retranslated from the Korean version once already translated from the original English version)

# 28) References of Three IOC Presidents (1980~2025)

## 7th IOC President Samaranch's Letters

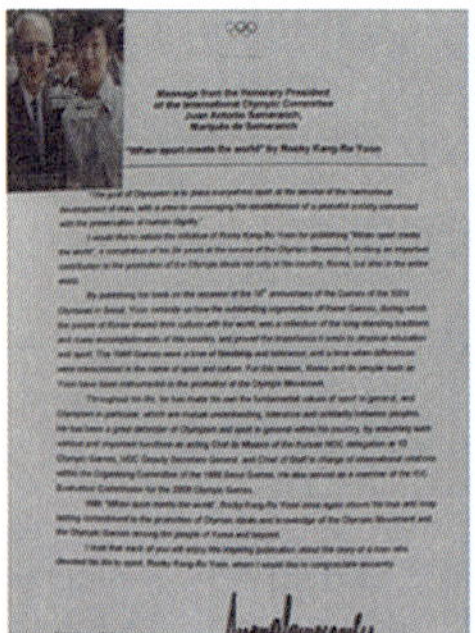

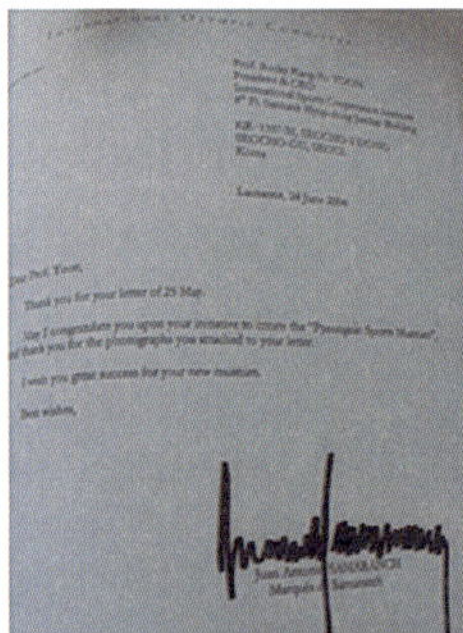

Lausanne, 24 June 2004

Dear Prof. Yoon,

Thank you for your letter of 25 May.

May I congratulate you upon your initiative to create the "Pyeongsan Sports Museum", and thank you for the photographs you attached to your letter.

I wish you great success for your new museum.

Best wishes,

Juan Antonio SAMARANCH
Marqués de Samaranch

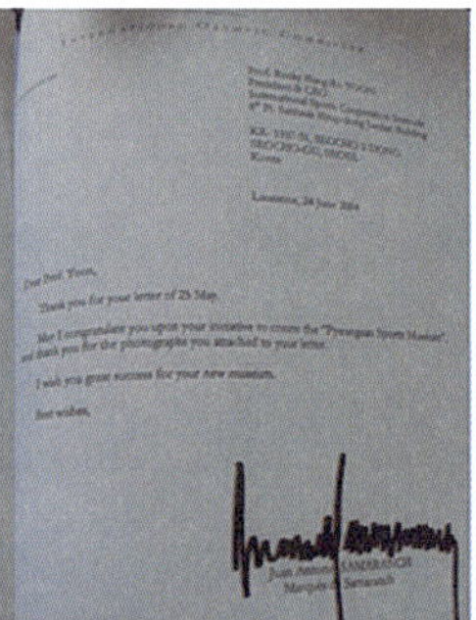

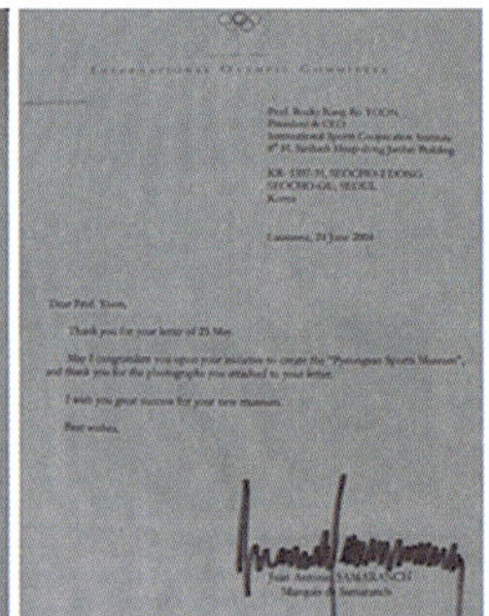

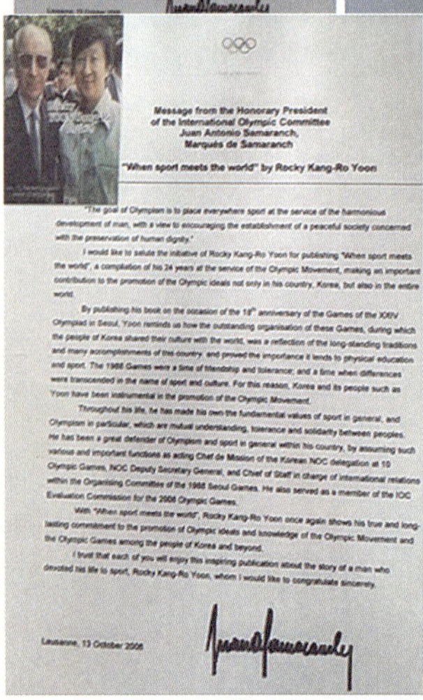

**Message from the Honorary President of the International Olympic Committee Juan Antonio Samaranch, Marqués de Samaranch**

**"When sport meets the world" by Rocky Kang-Ro Yoon**

"The goal of Olympism is to place everywhere sport at the service of the harmonious development of man, with a view to encouraging the establishment of a peaceful society concerned with the preservation of human dignity."

I would like to salute the initiative of Rocky Kang-Ro Yoon for publishing "When sport meets the world", a compilation of his 24 years at the service of the Olympic Movement, making an important contribution to the promotion of the Olympic ideals not only in his country, Korea, but also in the entire world.

By publishing his book on the occasion of the 18th anniversary of the Games of the XXIV Olympiad in Seoul, Yoon reminds us how the outstanding organisation of these Games, during which the people of Korea shared their culture with the world, was a reflection of the long-standing traditions and many accomplishments of this country, and proved the importance it lends to physical education and sport. The 1988 Games were a time of friendship and tolerance; and a time when differences were transcended in the name of sport and culture. For this reason, Korea and its people such as Yoon have been instrumental in the promotion of the Olympic Movement.

Throughout his life, he has made his own the fundamental values of sport in general, and Olympism in particular, which are mutual understanding, tolerance and solidarity between peoples. He has been a great defender of Olympism and sport in general within his country, by assuming such various and important functions as acting Chef de Mission of the Korean NOC delegation at 10 Olympic Games, NOC Deputy Secretary General, and Chief of Staff in charge of international relations within the Organising Committee of the 1988 Seoul Games. He also served as a member of the IOC Evaluation Commission for the 2008 Olympic Games.

With "When sport meets the world", Rocky Kang-Ro Yoon once again shows his true and long-lasting commitment to the promotion of Olympic ideals and knowledge of the Olympic Movement and the Olympic Games among the people of Korea and beyond.

I trust that each of you will enjoy this inspiring publication about the story of a man who devoted his life to sport, Rocky Kang-Ro Yoon, whom I would like to congratulate sincerely.

Lausanne, 13 October 2006

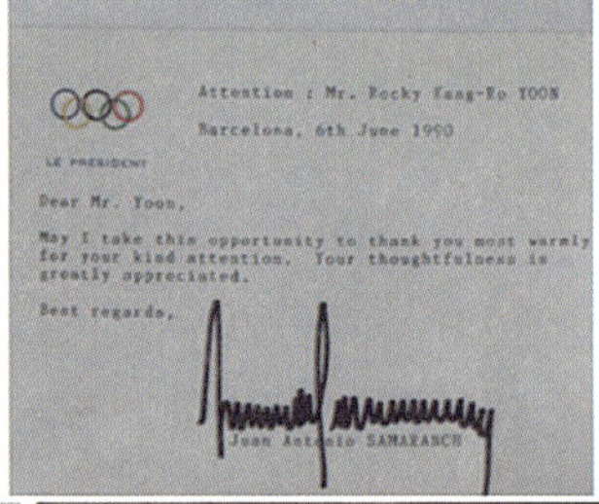

Attention : Mr. Rocky Kang-Ro YOON

Barcelona, 6th June 1990

LE PRESIDENT

Dear Mr. Yoon,

May I take this opportunity to thank you most warmly for your kind attention. Your thoughtfulness is greatly appreciated.

Best regards,

Juan Antonio SAMARANCH

## 29) Photo References of All ANOC Presidents(1979~President)

Mario Vazquez Rana (1979~2012) | Sheikh Ahmad (2012~2018) | Robin Mitchell (2018~ )

## 30) Photo References of IPC Presidents

### Rocky Yoon & IPC Presidents Sir. Phil Cravens(2001~2017) & Mr. Andrew Parsons(2017~)

1988년~1994년 | 1994년~2004년 | 2004년 ~ 현재

# 31) Photo References of GAISF Presidents

### Rocky Yoon & GAISF-SportAccord-GAISF(Global IFs Association)Presidents(1970's~2023/Thomas Keller-김운용-Hein Verbruggen-Marius Vizer-Patrick Bauman-Raffaele Chiulli-Ivo Ferriani)

## World Triathlon-Curling-Golf Three Women Presidents in total(Dec. 2020)

## Nicole Hoevertsz, Nawal El-Moutawakel. Gunilla Lindberg (IOC Members)

# 32) Photo References of OCA Presidents

## Summary(OCA Presidents)

**Sheikh Fahad(1982~1990)/Sheikh Ahmad(1991~2020 )/Randhir Singh(2020~ )**

## 33) Photo References of AIPS Presidents

### Rocky Yoon & Three World Sport Journalists Association(AIPS) Presidents(1980's~Present/Frank Talyer-Togay Bayatli-Gianni Merlo)

## 34) Photo References as Member of IOC Evaluation Commission for 2008 Olympics

### IOC Evaluation Commission Member for 2008 Olympics I

Olympic Games

THE GAMES OF THE XXIX OLYMPIAD IN 2008

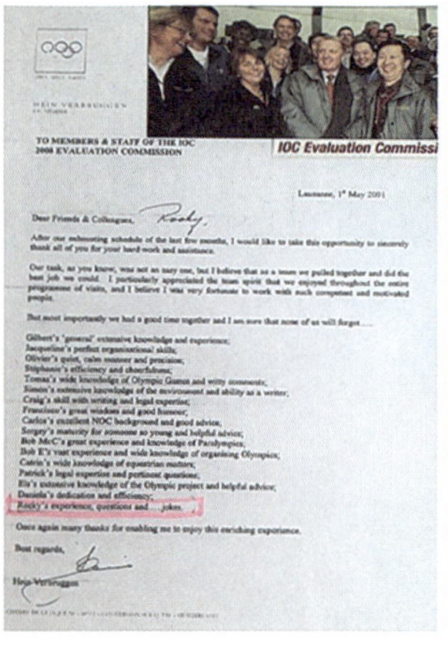

TO MEMBERS & STAFF OF THE IOC 2008 EVALUATION COMMISSION

IOC Evaluation Commissi

Lausanne, 1st May 2001

Dear Friends & Colleagues, Rocky,

After our exhausting schedule of the last few months, I would like to take this opportunity to sincerely thank all of you for your hard work and assistance.

Our task, as you know, was not an easy one, but I believe that as a team we pulled together and did the best job we could. I particularly appreciated the team spirit that we enjoyed throughout the entire programme of visits, and I believe I was very fortunate to work with such competent and motivated people.

But most importantly we had a good time together and I am sure that none of us will forget.....

Gilbert's "general" extensive knowledge and experience;
Jacqueline's perfect organisational skills;
Olivier's quiet, calm manner and precision;
Stephanie's efficiency and cheerfulness;
Tomas's wide knowledge of Olympic Games and witty comments;
Simon's extensive knowledge of the environment and ability as a writer;
Craig's skill with writing and legal expertise;
Francisco's great wisdom and good humour;
Carlos's excellent NOC background and good advice;
Sergey's maturity for someone so young and helpful advice;
Bob McC's great experience and knowledge of Paralympics;
Bob E's vast experience and wide knowledge of organising Olympics;
Catrin's wide knowledge of equestrian matters;
Patrick's legal expertise and pertinent questions;
Els's extensive knowledge of the Olympic project and helpful advice;
Daniela's dedication and efficiency;
Rocky's experience, questions and ....jokes.

Once again many thanks for enabling me to enjoy this enriching experience.

Best regards,

Hein Verbruggen

toronto

IOC Evaluation Commission Impressed by Toronto Bid

La Commission d'évaluation du CIO est impressionnée par la candidature de Toronto

La Comisión de Evaluación del COI impresionada con la candidatura de Toronto

## 35) Photo Reference of Sir. Craig Reedie, IOC Member, IOC Evaluation Commission Member for 2008 Olympics, Former WADA President and International Badminton Federation

## 36) Photo References of Two Kings

# Juan Carlos/King of Spain & Willem Alexander/King of the Netherlands

# Chinese President Jiang Zemin & Japanese Prime Minister Yoshiro Mori

## 37) Photo Reference of Mr. Peter Ueberroth, LAOOC1984 & USOC President

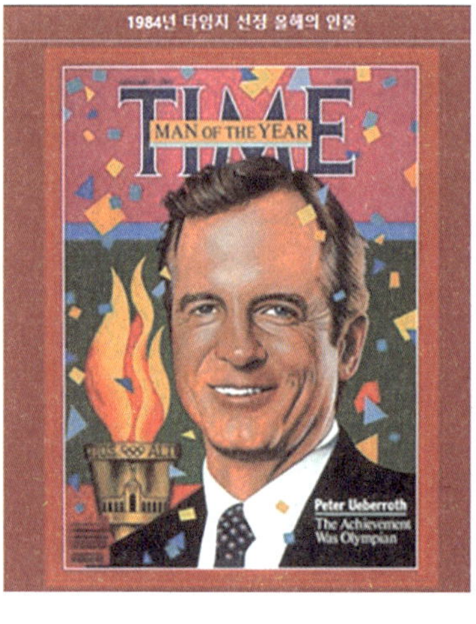

## 38) Photo References of the late Mr. Zhen Li-ang HE and Former IOC Vice President and IOC Member Zaiqing YU/China

## Sport Diplomacy : Chinese Olympic Family I

## Sport Diplomacy : Chinese Olympic Family II

## Sport Diplomacy: Japanese Olympic Family

# Sport Diplomacy: Chinese Taipei Olympic Family

## South-North Korea Sport Exchange(Visit to PyeongYang, Korea Unifying Delegation/Sydney2000 Olympics)

## OCA Leading Sport Diplomats

## Sport Diplomacy: Global NOCS(EOC Europe)

## Sport Diplomacy: Global NOCs(PASO Americas)

## Sport Diplomacy: Global NOCs(ANOCA Africa)

## Sport Diplomacy: Global NOCS(ONOC Oceania)

## Sport Diplomacy: Summer IFs Presidents I

# Sport Diplomacy: Summer IFs Presidents II

# Sport Diplomacy: Winter IFs (AIOWF) Presidents

# Sport Diplomacy Power=Global IOC Members I

# Sport Diplomacy Power=Global IOC Members II

# Sport Diplomacy Power=Global IOC Members III

# Sport Diplomacy Power=Global IOC Members IV

# Sport Diplomacy Power=Global IOC Members V

# Organizational Skills and Know-How(109th IOC Session Seoul 1999)

## Sport Diplomacy= Inter-Korean Exchange & Communications of Goodwill

## With DPR Korean NOC President and Secretary General(2002 Busan AG)

(북한 NOC 로고)

'남북체육회담' 의미·전망

# '스포츠 통일' 초안 만들었다

부산서 합의 '통일 아시아드' 결정체

종합대회 같이 참가 체육발전 도모

올림픽委로 실무협상 창구 단일화

## Two Mongolian Presidents & Genghis Khan Supported(Honorary Doctorate)

# Olympic Legacy (Pin Collections I)

# Olympic Legacy (Pin Collections II & Donation)

# First-ever Korea's Private Sport Museum(2004~2015)

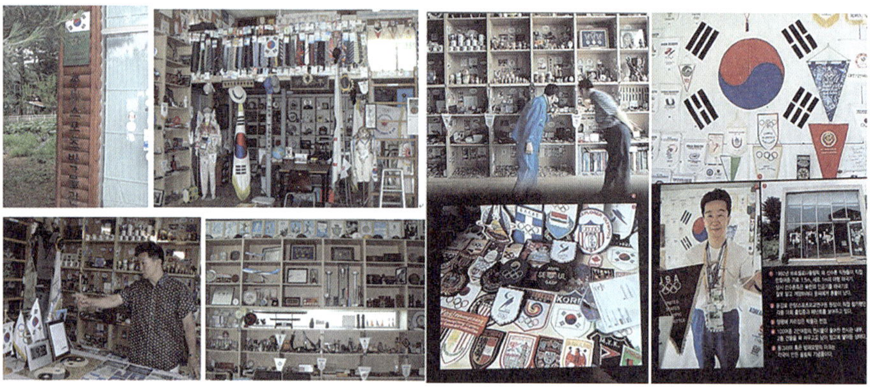

# Honorary Citizenship/2002 & Honorary Doctorate(Doctor Honoris Causa/2003)

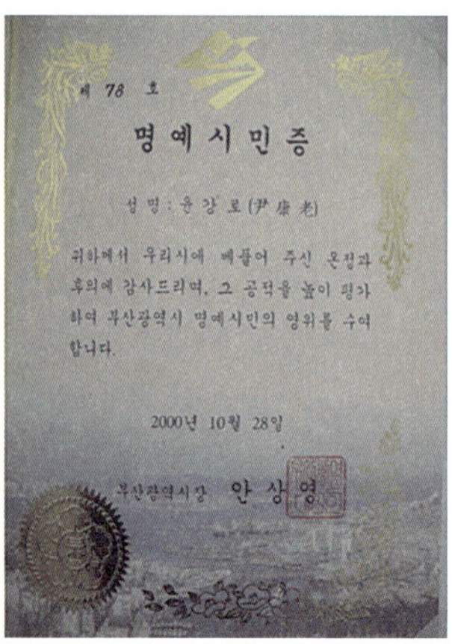

제 78 호

명예시민증

성명 : 윤강로(尹康老)

귀하께서 우리시에 베풀어 주신 온정과 후의에 감사드리며, 그 공적을 높이 평가하여 부산광역시 명예시민의 영위를 수여합니다.

2000년 10월 28일

부산광역시장 안 상 영

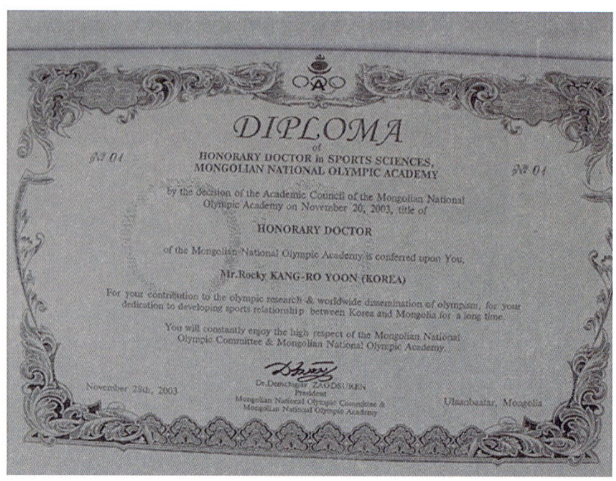

DIPLOMA

of

HONORARY DOCTOR in SPORTS SCIENCES,
MONGOLIAN NATIONAL OLYMPIC ACADEMY

№ 01

by the decision of the Academic Council of the Mongolian National Olympic Academy on November 20, 2003, title of

HONORARY DOCTOR

of the Mongolian National Olympic Academy is conferred upon You,

Mr.Rocky KANG-RO YOON (KOREA)

For your contribution to the olympic research & worldwide dissemination of olympism, for your dedication to developing sports relationship between Korea and Mongolia for a long time.

You will constantly enjoy the high respect of the Mongolian National Olympic Committee & Mongolian National Olympic Academy.

November 28th, 2003

Dr.Demchigjav ZAGDSUREN
President
Mongolian National Olympic Committee &
Mongolian National Olympic Academy

Ulaanbaatar, Mongolia

Prof. Rocky Yoon Kang-ro
... Bukhansan Raemian Apt
... Eunpyeong-gu
Seoul (03366)
KOREA

In loving memory of
Jacques
Count Rogge
1942 - 2021

Oprechte dank
voor uw steun en medeleven.

Merci sincèrement
pour votre soutien et marques de sympathie.

Sincere thanks
for your support and friendship.

Anne Rogge

# IOC President Rogge's Full Support(2004~2012)

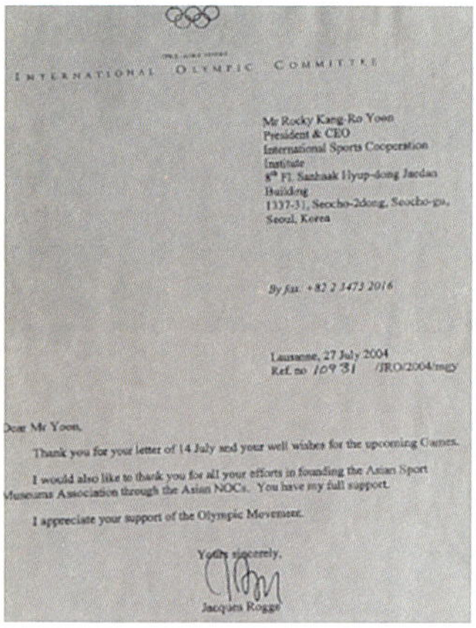

INTERNATIONAL OLYMPIC COMMITTEE

Mr Rocky Kang-Ro Yoon
President & CEO
International Sports Cooperation Institute
8th Fl. Sanhaak Hyup-dong Jaedan Building
1337-31, Seocho-2dong, Seocho-gu,
Seoul, Korea

By fax: +82 2 3473 2016

Lausanne, 27 July 2004
Ref. no 10931 /JRO/2004/mgy

Dear Mr Yoon,

Thank you for your letter of 14 July and your well wishes for the upcoming Games.

I would also like to thank you for all your efforts in founding the Asian Sport Museums Association through the Asian NOCs. You have my full support.

I appreciate your support of the Olympic Movement.

Yours sincerely,

Jacques Rogge

# In Memory of the Deceased Int'l & Global Sports Leaders

So far I have published about 20+ books during my 40 years' services in the Olympic Movement.

The International Sport Diplomacy Institute, equipped with its status as non-profit NGO, was created in 2004 right after I decided to tender a voluntary resignation from the Korean Olympic Committee as its Deputy Secretary General in order to further focus on the second PyeongChang Bid as Secretary General of the Bid Committee for the 2014 Olympic and Paralympic Winter Games following its first attempt for 2010 OWG which had been beaten by Vancouver 2010 bid by a narrow margin of 56:53 at the second round ballot of the IOC Session in Prague 2003.

The main Work Scope of the ISDI included but not limited to the compiling, summarizing and analyzing the international sporting trend and news on a daily basis along with the publication of the English News Letters titled "SOS" (Spot Light On Sport Life) on a weekly basis. And in 2008, I launched my blog titled "Sport World" delivering the summary with corresponding short analysis of the news and topics of the daily international sport world. The year 2024 will mark the 20th anniversary of the activities of the ISDI.

My first-ever book written in 2006 was titled “War without Gunfire” which dealt with stories and episodes I experienced at first hand in the global Olympic Movement. And the above book publication (book presentation) ceremony took place at the Press Center building downtown in Seoul.

At the book presentation ceremony, Hon. Seung-Soo HAN, who assumed the role as Chairman of the UN General Assembly-Foreign Affairs Minister-Korean Ambassador to the United States and National Assembly member was President of the PyeongChang2014 Bid Committee, who was, later on, appointed Prime Minister of the Republic of Korea. And he spoke well of me at his address with so many praises. At that time, I also served as Secretary General of the PyeongChang2014 Bid Committee. I still vividly remember like I smell the fresh paint! I would like to express my special thanks to H.E. Seung-Soo HAN.

While I was compiling documents, I found some of the recommendations as above on the occasion of my book publications including that of IOC President Thomas Bach as recently as the year 2020 about my latest book titled “True Records and Stories of Korea Sport Diplomacy, ‘The New Horizons’”. Reminiscing good old memories together with recent great honors of IOC Pierre de Coubertin Medal (2022) and the nomination as Member of IOC Culture and Heritage Commission (2024), I express my profound gratitude to IOC President Thomas Bach from the bottom of my heart.

Dedicated and Edited by Prof. Rocky Kang-Ro YOON

# Chapter 20:
## *Closing Message (The Last Page of the Book)*

In the quiet spaces between speeches and ceremonies, between policy papers and podiums, I found the real story: one of belief, of unity, of light shared between souls who never stopped chasing peace through sport.

This book is not just mine. It belongs to every athlete who dared, to every witness who hoped, and to one man whose torch never dimmed — IOC President Thomas Bach.

As he hands over the Olympic rings, I offer these pages as my own baton — a tribute, a prayer, and a pledge to keep walking beside the spirit that once walked beside me.

> *"These highlights are not just moments in a timeline. They're stars in the constellation of a presidency — and I was honored to reflect their light."*

Olympism is not carved only in stone monuments or etched in policy documents. It breathes in moments — quiet conversations, shared smiles, letters exchanged across oceans.

As Thomas Bach's Presidency came to its final bow, I looked not only at his achievements, but at our journey: walking together through corridors of history, policy, peace, and sport. This epilogue is where time slows — and gratitude speaks.

With deepest respect and gratitude,

"He taught me that greatness is not measured in applause, but in the people it touches."

— *Author's Reflection*

**Prof. Rocky Kang-Ro YOON**

President, International Sport Diplomacy Institute,

Advisor, Korean Sport and Olympic Committee (2025)

Recipient, IOC Pierre de Coubertin Medal (2022)

Recipient, ANOC Merit Award (Beijing General Assembly)

Member, IOC Culture and Olympic Heritage Commission (2024)

Olympic Communicator & Witness to Peace through Sport

Author of *"Thomas Bach,: The Olympic Reformer"* – A Tribute to IOC President Thomas Bach

Ambassador to IOC Recognized International Federation (FICTS: Federation Internationale Cinema Television Sportifs /2025~)

**Thomas Bach : The Olympic Reformer**

First Printed/October 15, 2025
First Published/October 20, 2025
Owner of Publication Right/Kim Young-Dae
Publisher/DKBooks
ISBN/979-11-7168-115-0



DKBooks
Publication registration number : 1-1003
2F, 45, Cheonjung-ro 42-gil, Gangdong-gu, Seoul, Republic of Korea
Tel : 82-2-485-1988, 82-2-485-2586~87 · Fax : 82-2-485-1488
e-mail: dkbookss@naver.com